Advancing Equity & Embracing Diversity in Early Childhood Education
Elevating Voices & Actions

Iliana Alanís & Iheoma U. Iruka, EDITORS
WITH Susan Friedman

National Association for the Education of Young Children
Washington, DC

National Association for the Education of Young Children

1401 H Street NW, Suite 600
Washington, DC 20005
202-232-8777 • 800-424-2460
NAEYC.org

NAEYC Books

Senior Director, Publishing & Content Development
Susan Friedman

Director, Books
Dana Battaglia

Senior Editor
Holly Bohart

Editor
Rossella Procopio

Senior Creative Design Manager
Henrique J. Siblesz

Senior Creative Design Specialist
Charity Coleman

Senior Creative Design Specialist
Gillian Frank

Publishing Business Operations Manager
Francine Markowitz

Through its publications program, the National Association for the Education of Young Children (NAEYC) provides a forum for discussion of major issues and ideas in the early childhood field, with the hope of provoking thought and promoting professional growth. The views expressed or implied in this book are not necessarily those of the Association.

Permissions

NAEYC accepts requests for limited use of our copyrighted material. For permission to reprint, adapt, translate, or otherwise reuse and repurpose content from this publication, review our guidelines at NAEYC.org/resources/permissions.

Figures 3.1 and 3.2 on pages 27 and 28 are reprinted, with permission, from Child Trends Databank, *Preschool and Prekindergarten* (Bethesda, MD: Child Trends, 2019).

Figure 3.3 on page 30 is reprinted from US Government Accountability Office (GAO), *Discipline Disparities for Black Students, Boys, and Students with Disabilities* (Washington, DC: GAO, 2018), 14.

Figure 20.1 on page 121 is reprinted, with permission, from Belinda Bustos Flores, Lorena Claeys, and Conra Gist, *Crafting Culturally Efficacious Teacher Preparation and Pedagogies* (Lanham, MD: Lexington Books, 2018), 31.

Photo and Illustration Credits
Copyright © NAEYC: cover
Courtesy of Isauro M. Escamilla: 95

Library of Congress Control Number: 2020951548

ISBN: 978-1-938113-78-9

Item 1155

Contents

Acknowledgments

We acknowledge the work of educators around the country who strive to build equitable classrooms, relationships, and policy for young children and their families. We recognize the impact an empowering pedagogy can have in our communities and the significance of educators who work toward advancing equity on a daily basis.

We thank the NAEYC staff for their continued support in these efforts, particularly our editor, Dana Battaglia, for bringing this important work to fruition and assisting us along the way. We also acknowledge the NAEYC Governing Board's commitment to equity for children and early childhood educators across the United States and thank the DAP/Diversity & Equity Workgroup who advised the board on the NAEYC's "Advancing Equity in Early Childhood Education" position statement, which inspired this book.

Lastly, we recognize our families who continue to support and encourage our work. *Gratitud por su apoyo y amor.*

Contributor List

Teresa Acevedo
is executive director and cofounder of Tucson Children's Project (TCP), which works to advance the rights and potential of all children and families. TCP works in community collaborations to expand the understanding of the Reggio Emilia approaches in one's own context. Teresa is the author of numerous articles related to early childhood education and coauthor of a locally constructed curriculum framework. Formerly, she was director of education for Head Start's Child-Parent Centers.

Jennifer Keys Adair, PhD
is associate professor of early childhood education and director of the Agency and Young Children Research Collective at the University of Texas at Austin. Her work centers on the impact of racism on children's agency. Her forthcoming book, *Segregation by Experience: Agency, Racism, and Early Learning,* with Dr. Kiyomi Sánchez-Suzuki Colegrove, was published by University of Chicago Press in early 2021. More information can be found at www.jenniferkeysadair.com.

Rosemarie Allen, EdD
is associate professor in the School of Education at Metropolitan State University of Denver. She is also the founder, president, and CEO of the Institute for Racial Equity and Excellence. Dr. Allen's areas of expertise include implicit bias, culturally responsive practices, racial equity, and anti-racism practices at the personal, institutional, and systemic levels.

Garnett S. Booker III
is a pre-K–3 teacher in Washington, DC. Originally from Wilmington, DE, he has been an early childhood teacher for over 10 years. Garnett has presented nationally and locally on various early childhood topics, including the importance of having males in early childhood programs and developmentally appropriate play behaviors in early childhood. He is passionate about advocating for the importance of the early childhood experience.

Barbara T. Bowman
is the Irving B. Harris Professor at Erikson Institute, where she teaches courses and supervises students. She was chief officer for early childhood education at the Chicago Public Schools (2004–2012) and a consultant to the US Department of Education (2009), and she served on the White House Initiative on Educational Excellence for African Americans (2014–2016). Bowman is a member of the Chicago Public Library Board of Directors and is also on the boards of a number of practice and policy organizations.

Anthony Broughton, PhD
is interim department chair at Claflin University, School of Education. Before his position at Claflin University, he worked for the South Carolina Department of Education as a 4K regional coordinator. Prior to that, he served as an administrator for the then NAEYC-accredited Benedict College Child Development Center.

Dina C. Castro, PhD

is professor and Velma E. Schmidt endowed chair in early childhood education at the University of North Texas. Her scholarship focuses on equity in the early care and education of bilingual children in immigrant, migrant, and indigenous communities. She is currently studying the extent to which early education policies governing curricula, programming, and teacher preparation address the characteristics and experiences of bilingual children. Internationally, she studies the experiences of transnational students in México and the United States as well as intercultural bilingual education in Latin America.

Jie-Qi Chen, PhD

is senior vice president for academic affairs and dean of faculty at Erikson Institute. She is also the founder of Erikson Institute's Early Math Collaborative, and serves on the NAEYC Governing Board. Dr. Chen has published 10 books and numerous articles. Her areas of expertise include cognitive development, early mathematic education, teacher change, classroom assessment, and educational implications of multiple intelligences theory.

Stephanie M. Curenton, PhD

is a tenured associate professor at Boston University. Her research focuses on positive child growth and development and dismantling health and education inequities for racially marginalized children and families. She created the Conversation Compass Communication Screener-Revised, a measure of children's classroom conversation skills, and the *Assessing Classroom Sociocultural Equity Scale*, a measure of classroom quality for racially marginalized students.

Felicia L. DeHaney, PhD

is director of program and strategy for the W.K. Kellogg Foundation. In this role, she supports the foundation's efforts to promote thriving children, working families, and equitable communities. She provides leadership and oversight to ensure alignment to the strategic framework resulting in positive systemic change within communities and programming efforts. DeHaney holds her bachelor's degree in psychology from Howard University, a master's degree in educational psychology from Columbia University's Teacher's College, and a PhD in educational psychology from Howard University.

Louise Derman-Sparks, MS

has worked in early childhood care and education for over 50 years as a preschool and college teacher, director, author, consultant, and social justice activist. The author and coauthor of several books and articles, Louise's first book, *Anti-Bias Curriculum* (NAEYC, 1989), developed with the ABC Task Force, brought the concepts and goals of the anti-bias approach into early childhood education discourse and practice. A Pacific Oaks College faculty emeritus, Louise continues her social justice activism.

Lillian Durán, PhD

is associate professor in the department of special education and clinical sciences at the University of Oregon. Her research is focused on improving instructional and assessment practices with dual language learners. She is currently a coprincipal investigator on an Institute of Education Sciences grant to develop a Spanish early language and literacy general outcome measure for screening and progress monitoring in preschool.

Tonia R. Durden, PhD

is clinical associate professor and coordinator of the Birth through 5 program at Georgia State University. Dr. Durden's primary scholarship and research trajectory focuses on exploring how to develop and support African American children's sociocultural development and create racially equitable learning experiences for children of color. As a teacher educator and researcher, the focus of her work also includes preparing preservice and in-service teachers to become culturally competent master teachers.

Isauro M. Escamilla, MA

is an early childhood educator in a Spanish-English dual language early childhood program in the San Francisco Unified School District. He is also adjunct faculty at San Francisco State University. Isauro has authored several articles and chapters for different books on narrative, inquiry, and documentation of children's learning. He's a doctoral candidate in the EdD Educational Leadership program at San Francisco State University.

Belinda Bustos Flores, PhD

is associate dean of professional preparation and partnerships and professor of bicultural-bilingual studies in the College of Education and Human Development at the University of Texas at San Antonio. Her research focuses on teacher development. Dr. Flores was the recipient of the American Educational Research Association (AERA) Hispanic Research Issues Elementary, Secondary, and Postsecondary Special Interest Group (SIG) Award in 2015 and the AERA Bilingual Education Research SIG Lifetime Achievement Award in 2019.

Janelle Beth Flores, MS, CCC-SLP

holds a master's degree in communication sciences and disorders from Texas Woman's University, a bachelor's degree in communication sciences and disorders from the University of Texas at Austin, and a bachelor's degree in biology with a concentration in neuroscience from the University of Texas at San Antonio. Her research interests include appropriate assessment and intervention practices with bilingual/diverse populations and utilizing therapy dogs for speech and language therapy.

Ximena Franco, PhD

is an advanced research scientist at the Frank Porter Graham (FPG) Child Development Institute at the University of North Carolina at Chapel Hill. She has held lead roles on several research projects focused on generating new knowledge about Spanish-English dual language learners, including developing culturally robust assessment and intervention strategies for teachers. Dr. Franco served for many years on the award-winning FPG RACE Committee, which created a racial equity professional development fund and print- and social media-based public information campaigns on issues of equity.

Michael Gonzalez

is director of recruiting and professional development at Metropolitan Montessori Schools. He has served on the board of directors for the Texas Association for the Education of Young Children (TXAEYC) for over 10 years, and currently serves as president. Michael also sits on the Steering Committee of the Greater Houston Chapter of the TXAEYC as the membership committee chair. A seasoned trainer in the field, Michael has delivered professional development to early childhood professionals over the course of his career in the field. He is designated as a Child Development Associate (CDA) Professional Development Specialist.

Mimi Gray, MA

is director of program development at Tucson Children's Project. In this role, she coordinates professional development opportunities that bring the study of the Reggio Emilia municipal schools to educators and policy advocates throughout Southern Arizona. She has worked in classrooms and held administrative positions in public schools, Head Start programs, and private early care and education programs, as well as in higher education.

Jillian Herink

is executive director of the Iowa Association for the Education of Young Children and has served in this position since 2017. Formerly, she served as superintendent of the Meskwaki Settlement School in Iowa. Jillian has spent a large part of her career advocating for students with unique learning needs, including second language learners and students with disabilities, and has worked primarily with underserved populations.

Socorro Herrera, PhD

is a professor in the Department of Curriculum and Instruction in the College of Education and executive director of the Center for Intercultural and Multilingual Advocacy at Kansas State University. Her research focuses on literacy opportunities with culturally and linguistically diverse students, reading strategies, and teacher preparation for diversity in the classroom. Dr. Herrera is the author of 10 textbooks and has been widely published in top journals in the field.

Steven Hicks

is a NAEYC Governing Board member (2020) and assistant state superintendent for the Division of Early Childhood at the Maryland State Department of Education. Prior to that, he served as senior advisor on early learning at the US Department of Education and was an early childhood educator for 20 years.

Zeynep Isik-Ercan, PhD

is professor of early childhood education and codirector of the Early Childhood Leadership Institute at Rowan University in New Jersey. Her research regularly appears in academic journals and covers topics such as culturally and linguistically diverse children, teachers, families, and communities; immigrant families with young children; culturally responsive teaching and intellectual development; and professional development of educators and leaders. She actively works with state organizations, schools, and educators through coaching and training programs.

Tamara Johnson

is a NAEYC Governing Board member (2020) and executive director of the Malaika Early Learning Center.

Debbie LeeKeenan, MEd

is an early childhood consultant and lecturer (www.antibiasleadersece.com) in Seattle, Washington. From 1996 to 2013, she was director and lecturer at the Eliot-Pearson Children's School, the laboratory school affiliated with the Eliot-Pearson Department of Child Study and Human Development at Tufts University. She is coauthor of *From Survive to Thrive: A Director's Guide for Leading an Early Childhood Program* and *Leading Anti-Bias Early Childhood Programs: A Guide for Change*.

Junlei Li, PhD

is the Saul Zaentz senior lecturer in early childhood education at Harvard University's Graduate School of Education. His research and practice focus on understanding and supporting the work of those who serve children and families on the frontlines of education and social services. He developed the Simple Interactions approach to help identify what ordinary people do extraordinarily well with children in everyday moments and made that the basis for promoting positive system change.

Daniel R. Meier, PhD

is professor of elementary education at San Francisco State University. He teaches in the MA program in early childhood education, the multiple subject teaching credential program, and the EdD program in educational leadership. Meier teaches courses in reading/language arts, multilingual development, narrative inquiry and memoir, qualitative research, and international education. He is the author, most recently, of *Supporting Literacies for Children of Color: A Strength-Based Approach to Preschool Literacy* (Routledge, 2020).

Jen Neitzel, PhD

is executive director of the Educational Equity Institute, which is focused on eliminating the educational and opportunity gaps within communities through systems-level change. Prior to this work, Jen was a research scientist and technical assistance provider at Frank Porter Graham (FPG) Child Development Institute at the University of North Carolina at Chapel Hill for 15 years. During her time at FPG, her work focused on implicit bias, disparities in suspensions and expulsions, trauma, and culturally responsive anti-bias practices. Jen presents frequently at state and national conferences and is widely published in peer-reviewed journals. She also is the author of the book *Achieving Equity and Justice in Education Through the Work of Systems Change*.

Karen Nemeth

is an author, consultant, and subject matter expert focusing on early childhood education for children who are dual language learners. She has held leadership roles at national organizations including NAEYC, the National Association for Bilingual Education, and the TESOL International Association. She currently works as a senior training and technical specialist – DLL for the National Center on Early Childhood Development, Teaching, and Learning as part of Zero to Three.

John Nimmo, EdD

is associate professor of early childhood education at Portland State University in Oregon. He is coauthor of three books: *Leading Anti-Bias Early Childhood Programs: A Guide for Change*; *Loris Malaguzzi and the Teachers: Dialogues on Collaboration and Conflict among Children, Reggio Emilia 1990*; and *Emergent Curriculum*. John is also coproducer of the international film *The Voices of Children* and is collaborating with Debbie LeeKeenan on an anti-bias education professional development video.

Iliana Reyes, PhD

is associate dean for academic affairs and community and global partnerships at the University of Arizona's College of Education. She specializes in a range of research and educational issues on early childhood education, including multilingualism and immigration and education with families, teachers, and young children. Previously, she worked as a researcher scientist at the Center for Research and Advanced Studies of the National Polytechnic Institute in Mexico City and as affiliated faculty at the University of Arizona Center for Latin American Studies and the Second Language and Acquisition Teaching Program. In her collaboration with Tucson Children's Project, she studies children's inquiry from a socio-constructivist approach to integrate family and community as integral part of children's learning.

Nicol Russell

is a NAEYC Governing Board member (2020) and vice president of implementation research for Teaching Strategies, LLC. In this role, Nicol works with the director of research to design and conduct research projects that tell the stories of early learning partners of Teaching Strategies. Previously, she served as the deputy associate superintendent for early childhood at the Arizona Department of Education and the director of the Arizona Head Start State Collaboration Office.

Shubhi Sachdeva

is a doctoral candidate in the Department of Curriculum and Instruction, specializing in early childhood education, at the University of Texas at Austin. Her experience in early education spans three countries: India, Taiwan, and the United States. Her research interests include global perspectives on childhood, sociocultural processes in early education, and equity and social justice issues in early education.

Hilary Seitz, PhD

is a professor of early childhood education at the University of Alaska Anchorage. Her research focuses on teaching pedagogies for teachers of young children, including STEAM methods, culturally responsive teaching, authentic assessment, and connecting to the community.

Dorothy L. Shapland, EdD

is assistant professor of special education, early childhood, and culturally and linguistically diverse education at Metropolitan State University of Denver. She is a founding member of the Division for Early Childhood's Inclusion, Equity, and Social Justice Committee. Dr. Shapland's areas of expertise include effective, intentional, anti-biased, culturally responsive, and trauma-informed teaching and learning in early education, and trauma-informed equity leadership for schools and centers.

Carla Thompson Payton

is vice president for program strategy for the W.K. Kellogg Foundation. In this role, she supports the foundation's efforts to promote thriving children, working families, and equitable communities. She provides leadership and management for the creative and strategic direction of programming from design through implementation, evaluation, and dissemination. Thompson Payton received her bachelor's degree from Syracuse University

in Syracuse, New York. She holds a master's degree in social work and a doctorate in educational leadership from the University of Pennsylvania in Philadelphia.

Shannon Wanless

is associate professor of applied developmental psychology and director of the Office of Child Development at the University of Pittsburgh's School of Education. She is a former YMCA camp director and Head Start teacher.

Alandra Washington, PhD

is vice president for transformation and organizational effectiveness at the W.K. Kellogg Foundation. In this role, she supports the foundation's efforts to promote thriving children, working families, and equitable communities. She provides leadership and management of enterprise wide transformation efforts, organizational redesign, change management, and efficient operations to maximize overall organizational performance excellence. Dr. Washington earned a bachelor's degree in business administration and a master's degree in public administration, both from Southern Illinois University at Edwardsville. She holds a doctorate in educational leadership and organizational analysis from Western Michigan University.

Dana Winters, PhD

is faculty and academic director of the Fred Rogers Center for Early Learning and Children's Media at Saint Vincent College and co-creator of the Simple Interactions approach to support children, families, and their helpers. She studies and advances the legacy of Fred Rogers by directing the Center's partnerships with educators and communities, including numerous federal, state, and foundation grants in early childhood education, family engagement, and statewide training and technical assistance.

Brian L. Wright, PhD

is associate professor and coordinator of the early childhood education program as well as coordinator of the middle school cohort of the African American Male Academy at the University of Memphis. He is author of *The Brilliance of Black Boys: Cultivating School Success in the Early Grades*, with contributions by Shelly L. Counsell, which won the National Association for Multicultural Education's 2018 Phillip C. Chinn Book Award.

Advancing Equity in Early Childhood Education

Position Statement adopted by the NAEYC National Governing Board April 2019

All children have the right to **equitable learning opportunities** that enable them to achieve their full potential as engaged learners and valued members of society. Advancing the right to equitable learning opportunities requires recognizing and dismantling the systems of bias that accord privilege to some and are unjust to others. Advancing the full inclusion of all individuals across all social identities will take sustained efforts far beyond those of early childhood educators alone. Early childhood educators, however, have a unique opportunity and obligation to advance equity. With the support of the early education system as a whole, they can create early learning environments that equitably distribute learning opportunities by helping **all** children experience responsive interactions that nurture their full range of social, emotional, cognitive, physical, and linguistic abilities; that reflect and model fundamental principles of fairness and justice; and that help them accomplish the goals of anti-bias education. Each child will

> demonstrate self-awareness, confidence, family pride, and positive social identities;

> express comfort and joy with human diversity, use accurate language for human differences, and form deep, caring human connections across diverse backgrounds;

> increasingly recognize and have language to describe unfairness (injustice) and understand that unfairness hurts;

> have the will and the skills to act, with others or alone, against prejudice and/or discriminatory actions.[1]

Early childhood education settings—including centers, family child care homes, and schools—are often among children's first communities beyond their families. These settings offer important contexts for children's learning. They should be environments in which children learn that they are valued by others, learn how to treat others with fairness and respect, and learn how to embrace human differences rather than ignore or fear them.

When early childhood educators use inclusive teaching approaches, they demonstrate that they respect diversity and value all children's strengths. Early childhood educators can model humility and a willingness to learn by being accountable for any negative impacts of their own biases on their interactions with children and their families. They can work to ensure that all children have equitable access to the learning environment, the materials, and the adult–child and child–child interactions that help children thrive. Early childhood educators can recognize and support each child's unique strengths, seeking through personal and collective reflection to avoid biases—explicit or implicit—that may affect their decision making related to children.

To effectively advance equity and embrace diversity and full inclusion, early childhood educators need work settings that also embrace these goals—not only for the children and families served but also for the educators themselves. Early childhood educators should be well prepared in their professional knowledge, skills, and dispositions to teach in diverse, inclusive settings. They also need to be supported by, and to advocate for, equity- and diversity-focused public policies. Each of these areas is addressed more fully in the recommendations below. Although the primary focus of this statement is on equitable learning opportunities for young children, we stress that such opportunities depend on equitable treatment of early childhood educators as well. We make these recommendations understanding the critical importance of building a recognized early childhood profession and a system with sufficient funding to ensure that all its members receive equitable compensation and professional recognition that reflect the importance of their work.

Recognizing that both institutional and interpersonal systems must change, our recommendations begin with a focus on individual reflection. Across all roles and settings, advancing equity requires a dedication to self-reflection, a willingness to respectfully listen to others' perspectives without interruption or defensiveness, and a commitment to continuous learning to improve practice. Members of groups that have historically enjoyed advantages must be willing to recognize the often-unintended consequences of ignorance, action, and inaction and how they may contribute to perpetuating existing systems of privilege. It is also important to recognize the many reactions associated with marginalization that begin in early childhood and range from internalization to resistance.[2]

The following general recommendations apply to everyone involved in any aspect of early childhood education.

Recommendations for Everyone

1. **Build awareness and understanding of your culture, personal beliefs, values, and biases.** Recognize that everyone holds some types of bias based on their personal background and experiences. Even if you think of yourself as unbiased, reflect on the impacts of racism, sexism, classism, ableism, heterosexism, xenophobia, and other systems of oppression affecting you and the people around you. Identify where your varied social identities have provided strengths and understandings based on your experiences of both injustice and privilege.

2. **Recognize the power and benefits of diversity and inclusivity.** Carefully observe and listen to others (children, families, colleagues). Expand your knowledge by considering diverse experiences and perspectives without generalizing or stereotyping.

3. **Take responsibility for biased actions, even if unintended, and actively work to repair the harm.** When you commit a biased action, be ready and willing to be held accountable. Resist the urge to become defensive, especially as a member of a privileged group. Before making judgments, take responsibility for recognizing what you don't know or understand and use the opportunity to learn and reflect. Be willing to constructively share feedback and discuss alternative approaches when observing potentially biased actions by others.

4. **Acknowledge and seek to understand structural inequities and their impact over time.** Take action when outcomes vary significantly by social identities (e.g., lopsided achievement test scores, number and frequency of suspensions or expulsions that disproportionately target African American and Latino boys, or engagement with certain materials and activities by gender). Look deeper at how your expectations, practices, curriculum, and/or policies may contribute (perhaps unwittingly) to inequitable outcomes for children and take steps to change them.

5. **View your commitment to cultural responsiveness as an ongoing process.** It is not a one-time matter of mastering knowledge of customs and practices, but an enduring responsibility to learn and reflect based on direct experiences with children, their families, and others.

6. **Recognize that the professional knowledge base is changing.** There is growing awareness of the limitations of child development theories and research based primarily on a normative perspective of White, middle-class children without disabilities educated in predominantly English-language schools.[3, 4] Keep up to date professionally as more strengths-based approaches to research and practice are articulated and as narrowly defined normative approaches to child development and learning are questioned. Be willing to challenge the use of outdated or narrowly defined approaches—for example, in curriculum, assessment policies and practices, or early learning standards. Seek information from families and communities about their social and cultural beliefs and practices to supplement your knowledge.

Recommendations for Early Childhood Educators[5]

Create a Caring, Equitable Community of Engaged Learners

1. **Uphold the unique value and dignity of each child and family.** Ensure that all children see themselves and their daily experiences, as well as the daily lives of others within and beyond their community, positively reflected in the design and implementation of pedagogy, curriculum, learning environment, interactions, and materials. Celebrate diversity by acknowledging similarities and differences and provide perspectives that recognize beauty and value across differences.

2. **Recognize each child's unique strengths and support the full inclusion of all children—given differences in culture, family structure, language, racial identity, gender, abilities and disabilities, religious beliefs, or economic class.** Help children get to know, recognize, and support one another as valued members of the community. Take care that no one feels bullied, invisible, or unnoticed.

3. **Develop trusting relationships with children and nurture relationships among them while building on their knowledge and skills.** Embrace children's cultural experiences and the languages and customs that shape their

learning. Treat each child with respect. Eliminate language or behavior that is stereotypical, demeaning, exclusionary, or judgmental.

4. **Consider the developmental, cultural, and linguistic appropriateness of the learning environment and your teaching practices for each child.** Offer meaningful, relevant, and appropriately challenging activities across all interests and abilities. Children of all genders, with and without disabilities, should see themselves and their families, languages, and cultures regularly and meaningfully reflected in the environment and learning materials. Counter common stereotypes and misinformation. Remember that the learning environment and its materials reflect what you do and do not value by what is present and what is omitted.

5. **Involve children, families, and the community in the design and implementation of learning activities.** Doing this builds on the funds of knowledge that children and families bring as members of their cultures and communities while also sparking children's interest and engagement. Recognizing the community as a context for learning can model citizen engagement.

6. **Actively promote children's agency.** Provide each child with opportunities for rich, engaging play and opportunities to make choices in planning and carrying out activities. Use open-ended activities that encourage children to work together and solve problems to support learning across all areas of development and curriculum.

7. **Scaffold children's learning to achieve meaningful goals.** Set challenging but achievable goals for each child. Build on children's strengths and interests to affirm their identities and help them gain new skills, understanding, and vocabulary. Provide supports as needed while you communicate—both verbally and nonverbally—your authentic confidence in each child's ability to achieve these goals.

8. **Design and implement learning activities using language(s) that the children understand.** Support the development of children's first languages while simultaneously promoting proficiency in English. Similarly, recognize and support dialectal differences as children gain proficiency in the Standard Academic English they are expected to use in school.[6]

9. **Recognize and be prepared to provide different levels of support to different children depending on what they need.** For example, some children may need more attention at certain times or more support for learning particular concepts or skills. Differentiating support in a strengths-based way is the most equitable approach because it helps to meet each child's needs.

10. **Consider how your own biases (implicit and explicit) may be contributing to your interactions and the messages you are sending children.** Also reflect on whether biases may contribute to your understanding of a situation. How might they be affecting your judgment of a child's behavior, especially a behavior you find negative or challenging? What messages do children take from your verbal and nonverbal cues about themselves and other children? Recognize that all relationships are reciprocal, and thus that your behavior impacts that of children.

11. **Use multi-tiered systems of support.** Collaborate with early childhood special educators and other allied education and health professionals as needed. Facilitate each professional establishing a relationship with each child to foster success and maximize potential.

Establish Reciprocal Relationships with Families

1. **Embrace the primary role of families in children's development and learning.** Recognize and acknowledge family members based on how families define their members and their roles. Seek to learn about and honor each family's child-rearing values, languages (including dialects), and culture. Gather information about the hopes and expectations families have for their children's behavior, learning, and development so that you can support their goals.

2. **Uphold every family's right to make decisions for and with their children.** If a family's desire appears to conflict with your professional knowledge or presents an ethical dilemma, work with the family to learn more, identify common goals, and strive to establish mutually acceptable strategies.

3. **Be curious, making time to learn about the families with whom you work.** This includes learning about their languages, customs, activities, values, and beliefs so you can provide a culturally and linguistically responsive and sustaining learning environment. It requires intentionally reaching out to families who, for a range of reasons, may not initiate or respond to traditional approaches (e.g., paper and pencil/electronic surveys, invitations to open houses, parent–teacher conferences) to interact with educators.

4. **Maintain consistently high expectations for family involvement, being open to multiple and varied forms of engagement and providing intentional and responsive supports.** Ask families how they would like to be involved and what supports may be helpful. Families may face challenges (e.g., fear due to immigration status, less flexibility during the workday, child care or

transportation issues) that may require a variety of approaches to building engagement. Recognize that it is your responsibility as an educator to connect with families successfully so that you can provide the most culturally and linguistically sustaining learning environment for each child.

5. **Communicate the value of multilingualism to all families.** All children benefit from the social and cognitive advantages of multilingualism and multiliteracy. Make sure families of emergent bilinguals understand the academic benefits and the significance of supporting their child's home language as English is introduced through the early childhood program, to ensure their children develop into fully bilingual and biliterate adults.

Observe, Document, and Assess Children's Learning and Development

1. **Recognize the potential of your own culture and background affecting your judgment when observing, documenting, and assessing children's behavior, learning, or development.** Approach a child's confusing or challenging behavior as an opportunity for inquiry. Consider whether these may be behaviors that work well for the child's own home or community context but differ or conflict with your family culture and/or the culture of your setting. How can you adapt your own expectations and learning environment to incorporate each child's cultural way of being? Also, consider the societal and structural perspectives: How might poverty, trauma, inequities, and other adverse conditions affect how children negotiate and respond to their world? How can you help each child build resilience?

2. **Use authentic assessments that seek to identify children's strengths and provide a well-rounded picture of development.** For children whose first language is not English, conduct assessments in as many of the children's home languages as possible. If you are required to use an assessment tool that has not been established as reliable or valid for the characteristics of a given child, recognize the limitations of the findings and strive to make sure they are not used as a key factor in high-stakes decisions.

3. **Focus on strengths.** Develop the skill to observe a child's environment from the child's perspective. Seek to change what you can about your own behaviors to support that child instead of expecting the child to change first. Recognize that it is often easier to focus on what a child *isn't* doing compared with peers than it is to see what that child *can* do in a given context (or could do with support).

Advocate on Behalf of Young Children, Families, and the Early Childhood Profession

1. **Speak out against unfair policies or practices and challenge biased perspectives.** Work to embed fair and equitable approaches in all aspects of early childhood program delivery, including standards, assessments, curriculum, and personnel practices.

2. **Look for ways to work collectively with others who are committed to equity.** Consider it a professional responsibility to help challenge and change policies, laws, systems, and institutional practices that keep social inequities in place.

Recommendations for Administrators of Schools, Centers, Family Child Care Homes, and Other Early Childhood Education Settings

1. **Provide high-quality early learning services that demonstrate a commitment to equitable outcomes for all children.** Arrange budgets to equitably meet the needs of children and staff. Recognize that high-quality programs will look different in different settings because they reflect the values, beliefs, and practices of specific children, families, and communities.

2. **Take proactive steps with measurable goals to recruit and retain educators and leaders who reflect the diversity of children and families served and who meet professional expectations.** All children benefit from a diverse teaching and leadership staff, but it is especially important for children whose social identities have historically been marginalized to see people like them as teachers and leaders.

3. **Employ staff who speak the languages of the children and families served.** When many languages are spoken by the families served, establish relationships with agencies or organizations that can assist with translation and interpretation services. Avoid using the children themselves as translators as much as possible. Families may also be able to identify someone they are comfortable including in conversations.

4. **Ensure that any formal assessment tools are designed and validated for use with the children being assessed.** Key characteristics to consider include age, culture, language, social and economic status, and ability and disability. Assessors should also be proficient in the language and culture in which the assessment is conducted. If appropriate assessment tools are not available for all children, interpret the results considering these limitations.

5. **Recognize the value of serving a diverse group of children and strive to increase the range of diversity among those served.** Race, ethnicity, language, and social and economic status are some dimensions by which early childhood education settings have historically been segregated.

6. **Provide regular time and space to foster a learning community among administrators and staff regarding equity issues.** Include opportunities for all individuals to reflect about their own cultural attitudes and behaviors as well as to uncover and change actions that reflect implicit bias and microaggressions toward children, families, school staff, and administrators.

7. **Establish collaborative relationships with other social service agencies and providers within the community.** Support and give voice to diverse perspectives to strengthen the network of resources available to all children and families.

8. **Establish clear protocols for dealing with children's challenging behaviors and provide teaching staff with consultation and support to address them effectively and equitably.** To consider potential effects of implicit bias, regularly collect and assess data regarding whether certain policies and procedures, including curriculum and instructional practices, have differential impacts on different groups of children. Set a goal of immediately limiting and ultimately eliminating suspensions and expulsions by ensuring appropriate supports for teachers, children, and families.

9. **Create meaningful, ongoing opportunities for multiple voices with diverse perspectives to engage in leadership and decision making.** Recognize that implicit biases have often resulted in limited opportunities for members of marginalized groups. Consider and address factors that create barriers to diversified participation (e.g., time of meetings, location of meetings, languages in which meetings are conducted).

Recommendations for those Facilitating Educator Preparation and Professional Development

1. **Prepare current and prospective early childhood educators to provide equitable learning opportunities for all children.** Ensure that prospective educators understand the historical and systemic issues that have created structural inequities in society, including in early childhood education. Ensure that their preparation and field experiences provide opportunities to work effectively with diverse populations.

2. **Prepare prospective early childhood educators to meet the Professional Standards and Competencies for Early Childhood Educators** (formerly NAEYC's Professional Preparation Standards). Ensure that curriculum and field experiences reflect a focus on diversity, full inclusion, and equity within each of the competencies to cultivate culturally and linguistically responsive practices.

3. **Work with students, community leaders, and public officials to address barriers to educational attainment in the specific community you serve.** Pay special attention to assumptions about academic skill attainment in communities with inadequate public schools, transportation barriers (e.g., limited public transit), financial constraints (e.g., student loans, tuition balances, outstanding bookstore bills), course scheduling during the working day, lack of child care, and the like. Design educational programs that put students' needs first and take identified barriers into account while also working to remove those barriers (e.g., loan forgiveness programs, evening and weekend courses, extended bus or train service, child care services aligned with course and professional development offerings).

4. **Implement transfer and articulation policies that recognize and award credits for students' previous early childhood courses and degrees as well as demonstrated competency through prior work experience.** This will support a wide range of students in advancing their postsecondary credentials.

5. **Work actively to foster a sense of belonging, community, and support among first-generation college students.** Cohorts and facilitated support from first-generation graduates can be especially useful.

6. **Set and achieve measurable goals to recruit and retain a representative faculty across multiple dimensions.** Consider establishing goals related to race, ethnicity, age, language, ability and disability, gender, and sexual orientation, among others.

7. **Provide regular time and space to foster a learning community among administrators, faculty, and staff.** Create opportunities for reflection and learning about cultural respect and responsiveness, including potential instances of implicit bias and microaggressions toward both children and adults.

8. **Ensure that all professional standards, career pathways, articulation, advisory structures, data collection, and financing systems in state professional development systems are subjected to review.** Assess whether each of the system's policies supports workforce diversity by reflecting the children and families served and offering equitable access to professional development. Determine whether these systems serve to increase compensation parity across early childhood education settings and sectors, birth through age 8.

Recommendations for Public Policymakers

1. **Use an equity lens to consider policy impacts on all children and on the bonds between them and their families.** Work to change any policy that either directly or through unintended negative consequences undermines children's physical and emotional well-being or weakens the bonds between children and their families.

2. **Increase financing for high-quality early learning services.** Ensure that there are sufficient resources to make high-quality early childhood education universally accessible. Every setting should have the resources it requires to meet the needs of its children and families. This includes ensuring equitable access to high-quality higher education and compensation for a qualified workforce. See the NASEM report *Transforming the Financing of Early Care and Education* for more details.[7]

3. **Revise early learning standards to ensure that they reflect the culturally diverse settings in which educators practice.** Provide ongoing, in-depth staff development on how to use standards in diverse classrooms. Quality rating and improvement systems should further the principles of equity across all aspects of education, including curriculum, instruction, full inclusion, family engagement, program design, and delivery.

4. **Make sure policies promote the use of authentic assessments that are developmentally, culturally, and linguistically appropriate for the children being assessed and use valid and reliable tools designed for a purpose consistent with the intent of the assessment.** Assessments should be tied to children's daily activities, supported by professional development, and inclusive of families; they should be purposefully used to make sound decisions about teaching and learning, to identify significant concerns that may require focused intervention for individual children, and to help programs improve their educational and developmental interventions.

5. **Increase opportunities for families to choose early childhood programs that serve diverse populations of children.** Incentivize these choices and seek to provide supports such as transportation. These supports will help to reduce the segregation of programs (primarily by race, language, ability, and class), which reflects segregated housing patterns and fuels persistent discrimination and inequities.

6. **Include community-based programs and family child care homes in state funding systems for early childhood education.** Ensure that these systems equitably support community-based programs and engage community members and families in activist and leadership roles. Support the educators who work in community-based programs so they can meet high-quality standards while allowing families to choose the best setting for their needs.

7. **Ensure sufficient funding for, access to, and supports for children, teachers, and administrators to respond to children's behaviors that others find challenging.** Mental health supports and prevention-oriented interventions can help meet each child's needs, including mental health challenges, without stigmatization, and eliminate the use of suspensions and expulsions across all early childhood settings.

8. **Establish comparable compensation (including benefits) across settings for early childhood educators with comparable qualifications, experience, and responsibilities.** Focusing only on comparable compensation for those working in pre-K settings will deepen disparities felt by educators working with infants and toddlers, who are disproportionately women of color. Including educators working with infants and toddlers in compensation policies is a fundamental matter of equity.

9. **Incorporate the science of toxic stress and adverse childhood experiences (ACEs) into federal and state policies and programs.** Trauma-informed care and healing-centered approaches can support resilience and help mitigate the effects of toxic stress and ACEs, which affect children of all social groups but disproportionately affect children of marginalized groups.

10. **Promote national, state, and local policies that promote and support multilingualism for all children.** This can include funding for early learning dual-language immersion programs, early childhood educator professional development for teaching and supporting emergent bilinguals, and the inclusion of multi/dual language promotion in quality rating and improvement systems.

11. **Set a goal of reducing the US child poverty rate by half within a decade.** A 2019 National Academies of Sciences report provides a consensus approach to achieving this goal through specific policies such as supporting families' financial well-being and stability, ensuring universal child health insurance, and providing universal access to early care and education.[8]

The Evidence for this Position Statement

The recommendations are based on a set of principles that synthesize current early childhood education research through the lenses of equity and NAEYC's core values.[9]

Principles of Child Development and Learning

1. **Early childhood (birth through age 8) is a uniquely valuable and vulnerable time in the human life cycle.** The early childhood years lay the foundation and create trajectories for all later learning and development.[10, 11, 12]

2. **Each individual—child, family member, and early educator—is unique.** Each has dignity and value and is equally worthy of respect. Embracing and including multiple perspectives as a result of diverse lived experiences is valuable and enriching for all.

3. **Each individual belongs to multiple social and cultural groups.**[13] This creates richly varied and complex social identities (related to race, gender, culture, language, ability and disability, and indigenous heritage identities, among others). Children learn the socially constructed meanings of these identities early in life, in part by recognizing how they and others who share or do not share them are treated.[14, 15, 16, 17, 18, 19] Early childhood educators and early childhood programs in centers, homes, and schools play a critical role in fostering children's development of positive social identities.[20, 21, 22]

4. **Learning is a social process profoundly shaped by culture, social interactions, and language.**[23, 24] From early infancy, children are hardwired to seek human interaction.[25] They construct knowledge through their interactions with people and their environment, and they make meaning of their experiences through a cultural lens.[26, 27]

5. **Language and communication are essential to the learning process.** Young children who are exposed to multiple linguistic contexts can learn multiple languages, which carries many cognitive, cultural, economic, and social advantages.[28] This process is facilitated when children's first language is recognized as an asset and supported by competent speakers through rich, frequent, child-directed language as the second language is introduced.[29, 30, 31]

6. **Families are the primary context for children's development and learning.**[32] Family relationships precede and endure long after children's relationships with early childhood educators have ended. Early childhood educators are responsible for partnering with families to ensure consistent relationships between school and home. This includes recognizing families as experts about their children and respecting their languages.[33] It means learning as much as possible about families' cultures in order to incorporate their funds of knowledge into the curriculum, teaching practices, and learning environment.[34] It also means actively working to support and sustain family languages and cultures.[35] Finally, it means recognizing and addressing the ways in which early childhood educators' own biases can affect their work with families, to ensure that all families receive the same acknowledgment, support, and respect.[36]

7. **Learning, emotions, and memory are inextricably interconnected in brain processing networks.**[37] Positive emotions and a sense of security promote memory and learning. Learning is also facilitated when the learner perceives the content and skills as useful because of their connection to personal motivations and interests. Connections to life experiences and sense of mastery and belonging are especially important for young children.

8. **Toxic stress and anxiety can undermine learning.**[38] They activate the "fight or flight" regions of the brain instead of the prefrontal cortex associated with higher order thinking. Poverty and other adverse childhood experiences are major sources of toxic stress and can have a negative impact on all aspects of learning and development.[39, 40] Protective factors that promote resilience in the face of adversity include supportive adult-child relationships, a sense of self-efficacy and perceived control, opportunities to strengthen adaptive skills and self-regulatory capacity, cultural traditions, and sources of faith and hope.[41]

9. **Children's learning is facilitated when teaching practices, curricula, and learning environments build on children's strengths and are developmentally, culturally, and linguistically appropriate for each child.**[42, 43, 44, 45, 46, 47] That is, teaching practices, curricula, and learning environments are meaningful and engaging for every child and lead to challenging and achievable goals.

10. **Reflective practice is required to achieve equitable learning opportunities.** Self-awareness, humility, respect, and a willingness to learn are key to becoming a teacher who equitably and effectively supports all children and families.[48]

The Social-Cultural Context of Child Development and Learning

It is essential to understand that child development and learning occur within a social-cultural, political, and historical context.[49] Within that context, each person's experiences may vary based on their social identities and the intersection of these identities. Social identities bring with them socially constructed meanings that reflect biases targeted to marginalized groups, resulting in differential experiences of privilege and injustice.[50] These systems can change over time, although many have remained stubbornly rooted in our national ethos.

Traditionally, the dominant narrative in the United States—in our history, scientific research, education, and other social policy and media—has reflected the ways in which society has granted or denied privilege to people based on certain aspects of their identity. Whiteness, for example, confers privilege, as does being male. Other aspects of identity that society tends to favor with easier access to power structures include being able-bodied, US born, Christian, heterosexual, cisgender, thin, educated, and economically advantaged.[51] Conversely, other aspects of identity tend to be associated with societal oppression, experienced, for example, by those who are members of indigenous societies and those who do not speak fluent, standard English. By naming such privilege and acknowledging the intersection of privilege and oppression, the intent is not to blame those who have benefited, but to acknowledge that privilege exists and that the benefits are unfairly distributed in ways that must be addressed.

Dominant social biases are rooted in the social, political, and economic structures of the United States. Powerful messages—conveyed through the media, symbols, attitudes, and actions—continue to reflect and promote both explicit and implicit bias. These biases, with effects across generations, stem from a national history too often ignored or denied—including trauma inflicted through slavery, genocide, sexual exploitation, segregation, incarceration, exclusion, and forced relocation. Deeply embedded biases maintain systems of privilege and result in structural inequities that grant greater access, opportunity, and power to some at the expense of others.[52]

Few men enter the field of early childhood education, reflecting the historic marginalization of women's social and economic roles—which has had a particularly strong impact on women of color. Comprising primarily women, the early childhood workforce is typically characterized by low wages.[53] It is also stratified, with fewer women of color and immigrant women having access to higher education opportunities that lead to the educational qualifications required for higher-paying roles.[54] Systemic barriers limit upward mobility, even when degrees and qualifications are obtained.[55] As a result, children are typically taught by White, middle-class women, with women of color assisting rather than leading. Some evidence, especially with elementary-grade children, suggests that a racial and gender match between teachers and children can be particularly beneficial for children of color without being detrimental to other children.[56, 57, 58, 59]

The professional research and knowledge base is largely grounded in a dominant Western scientific-cultural model that is but "one perspective on reality and carries with it its own biases and assumptions."[60] These shortcomings of the knowledge base reflect the historical issues of access to higher levels of scholarship for individuals of color and the need to expand the pipeline of researchers who bring different lived experiences across multiple social identities. It is important to consider these biases and their impact[61] on all aspects of system delivery, including professional development, curriculum, assessment, early learning standards,[62] and accountability systems.

The research base regarding the impact of implicit bias in early childhood settings is growing.[63] Teachers of young children—like all people—are not immune to such bias. Even among teachers who do not believe they hold any explicit biases, implicit biases are associated with differential judgments about and treatment of children by race, gender, ability and disability, body type, physical appearance, and social, economic, and language status—all of which limit children's opportunities to reach their potential. Implicit biases also result in differential judgments of children's play, aggressiveness, compliance, initiative, and abilities. These biases are associated with lower rates of achievement and assignment to "gifted" services and disproportionately higher rates of suspension and expulsion, beginning in preschool, for African American children, especially boys. Studies of multiple racial and ethnic subgroups in different contexts point to the complexity of the implicit bias phenomenon, with different levels and types of bias received by different subgroups.[64] Children's expression of implicit bias has also been found to vary across countries, although some preference for Whites was found even in nations with few White or Black residents.[65]

By recognizing and addressing these patterns of inequity, society will benefit from tapping the potential of children whose families and communities have been systematically marginalized and oppressed. Early childhood educators, early learning settings, higher education and professional development systems, and public policy all have important roles in forging a new path for the future. By eliminating systemic biases and the structures that sustain them, advancing equity, and embracing diversity and inclusivity, we can strengthen our democracy as we realize the full potential of all young children—and, therefore, of the next generation of leaders and activists.

Conclusion

A large and well-established body of knowledge demonstrates that high-quality early childhood programs promote children's opportunities for lifelong success and that public investments in such programs generate savings that benefit the economy.[66] As a result, in the United States and around the world, leaders across all political persuasions are making greater investments in early childhood services with broad public support. But more remains to be done.

We must build on these investments and work to advance equity in early childhood education by ensuring equitable learning opportunities for all young children. This position statement outlines steps needed to (1) provide high-quality early learning programs that build on each child's unique set of individual and family strengths, cultural background, language(s), abilities, and experiences and (2) eliminate differences in educational outcomes as a result of who children are, where they live, and what resources their families have. All children deserve the opportunity to reach their full potential.

Acknowledgments

NAEYC appreciates the work of the Developmentally Appropriate Practice/Diversity and Equity Workgroup and the Early Learning Systems Committee, who participated in the development of this statement (asterisk denotes service in both groups): Elisa Huss-Hage (Chair),* Iliana Alanís,* Chris Amirault,* Amy Blessing, Garnett S. Booker III, Dina C. Castro,* Lillian Durán, Isauro M. Escamilla Calan,* Linda M. Espinosa, Kelly Hantak,* Iheoma U. Iruka, Tamara Johnson,* Sarah LeMoine, Megan Pamela Ruth Madison,* Ben Mardell, Lauren E. Mueller, Krista Murphy,* Bridget Murray,* Alissa Mwenelupembe,* Hakim Rashid, Aisha Ray, Jeanne L. Reid, Shannon Riley-Ayers,* Christine M. Snyder,* Jan Stevenson,* Crystal Swank,* Ruby Takanishi, Tarajean Yazzie-Mintz,* and Marlene Zepeda.

The workgroup and committee were primarily supported by staff members Barbara Willer, Lauren Hogan, and Marica Cox Mitchell. NAEYC also acknowledges the support of the Bainum Family Foundation toward this project. Finally, NAEYC thanks the many NAEYC members and others who provided input and feedback as this statement was developed.

Definitions of Key Terms

ability—The means or skills to do something. In this position statement, we use the term "ability" more broadly than the traditional focus on cognition or psychometric properties to apply across all domains of development. We focus and build on each child's abilities, strengths, and interests, acknowledging disabilities and developmental delays while avoiding ableism (see also *ableism* and *disability* below).

ableism—A systemic form of oppression deeply embedded in society that devalues disabilities through structures based on implicit assumptions about standards of physical, intellectual, and emotional normalcy.[67, 68]

agency—A person's ability to make choices and influence events. In this position statement, we emphasize each child's agency, especially a child's ability to make choices and influence events in the context of learning activities, also referred to as autonomy or child-directed learning.[69, 70]

bias—Attitudes or stereotypes that favor one group over another. **Explicit biases** are *conscious* beliefs and stereotypes that affect one's understanding, actions, and decisions; **implicit biases** also affect one's understanding, actions, and decisions but in an unconscious manner. Implicit biases reflect an individual's socialization and experiences within broader systemic structures that work to perpetuate existing systems of privilege and oppression. An **anti-bias** approach to education explicitly works to end all forms of bias and discrimination.[71]

classism—A systemic form of oppression deeply embedded in society that tends to assign greater value to middle and upper socioeconomic status and devalue the "working" class.

culture—The patterns of beliefs, practices, and traditions associated with a group of people. Culture is increasingly understood as inseparable from development.[72, 73] Individuals both learn from and contribute to the culture of the groups to which they belong. Cultures evolve over time, reflecting the lived experiences of their members in particular times and places.

disability and developmental delay—Legally defined for young children under the Individuals with Disabilities Education Act (IDEA), disabilities include intellectual disability; hearing, speech or language, visual, and/or orthopedic impairment; autism; and traumatic brain injury. Under IDEA, states define developmental delays to include delays in physical, cognitive, communication, social or emotional, or adaptive development. These legal definitions are important for determining access to early intervention and early childhood special education services. The consequences of the definition can vary based on the degree to which they are seen as variations in children's assets or the degree to which they are seen as deficits.[74] (See also *ableism* and *ability*, above.)

diversity—Variation among individuals, as well as within and across groups of individuals, in terms of their backgrounds and lived experiences. These experiences are related to social identities, including race, ethnicity, language, sexual orientation, gender identity and expression, social and economic status, religion, ability status, and country of origin. The terms *diverse* and *diversity* are sometimes used as euphemisms for *non-White*. NAEYC specifically rejects this usage, which implies that Whiteness is the norm against which diversity is defined.

equity—The state that would be achieved if individuals fared the same way in society regardless of race, gender, class, language, disability, or any other social or cultural characteristic. In practice, equity means all children and families receive necessary supports in a timely fashion so they can develop their full intellectual, social, and physical potential.

Equity is not the same as *equality*. Equal treatment given to individuals at unequal starting points is inequitable. Instead of equal treatment, NAEYC aims for equal opportunity. This requires considering individuals' and groups' starting points, then distributing resources equitably (not equally) to meet needs. Attempting to achieve equality of opportunity without considering historic and present inequities is ineffective, unjust, and unfair.[75]

equitable learning opportunities—Learning opportunities that not only help each child thrive by building on each one's unique set of individual and family strengths—including cultural background, language(s), abilities and disabilities, and experiences—but also are designed to eliminate differences in outcomes that are a result of past and present inequities in society.

funds of knowledge—Essential cultural practices and bodies of knowledge embedded in the daily practices and routines of families.[76]

gender identity—A social concept that reflects how individuals identify themselves. Traditionally viewed as a binary category of male/female linked to an individual's sex, gender identity is viewed by current science as fluid and expansive. **Cisgender** individuals develop a gender identity that matches their legal designation. **Transgender** individuals are those whose gender identity and/or expression differs from cultural expectations based on their legal designation at birth.[77]

historical trauma—"The cumulative emotional and psychological wounding over the lifespan and across generations, emanating from massive group trauma experiences."[78] Examples of historical trauma include the multigenerational effects of white supremacy reflected in colonization, genocide, slavery, sexual exploitation, forced relocation, and incarceration based on race or ethnicity.

inclusion—Embodied by the values, policies, and practices that support the right of every infant and young child and their family, regardless of ability, to participate in a broad range of activities and contexts as full members of families, communities, and society. The desired results of inclusive experiences for children with and without disabilities and their families include a sense of belonging and membership, positive social relationships and friendships, and development and learning to help them reach their full potential.[79] Although the traditional focus of inclusion has been on addressing the exclusion of children with disabilities, full inclusion seeks to promote justice by ensuring equitable participation of all historically marginalized children.[80]

intersectionality—The overlapping and interdependent systems of oppression across, for example, race, gender, ability, and social status. Intersectionality encourages us to embrace and celebrate individuals' multiple social identities. It also highlights the complex and cumulative effects of different forms of structural inequity that can arise for members of multiple marginalized groups.

LGBTQIA+—An acronym for lesbian, gay, bisexual, transgender, queer or questioning, intersex, asexual, and more, reflecting the expansive and fluid concepts of sexual orientation, gender identity, and gender expression.

marginalization—The process by which specific social groups are pushed to the edges or margins of society. Marginalized groups are treated as less important or inferior through policies or practices that reduce their members' economic, social, and political power.

microaggressions—Everyday verbal, nonverbal, or environmental messages that implicitly contain a negative stereotype or are in some way dehumanizing or othering. These hidden messages serve to invalidate the recipients' group identity, to question their experience, to threaten them, or to demean them on a personal or group level. Microaggressions may result from implicit or explicit biases. People who commit microaggressions may view their remarks as casual observations or even compliments and may not recognize the harm they can cause.[81]

norm, normative—The definition of certain actions, identities, and outcomes as the standard ("the norm" or "normal"), with everything else as outside the norm. For example, the terms *White normativity* or *heteronormative* refer to instances in which Whiteness and heterosexuality are considered normal or preferred. Such norms wrongly suggest that all other races and sexual orientations are outside the norm or are less preferable. Art activities focused on filling out a family tree, with designated spaces for "mommy," "daddy," "grandma," and "grandpa," for example, may assume a two-parent, heterosexual household as the normative family structure. (While some research-based norms provide guidance regarding healthy child development and appropriate educational activities and expectations, these norms have too often been derived through research that has only or primarily included nonrepresentative samples of children or has been conducted primarily by nonrepresentative researchers. Additional research, by a more representative selection of researchers and theorists, is needed to develop new norms that will support equitably educating all children.)

oppression—The systematic and prolonged mistreatment of a group of people.

privilege—Unearned advantages that result from being a member of a socially preferred or dominant social identity group. Because it is deeply embedded, privilege is often invisible to those who experience it without ongoing self-reflection. Privilege is the opposite of marginalization or oppression that results from racism and other forms of bias.

race—A social-political construct that categorizes and ranks groups of human beings on the basis of skin color and other physical features. The scientific consensus is that using the social construct of race to divide humans into distinct and different groups has no biological basis.[82]

racism—A belief that some races are superior or inferior to others. Racism operates at a systemic level through deeply embedded structural and institutional policies that have favored Whiteness at the expense of other groups. On an individual level, racism can be seen in both explicit and implicit prejudice and discrimination. Both individual and institutional acts of bias work to maintain power and privilege in the hands of some over others.[83]

resilience—The ability to overcome serious hardship or adverse experiences. For children, resilience is promoted through such protective factors as supportive relationships, adaptive skill building, and positive experiences.[84]

sexism—A belief that some gender identities are superior or inferior to others. Sexism operates at a systemic level through deeply embedded structural and institutional policies that have assigned power and prestige to cisgender men and caring and nurturing roles with little economic reward to cisgender women, to the detriment of all.

stereotype—Any depiction of a person or group of people that makes them appear less than fully human, unique, or individual or that reinforces misinformation about that person or group.

structural inequities—The systemic disadvantage of one or more social groups compared to systemic advantage for other groups with whom they coexist. The term encompasses policy, law, governance, and culture and refers to race, ethnicity, gender or gender identity, class, sexual orientation, and other domains.[85]

White fragility—A concept based on the observation that White people in North America and other parts of the world live in a social environment that protects and insulates them from race-based stress, heightening their expectations for racial comfort and lowering their ability to tolerate racial stress. Even small amounts of racial stress can be intolerable to White people and can trigger defensive actions designed to restore the previous equilibrium and comfort.[86]

xenophobia—Attitudes, prejudices, or actions that reject, exclude, or vilify individuals as foreigners or outsiders. Although often targeted at migrants, refugees, asylum seekers, and displaced persons, xenophobia is not limited to these individuals but may be applied to others on the basis of assumptions.

For endnote references, please visit **NAEYC.org/equity**

Introduction

Iliana Alanís, Iheoma U. Iruka, and Susan Friedman

> All children have the right to equitable learning opportunities that help them achieve their full potential as engaged learners and valued members of society. Thus, all early childhood educators have a professional obligation to advance equity. They can do this best when they are effectively supported by the early learning settings in which they work and when they and their wider communities embrace diversity and full inclusion as strengths, uphold fundamental principles of fairness and justice, and work to eliminate structural inequities that limit equitable learning opportunities.
>
> —NAEYC, "Advancing Equity in Early Childhood Education"

These opening words to NAEYC's "Advancing Equity in Early Childhood Education" position statement encapsulate what the early childhood education system must do to ensure the rights of all children to learn and thrive. The primary purpose of this book is to bring this position statement to life by showing how teachers, administrators, researchers, faculty, and the broader community can enact equity practices in daily life by addressing racial inequalities and social injustices that are systemic in every aspect of education (children's development and learning). To achieve this, we, the early childhood education community, must also understand our role within the bigger context of what social justice and equity means for everyone.

Advocating for Social Justice for All

Social justice is defined as the active promotion of a just society by challenging systemic and institutional racism, inequality, and oppression. In recent decades, the United States has experienced a major shift in the racial and ethnic makeup of the population of young children. In particular, US Census Bureau figures show a dramatic increase in the population of children of color (Ortman & Guarneri 2009). The US Census Bureau estimates now indicate that more than half of the children born in the United States are non-White and that young racially, ethnically, and linguistically minoritized children continue to rise in number. These estimates predict that by 2050 children from various racial and ethnic groups will no longer be the minority population. Projections indicate that the Latino/a population will more than double by 2050, while the Asian population is projected to increase by 79 percent (Ortman & Guarneri 2009). It is important to note that even in the absence of immigration, the size of the Latino/a population is expected to increase substantially. We have also seen fluctuations in the rates of children living in poverty. After a decline in child poverty rates to a low of 17 percent in 2000, we have seen a rapid rise in poverty following the recession and the loss of housing values (and wealth accumulation), especially for families of color.

During this recent history, much attention has been given to disparities in academic outcomes and measures of well-being of children in the population. In spite of the attention, little progress has been made in reducing the disparities for children of color, children from immigrant backgrounds, and children living in households and communities with low resources. The United States' ability to improve the outcomes and productivity of almost 50 percent of its future workforce (i.e., young children of color) is inextricably tied to its addressing institutional racism, oppression, and historical and contemporary trauma.

These changes in demographics coupled with the historical legacy of racism and discrimination still continue to impact Black, Native American, Latino/a, and Asian communities, revealing the urgency for early childhood teachers and administrators to analyze their ideologies, values, and motivations that enlighten their role as educators as well as the sociocultural politics they promote in the classroom. Through critical reflection, teachers recognize the power of their own agency in order to act upon such questions as

1. What notions of authority should structure teaching and learning?

2. Who should early education settings and schools serve?

3. How and why does race and ethnicity manifest in the classroom and teaching?

These questions compel educators to engage in a process of self-critique while simultaneously highlighting the central role they play in any viable attempt to develop equitable schooling. Through this process, educators gain the consciousness to interpret and address inequitable schooling events with ideological purpose and intentionality.

Advancing equity in early childhood education requires understanding the broader societal contexts and biases, and the ways in which historical and current inequities have shaped our education systems in the United States, as they have shaped our nation. Children, families, communities, and educators experience an uneven distribution of privilege and power that affects every aspect of their work and interactions with others. It is important for educators to understand that the schooling experiences of children may be qualitatively different depending on their culture, race, home language, ability, gender expression, or other aspects of identity. These differences can propel them down a path of insecurity and have a negative effect on their future accomplishments.

Vast research indicates that children benefit from qualified and reflective teachers who provide developmentally and linguistically appropriate, culturally relevant, responsive, and sustaining experiences and interactions in curricula and instruction (IOM & NRC 2015; NASEM 2017). Educators who have a strong understanding of the developmental nature of children's learning as well as the sociocultural and political aspects of learning are equipped to create effective and affirming environments, instructional activities, and assessments.

NAEYC's "Advancing Equity in Early Childhood Education" position statement challenges us to think critically about the care and education of young children in this country.

We come back to these words from the position statement that unequivocally state the responsibility we share in creating a society where equity is more than a lofty goal but a key aspect of the profession: "All children have the right to equitable learning opportunities. . . . All early childhood educators have a professional obligation to advance equity" (NAEYC 2019, 1).

About the Book

This compilation of work brings the voices of early childhood scholars and professionals to the forefront as we highlight their experiences and expertise to advance the movement toward more equitable early childhood education, systems, and practices. The information presented by the authors of these chapters expands on one or more recommendations from the position statement, recognizing that many recommendations are related and interconnected and align with NAEYC's revised "Developmentally Appropriate Practice" position statement and the revised "Standards and Competencies for Early Childhood Educators."

Collectively, the chapters in this text shed light on various pedagogical practices and policies that influence the educational experiences of generations of young children and their teachers. We have purposefully included pieces to extend the conversations related to equitable learning and teaching by emphasizing the past, present, and future of early childhood education. We include work from various scholars and educators across the United States, who advance equity on a daily basis in their work with children and families, preservice teachers, policymakers, and other key stakeholders. Grounded in theoretical frameworks and current research, the authors focus on the need to address historical ills and bias framing and negotiate paradigm shifts as we develop strategies and implement recommendations for equitable schooling. We value, respect, and affirm the diversity and intersectionality of children, families, and the educators who care for and teach them, and recognize that this book is unable to address all of the diversity, equity, and inclusion issues in early childhood. Rather, readers should see the chapters in this volume as the beginning, and not the end, of how the education field can implement the recommendations from the equity statement.

How the Book Is Organized

The book is organized in three parts.

Part 1: Reflections on Equity. This part is divided into two sections, "Section 1: Reflections on Ourselves" and "Section 2: Reflections on Our Profession." Section 1 is a compilation of personal responses to a questionnaire on equity from leaders in early childhood education (ECE), including NAEYC affiliate leaders and NAEYC Governing Board members. Section 2 is a collection of chapters that discuss past and current practices in ECE within equitable educational and professional contexts.

Part 2: Responsive Pedagogical Practices. The chapters included in this part focus on exemplary developmentally, culturally, and linguistically responsive pedagogical practices within diverse early childhood contexts.

Part 3: Moving Forward as a Profession. This part includes chapters that reveal and discuss shortcomings of a traditional monolithic professional knowledge base, opening a space for personal reflection and offering recommendations for administrators to support early childhood educators in this process, including recommendations for faculty within teacher preparation programs. Lastly, it provides a call to action for each of us to advocate for equitable policies that support the ECE system as a whole.

Each part begins with an introduction that gives an overview of the purpose of its collection of chapters. These introductions include broad reflection questions to promote a deeper connection to the work at an individual level.

Taking Up the Call

The focus on early childhood education across the United States, as well as globally, provides us with many opportunities to shape the future as we consider how educators are prepared with pedagogies that are anti-bias, culturally and linguistically responsive, and sustaining. Early childhood educators, administrators, faculty at institutes of higher education, researchers, and policymakers all play an important role in creating equitable spaces and systems for the future. Systemic changes are not possible without committed educators who understand the process of learning and the ramifications of inequitable schooling for young learners, their families, and the educators that serve them. The best teachers are those who are committed to continuing to learn about their academic areas, their students, and the world, and incorporate it in their practices and pedagogical approaches. Individual reflection and a willingness to learn are key to becoming an educator who effectively supports all children and families.

Note: Please see "Appendix: A Note on Terminology Used in this Book" for a list of key terms and explanations.

Reflection Questions

As you read the introduction and begin this book, we encourage you to reflect on the following questions:

1. How do you define *equity*?

2. What does it mean to ensure equitable learning opportunities for children?

3. What are the barriers to equitable learning opportunities?

4. What control, power, and privilege do you have to ensure that children are provided with equitable learning opportunities?

References

IOM (Institute of Medicine) & NRC (National Research Council). 2015. *Transforming the Workforce for Children Birth Through Age 8: A Unifying Foundation.* Report of the National Academies of Sciences, Engineering, and Medicine. Washington, DC: National Academies Press. doi:10.17226/19401.

NAEYC. 2019. "Advancing Equity in Early Childhood Education." Position statement. Washington, DC: NAEYC. www.naeyc.org /resources/position-statements/equity.

NASEM (National Academies of Sciences, Engineering, and Medicine). 2017. *Promoting the Educational Success of Children and Youth Learning English: Promising Futures.* Report. Washington, DC: National Academies Press. doi:10.17226/24677.

Ortman, J.M., & C.E. Guarneri. 2009. "United States Population Projections: 2000 to 2050." Washington, DC: US Census Bureau. www.census.gov/library/working-papers/2009/demo /us-pop-proj-2000-2050.html.

This part of the book is divided into two sections. "Section 1: Reflections on Ourselves" is a collection of personal reflections from educators, NAEYC affiliate leaders, and NAEYC Governing Board members on their own experiences with bias and racism, and how they work toward equity in their daily lives. Each responded to a series of questions about their backgrounds, experiences, and methods for working toward a more equitable early childhood education system.

"Section 2: Reflections on Our Profession" is a collection of chapters that provides historical and present-day contexts for early childhood education's role in anti-bias and anti-racist education. To begin this discussion and set the stage for the rest of the book, the first chapter in this part, written by Barbara Bowman, calls attention to how history helps to form the present and the future, and by ignoring the history one ignores the pain, trauma, and culture that make up the current experiences of children, families, and communities. For example, she provides a history of how African American English Vernacular (AAEV), or Black English, developed through the enslavement period. That is, AAEV was created by enslaved Africans who came from different tribes with different languages to help them communicate with each other. By dismissing Black English as less than disregards the pain and history of Black people and supports a deficit lens that views people speaking this language as unintelligent, though there is evidence that AAEV contains elements of many languages and is a language system (Craig et al. 2003; Washington & Craig 2002).

Reflection Questions

As you read the chapters in Part 1, we encourage you to reflect on the following questions:

1. How does history shape current and future practices in early childhood?

2. How has language changed to reflect a strengths-based perspective rather than a deficit perspective?

3. What vocabulary have educators incorporated into how they describe their teaching (such as *funds of knowledge* or *anti-racist teaching*) which reflect an evolving perspective?

References

Craig, H.K., C.A. Thompson, J.A. Washington, & S.L. Potter. 2003. "Phonological Features of Child African American English." *Journal of Speech, Language, and Hearing Research* 46 (3): 623–635. doi:10.1044/1092-4388 (2003/049).

Washington, J.A., & H.K. Craig. 2002. "Morphosyntactic Forms of African American English Used by Young Children and Their Caregivers." *Applied Psycholinguistics* 23 (2): 209–231. doi:10.1017/S0142716402002035.

SECTION 1
Reflections on Ourselves

CHAPTER 1
Looking Inward
Reflections from Early Education Professionals on Their Journey to Reduce Bias and Racism

Iheoma U. Iruka, with Anthony Broughton, Michael Gonzalez, Jillian Herink, Steven Hicks, Tamara Johnson, Jen Neitzel, Karen Nemeth, Nicol Russell, and Shannon Wanless

NAEYC's "Advancing Equity in Early Childhood Education" position statement provides a blueprint for what the early childhood education system needs to do to ensure that all children have access to high-quality, culturally affirming, and sustaining early learning experiences. This position statement also underscores how the broader societal context in the United States, including historical and current inequities, shape the field and the profession, as well as the nation. It also recognizes that educators cannot address inequities by trying to "fix" children and their families; rather the work must start with individuals looking inward:

> Our recommendations begin with a focus on individual reflection. Across all roles and settings, advancing equity requires a dedication to self-reflection, a willingness to respectfully listen to others' perspectives without interruption or defensiveness, and a commitment to continuous learning to improve practice. (NAEYC 2019, 5)

One of the first recommendations from the position statement is for everyone to

> Build awareness and understanding of your culture, personal beliefs, values, and biases. Recognize that everyone holds some types of bias based on their personal background and experiences. Even if you think of yourself as unbiased, reflect on the impacts of racism, sexism, classism, ableism, heterosexism,

xenophobia, and other systems of oppression affecting you and the people around you. Identify where your varied social identities have provided strengths and understandings based on your experiences of both injustice and privilege. (NAEYC 2019, 6)

For this chapter, the book editors asked a group of diverse early childhood education professionals to walk us through their journey of self-reflection about their roles and approaches in ensuring a more equitable early education system by answering a set of questions. The questions were designed to help the education professionals think more intentionally about these issues. In their answers, they talk about their own experiences with marginalization and privilege, provide some information about bias and how to become aware of and counter it, and share lessons to help others in their own journeys. The book editors encourage others to reflect on these questions as they engage in this work with their colleagues, friends, and other professional groups.

A note from the editors: The contributors and their contributions, which appear in alphabetical order, provide many perspectives on what equity means. We appreciate their reflections and candor as they help us understand their culture, personal beliefs, values, and biases. We also acknowledge their continual personal engagement with this important work.

The Questions

1. What is your area of work and expertise?

2. Why are you engaged in this work? What do you see as the outcome for children?

3. How do you define *equity*? What do you see as the markers of equity?

4. When did the issue of equity (and anti-bias/anti-racist education) become a focus of your work?

5. Are there particular incidents or experiences that made you more focused on the issue of equity? What privilege do you have and how does it play out in your work or daily experiences?

6. What tools or strategies do you use in your work or personal life that strengthen your knowledge and behavior regarding equity (and anti-bias/anti-racism)?

7. What, if anything, do you do to strengthen equity and counter anti-bias/anti-racism in your work?

8. Are there tools, strategies, workshops, or readings that you would suggest to early childhood professionals to strengthen their knowledge and skills in this area?

The Voices

Anthony Broughton, NAEYC Governing Board member (2020) and Interim Department Chair at Claflin University, School of Education

Michael Gonzalez, President of the Governing Board of the Texas Association for the Education of Young Children

Jillian Herink, Executive Director for the Iowa Association for the Education of Young Children

Steven Hicks, NAEYC Governing Board member (2020) and Assistant State Superintendent for the Division of Early Childhood at the Maryland State Department of Education

Tamara Johnson, NAEYC Governing Board member (2020) and Executive Director of the Malaika Early Learning Center

Jen Neitzel, Executive Director of the Educational Equity Institute

Karen Nemeth, Senior Training and Technical Specialist — DLL for the National Center on Early Childhood Development, Teaching, and Learning as part of Zero to Three

Nicol Russell, NAEYC Governing Board member (2020) and Vice President of Implementation Research for Teaching Strategies, LLC

Shannon Wanless, Associate Professor of Applied Developmental Psychology and Director of the Office of Child Development at the University of Pittsburgh's School of Education

For more information about these contributors, please see the Contributor List located in the front of the book.

Question 1: What is your area of work and expertise?

Anthony Broughton: My area of work is in equity and excellence in early childhood education and culturally responsive/sustaining pedagogies.

Michael Gonzalez: My area of work is in the early childhood field with professional development. My work began 20 years ago as a toddler teacher. My experiences as an administrator, parent, consultant, student, and educator made me who I am today and who I will become. I am now a coach for early childhood professionals in the Houston area.

Jillian Herink: Educational leadership is my area of expertise. Currently, my role is executive director for the Iowa Association for the Education of Young Children (Iowa AEYC). Prior to this position, I was the superintendent of the only Native American school in Iowa. In my educational leadership and teaching experience, I worked extensively with second language instructional practices and educational supports for least restrictive environments.

Steven Hicks: I oversee child care, mixed-delivery state pre-K, assessment, curriculum, Head Start Collaboration, early childhood advisory councils, Judy Center Early Learning Hubs, professional development and training, family engagement, early childhood systems, and

Maryland EXCELS, the quality rating and improvement system. Prior to that, I served as senior advisor on early learning at the US Department of Education and was an early childhood educator for 20 years.

Tamara Johnson: My areas of work and expertise are leadership, organizational development, and empowering people, all of which focus on work with children and families.

Jen Neitzel: I am engaged in providing professional development to educators on implicit bias, structural racism, and culturally responsive anti-bias practices through a practice-based coaching train-the-trainer framework. With this approach, the system is altered in a way that practices are sustained over time, and policies can be changed to support implementation. I also have become more focused on addressing systems change through a community organizing approach in which power is shared across community members to produce meaningful change that is sustained over time.

Karen Nemeth: I am an author, consultant, and subject matter expert on early childhood education for children who are dual language learners (DLLs). My masters in learning, cognition, and development focused on first and second language acquisition. I have published more than 40 articles on this topic and more than 10 books including edited volumes, two NAEYC books, e-books for families, an app, and children's storybooks. I currently work as the senior training and technical specialist — DLL for the National Center on Early Childhood Development, Teaching, and Learning.

Nicol Russell: Currently, I work as a leader and researcher for an early childhood educational technology company. My expertise is in early childhood programming and policy, with a passion for supporting administrators with their implementation practices.

Shannon Wanless: All of my work focuses on the intersection between scholarship and practice. The translation from research findings to implementation can raise new issues that require the expertise of practitioners and policymakers to adapt and transform recommendations to be successful in real-world contexts serving a wide range of people. I focus my work on trying to push the world toward being a place where young children and their important adults can thrive. This means using social-emotional competence and cultural responsivity to address our collective need for humanity in schools and communities. It also means focusing on building adult capacity to see racism, power, and

oppression happening in the systems they work in and to act to counter them. In Pittsburgh, like in many places, racial inequity is a major force driving the challenges children face in our city.

Question 2: Why are you engaged in this work? What do you see as the outcome for children?

Anthony Broughton: I have witnessed firsthand as a Black male the inequities that are pervasive in our national education system that continue to omit the diasporic literacies of Black people and people of color. I have grappled with my identity and have dealt firsthand with the miseducation that Dr. Carter G. Woodson articulated in his work. As a result of engaging in equity and social justice-oriented work, I envision *all* children having the opportunity to thrive as a result of liberatory teaching approaches, positive self-identity development, and curricula that center diasporic literacies.

Michael Gonzalez: It began with wanting to teach middle school. I chose early education as my degree focus and had to do lab assignments in a child care center. My professor, who was also the director of the lab school at the community college I attended, suggested it was easier for me to do my assignments there. I had a blast, as did the children, and my professor offered me a job. I saw the rewards of working in early childhood education and never left.

Jillian Herink: I am engaged in this work to help to create systems changes that will increase the education, skills, and stability of the early childhood workforce, which will in turn impact children during the most critical time of development, 0–8 years old.

Steven Hicks: I am driven by the belief that all children are entitled to the resources they need to achieve success in school and in life regardless of their economic status, ability, or language competency.

Tamara Johnson: I am engaged in this work because all children deserve excellence in education. Early education builds a solid foundation for educational and lifelong success.

Jen Neitzel: I became involved in equity work through my previous job at the Frank Porter Graham Child Development Institute, where I focused on the role of implicit bias in disciplinary practices for young children. As a result of this work, I became more engaged in educating myself about structural racism and white supremacy. With this knowledge, I was more committed to helping to disrupt the systems. Within an equitable education system, children and families have equal access to high-quality instruction, including resources, supports, and effective teaching. Outcomes for children of color within an equitable educational system include limited suspensions/expulsions, grade-level learning outcomes, increased knowledge about the history of our country, enhanced social-emotional competence, and positive racial identity. For White children, outcomes include positive racial identity, enhanced social-emotional competence, and increased knowledge about the history of our country. The goal is to eliminate the opportunity and achievement gaps, as well as to restructure the educational system so that social-emotional competence and positive racial identity become as much of a priority as learning outcomes.

Karen Nemeth: Throughout my career, I have worked with child care and preschool programs that serve increasingly diverse populations in terms of language and culture. When I first started this work, there was only one resource aimed specifically at teaching young children who are growing up in homes with two or more languages. Over the past 15 years, a growing body of research began to inform our practices, and I took on the role of listening to what teachers need and finding ways to translate the research into resources teachers can use effectively. To accomplish this, I built many partnerships and took active roles in several key organizations. As the population of children who are DLLs grew to about a third of young children, I knew that the field needed to make significant changes quickly to make sure these children could learn and develop toward a successful future. At the same time, research was revealing that many aspects of language and early literacy were not being adequately supported in preschool for any children—even monolingual children. I realized that we can accomplish two goals with one effort: by addressing the needs of the field to upgrade knowledge and skills to become effective teachers of children who are DLLs, we could leverage that increased knowledge and skill to improve supports for language and early literacy for *all* children.

Nicol Russell: I am engaged in this work because advancing equity is big, heavy work and it will require each of us doing our part to make it happen. In Hawaiian, we call this our *kuleana*, our responsibility, and it is simultaneously about the individual and the collective responsibilities we have. In this instance, it is our kuleana to advance equity and if we are successful, the outcome for children is a more fair and just society now and in the future.

Shannon Wanless: Children thrive when they are raised in the context of loving and responsive relationships where they feel safe, seen, heard, and connected. Although I continue to support adults so that they can have authentic and meaningful relationships with children, I have also come to realize that there are major systemic, structural, and intra/interpersonal barriers to adults being fully present and outwardly loving with children—and these often have to do with racism. So, I have embarked on a new learning path to understand what those barriers are, why they are present, and how to get rid of them. The less racial discrimination that adults experience, the more they will be available and have the resources to support their children's development.

Question 3: How do you define *equity*? What do you see as the markers of equity?

Anthony Broughton: I define *equity* as fairness in opportunities, access, interactions, treatment, and policies with a commitment to deconstructing systems that normalize oppression. Markers of equity would be the normalization of repudiating policies and practices that normalize oppression. In essence, markers would be a demonstration of moving beyond empathizing with issues of inequities toward responding and eradicating them.

Michael Gonzalez: I define *equity* as being equal or to be included. I hadn't really focused on it specifically until just last year—about how to include someone. Not to just be there, but how to participate and have inclusive resources and safe spaces.

Jillian Herink: I define *equity* as fair and impartial; it is when people have the same opportunities relative to their need. I think that markers of equity are the supports in place that align with needs and remove barriers. I believe these markers vary greatly depending on the situation and the need.

Steven Hicks: *Equity* is ensuring that all persons receive the supports they need to thrive, even if this does not mean equal distribution of resources. We can measure our success by looking at the metrics achieved. When one group does not achieve, we must recalibrate our actions.

Tamara Johnson: I define *equity* as being fair. To me the markers of equity include, but are not limited to, race, gender, class, sexuality, and age.

Jen Neitzel: To me, equity is when all the barriers to equal access have been removed; resources are distributed based on need (not property taxes); and policies and practices are altered to promote equitable outcomes for all children. Markers of equity include distribution of resources; access to high-quality instruction (including Advanced Placement courses, materials, and effective teachers); decreased suspension/expulsion rates; and equitable outcomes on grade-level measures across socioeconomic status and race/ethnicity. I also think that a huge marker of equity is in how we view children and families living in deep poverty, most of whom are Black because of the intersection of race and poverty in our country. When we can meet families where they are rather than where we think they should be (which is based on White norms), then we will be closer to equity. When we can engage families as one human being to another rather than "fixer" and "person needing to be fixed," we will be closer to equity. We must move out of the paternalistic way of thinking within education that has deep roots within the history of our nation. When we can begin to shift our way of thinking from a focus on present problems to healing the past, we will be closer to equity.

Karen Nemeth: For my own area of focus, I am constantly concerned with issues of equity that relate to language differences for young children, families, and early childhood educators. In that context, equity is about making sure that each child, family, and early childhood educator gets the support they need to succeed in ways that enable their full access to information and opportunities to express themselves. Every young child needs to learn content, concepts, and skills. It is our responsibility to make sure that language differences do not reduce a child's access to that learning. Also, we have a responsibility to build relationships with each and every family across cultural and language differences because that is critical to the success of each child. And, as programs are hiring an increasingly diverse workforce to meet the needs of the diverse population, we have a responsibility to support that workforce by celebrating their unique identities, cultural funds of knowledge, and linguistic assets.

Nicol Russell: In my mind, *equity* is both a noun and a verb. As a noun, equity is an outcome achieved when each person is able to access what they need without barriers put in place because of their identity, background, geographical location, social-economic status, or any characteristic. As a verb, equity is an ongoing process, alive and dynamic, looking for ways to make the world more just for all. This could be achieved through the destruction of barriers and/or through the creation of pathways (i.e., policies) to access the system in more fair ways.

Shannon Wanless: I define *equity* as all children and families having access to what they need to thrive. They may all need different things, and different amounts of those things, but whatever they need, it is available to them. In addition, systems in our communities (e.g., schools, health care, housing) should be set up with the goal of eliminating obstacles to thriving, rather than being solely focused on helping people deal with the realities of living with those obstacles. For example, we would not need as many behavioral consultants to support teachers in classrooms if the classrooms were set up to provide (1) children with adequate exercise, nutrition, a sense of safety and trust, and meaningful opportunities to play and learn; and (2) teachers with adequate professional development and resources to deliver effective instruction that is culturally and racially responsive and free of implicit and explicit bias. In such a world, we would have a school system that met our definition of equity: all children and families would have access to everything they needed to thrive at school.

Question 4: When did the issue of equity (and anti-bias/anti-racist education) become a focus of your work?

Anthony Broughton: The issue of equity became the focus of my work as a result of the development of my critical consciousness. I was immersed in critical scholarship while pursuing my doctorate in early childhood education and engaging with the Center for the Education and Equity of African American Students at the University of South Carolina. The work of scholars in the areas of critical race theory, African diasporic literacy, culturally relevant/sustaining pedagogies, and critical pedagogy jolted a great awakening in me that made me conscious of the ways that I was impacted mentally and physically by systemic racism through education. As a then kindergarten and first grade teacher, I embraced my ethical responsibility to attempt to interrupt systems of oppression that play out in early childhood education and throughout the American education system at large.

Michael Gonzalez: It began as early as my first year as a director with a corporate early childhood program. I was a male in the field, Hispanic, and my location was a school that was predominately Black. There were occasions when race was brought up. The early education center's parents and staff were mostly Black in multiple programs. A family who is White asked me once about working in a school where "all your kids and workers are Black." I wondered why. My answer was that we hire based on experience, customer service, and quality not their skin color. We accept anyone who wants to enroll in our program.

Jillian Herink: For me professionally, "equity" became a focus of my work in 2002 when I was a math teacher and had Latino/a students struggling to learn content due to language barriers. I was allowed to create a class for students who spoke Spanish as a primary language, and I began to instruct a math class utilizing both Spanish and English and working to create math classes where students speaking other languages as a primary language could succeed. For multiple years, I also served as the teacher for the least restrictive math class for students with disabilities, and I worked to build practices and incorporate strategies for all students that gave them equitable learning opportunities.

Steven Hicks: I grew up poor. There were times when we had no electricity, no gas, nor food except for what my mother could grow in our garden and cook as dinner in the fireplace, blackening all her pans. I ate the free lunch at school, my mother bought groceries with food stamps, and for many years, we did not have a car. My seven sisters have married immigrants, including legal residents and undocumented persons. My brothers-in-law are White, Latino, and Black. I was a harassed gay youth and wasn't able to marry my husband until it was made legal in California. Later, gay marriage became legal in the United States. For 20 years, I taught in South Central Los Angeles. I visited my students and families during home visits and saw how bias, racism, and injustice affect the development and learning of my Black and Brown students and undermine the ability of their parents to help them thrive.

Tamara Johnson: If I think back to before I began my career in early education, my lens of equity in education started in high school. I had gone to suburban schools just about my entire life, and early in my senior year I transferred to a public school. There was at least a two-year lag in the educational instruction and resources. I graduated early, but once I left and started working, I totally understood from that experience alone why life was different for people. Education is key to success in life.

Jen Neitzel: Equity became the main focus of my work about four years ago when I was employed at the Frank Porter Graham Child Development Institute at the University of North Carolina at Chapel Hill. I developed a greater awareness, not only about the current research, but also how systems work and the complexity of the problem. This is not going to be an easy fix, and I feel that we all must proceed with caution so that we are not perpetuating the problem through the implementation of Band-Aid interventions that do not address root causes. True equity work requires that we have a deep understanding of the issues as well as how we can be complicit in upholding the structures that ensure disparate outcomes for children and families.

Karen Nemeth: This part of the understanding of equity became an issue in my work more than 20 years ago as I observed so many classrooms where children from language backgrounds other than English were ignored, unengaged, or even bullied. I'll never forget visiting an infant care program where I watched caregivers respond enthusiastically when English-speaking babies attempted to say words but give no reaction to babies who were trying to say words in unfamiliar languages. I still can't forget the sadness of a bright young toddler clearly practicing their blossoming language skills with such openness and promise, only to be met with blank stares and silence. I heard a master teacher in a program with 95 percent Spanish speakers insist that she did not know any Spanish and she didn't intend to learn. Many more early childhood educators express motivation and concern but are not sure what is the best way to teach young children who are DLLs. This cannot persist in our field.

Nicol Russell: For me, the issues of equity and anti-racist/anti-bias education have always been present in my work. As a woman of color who grew up in a multiracial household in an Indigenous, rural community where markers of poverty were ever-present, these same issues affected everything from where I lived to how I was educated. So even before I became an educator, I was determined to let my experiences be integral to how I developed as a professional. Along my professional journey, I could often be counted on to ask, "And what about these children?"—*these children* being children from Indigenous families, children with disabilities, children in poverty, children from single family households—in discussions about early childhood education. These could be discussions about policymaking, funding, access, quality improvement, workforce development, and more. In my mind, my responsibility was to bring voice to whoever's voice(s) I felt were not being heard.

Shannon Wanless: I have always been drawn to and aware of the major role that culture plays in the way children perceive others and the way others perceive them. As a sociology major and a lover of travel, I was fascinated by cultures that were not my own, but I did not have the tools or awareness to turn that interest on understanding myself and my own positionality. For most of my life, I did not consider how the historical and contemporary power dynamics in a society can create injustices that my own White culture taught me to ignore—and taught me to create counternarratives around when I was confronted with injustice.

Three years ago, I began to partner with a dynamic team at the Office of Child Development, which has now become the P.R.I.D.E. (Positive Racial Identity Development in Early Education) Team, led by Dr. Aisha White. They were talking about how children's racial identities develop and how to create supports for families and educators who want to support positive racial identity development for young Black children. Being part of this team, and simultaneously being exposed to race-focused speakers brought in by my School of Education's Center for Urban Education, gave me many learning opportunities to begin to see my work with a racialized lens.

Question 5: Are there particular incidents or experiences that made you more focused on the issue of equity? What privilege do you have and how does it play out in your work or daily experiences?

Anthony Broughton: I still grapple with the dominance of Eurocentric worldviews, values, and perspectives in the field of early childhood education—and education as a whole. I am exhausted with seeking diasporic literacies to embed in the curriculum that were stolen and destroyed by European colonizers while simultaneously advocating for representation, access, and other educational professionals to see the possibilities of *all* children. When I entered the profession as a Black man in early childhood education, I experienced many microaggressions and, in some cases, racist statements that insinuated that I was incompetent to work in early childhood. Some people interrogated, "Why would a male want to work with young children?" I ignored their comments in many instances and retorted in some instances because I understood the necessity of young children being exposed to Black male educators at an early age in a White female dominated field. My privilege as a Black male plays out every day because while I fight for equity daily, I'm confronted with issues of equity on a daily basis. For instance, after a long day teaching, I wonder if I will be viewed as a suspect as I jog in my neighborhood. Will they know I'm an educator? Being a male in education comes with the privilege of being perceived as strong and dominant, and in some instances a commodity because we are rare. However, that privilege is often weaponized against Black men in early childhood settings.

Michael Gonzalez: I would go back to the examples given on question 4, but personally, it was with my stepfather. He wasn't my biological father, but he was my dad. He accepted my brother and me with no questions asked. He would make comments about Black people and race. Now he grew up in Diboll, Texas, and it was quite common there. He did, however, outgrow this attitude as we his children (three of us) began dating and didn't think about the color of the other person's skin. However, it did worry me when I would bring my date to the house and see how he would react. I guess for me, my privilege has been that I ignored my environment and focused on people and their personalities. How we got along. But, of course, as I grew up and worked, I saw there was bias. For example, I worked in retail, and we would watch for people in big pants and ball caps and check their bags to see if they were stealing. We had a bias on the way certain people dressed, even though we knew that anyone can steal. I really had to step back sometimes and just ask myself what I was thinking and if it was right.

Jillian Herink: I have several incidents as a parent and as an educator. I am the parent of a child with Asperger syndrome, I taught many students that had limited English proficiency, and I was an administrator at the only Native American school, all of which gave me different experiences with inequity, prejudice, racism, and systematic barriers.

I myself am White, English speaking, college educated, and middle class. I grew up with two married parents in stable household, no alcoholism or domestic abuse, and I grew up in a White neighborhood. I had limited experiences with people that had many barriers. As a teenager, I began to work with children and young adults who had disabilities, either mental or physical. From that work, I decided that I needed and wanted to find out and understand what others were up against and what their barriers were. I am still learning.

Steven Hicks: See my answer to question 4. I'm male, White, and make over $100K. I have more privilege than 95 percent of the planet. I have an obligation to use my privilege to advance the livelihood of others in my neighborhood, state, country, and world.

Tamara Johnson: See my answer to question 4. I believe my privilege is that I am the fair-skinned young lady who is well spoken and quiet. How this plays out in my work experiences is that I tend to be the one that others look to first to participate or speak on behalf of groups.

Jen Neitzel: Engaging in equity work requires a certain level of self-reflection so that we can develop greater awareness about our own experiences, including why we do the work that we do and how we are complicit in upholding the structures that advantage White children and families. White people, in particular, must be intentional in unlearning their "Whiteness." Otherwise, their good intentions lead to paternalism, White saviorism, and an ignorance about how their behaviors and decisions are counterproductive to equity work. As a White, middle-class woman, I have an enormous amount of privilege and power just because of the color of my skin. Through my work, I have become more aware of how White people operate within systems in ways that uphold power structures and dynamics. We White people have a tendency to take up all of the oxygen in the room and leave little room for other opinions or solutions. Because of this, I am very intentional in my interactions with Black colleagues, particularly Black women, so that I engage in more listening and waiting before inserting myself into the discussion. I think that I have a responsibility to make space for those who often do not have their voices heard simply because of the way in which our culture has operated for centuries. In addition, I feel that I have an obligation to walk behind or beside, but not in front of, people of color who also are engaged in this work. There is a deep need for true collaboration and relationship building so that we also can create equitable workspaces where all voices are heard and listened to. Finally, I feel that I have an obligation to use my privilege to elevate more people of color throughout my life. Because of my privilege, I have access to spaces that many of my colleagues, particularly those who have had lived experiences, cannot access because of structural racism. I can use my privilege to open doors and bring my Black and Brown friends along with me. We White people working in education have much work to do. It is not enough to be "woke." We must all be committed to engaging in deep self-reflection about how our White

fragility plays out in our daily lives (e.g., talking over Black colleagues), how we engage in paternalism and White saviorism (e.g., having all of the answers, implementing Band-Aid interventions), and how our actions are driven by White guilt and shame. Without this, we are in danger of being complicit in upholding the status quo.

Karen Nemeth: In order to confront these inequities and find new ways to support change, I work continuously on my own biases and experiences. This is not a one-workshop kind of work! As I have worked on participating and collaborating throughout the field, I have heard so many different perspectives about what really is developmentally appropriate practice and how that may vary across states, cultures, and countries. I have a particular area of privilege because I grew up as a White child in a suburb of New York City with a mother who was a lifelong early childhood educator with her background from Bank Street College. I am aware that I make assumptions about early childhood education and family life that are not available or comfortable for everyone.

Nicol Russell: Experience 1: I spoke multiple languages (Hawaiian, English, and Hawaiian Pidgin English), and it significantly affected how I was treated by teachers who had lower expectations for Indigenous, Black, and other non-White or non-Asian students.

Experience 2: I was raised in a financially poor family in a financially poor community. The lack in access to basic necessities I experienced made me want to be sure to always think about like students I was teaching. I specify the kind of poorness I experienced because it isn't as if I feel my childhood lacked anything important like love, kindness, joy, or memorable experiences. Rather, it is the kind that happens when greed and capitalism put basic necessities out of reach for the working poor.

Experience 3: My mother died when I was 14 years old. We watched her suffer from the effects of pancreatic cancer, cared for her while my father worked a graveyard shift to keep us from being even poorer, and then had to cope with the grief of living without her. I think about children experiencing that kind of life-altering trauma and grief and the kinds of supports they need—the kind I needed and didn't get—from their teachers and schools. More equity means they get support too.

As an adult, I know I have privilege now that I've never had before. I have multiple degrees that have given me access to employment opportunities I never would have had without them. I am privileged with status as an "expert" based on this education and these work experiences. Each day, I bring that privilege to my work as a researcher. As an employee of a well-known, frequently used publisher of early childhood curriculum and assessment resources, my privilege allows me opportunities to influence what is taught to teachers and administrators and what they, in turn, teach children. I recognize that it is a tremendous responsibility and take it seriously as I help shape the lens through which our research is conducted.

Shannon Wanless: There was not one particular incident or experience, but the culmination of many happenings at once through my involvement with the P.R.I.D.E. team. First, as part of this racially diverse team and with an increasing number of Black colleagues in my School of Education, I had the opportunity to get to hear their stories of being Black, particularly in Pittsburgh. Those relationships seem very honest and open to me and they are helping me see the world from a new perspective, including my own role in it. Second, as part of my work on P.R.I.D.E., our team had the opportunity to dig deeper into US history, and I learned for the first time how many repeated and extreme events kept Black people from thriving in this country. The frequency and intensity and intentionality were honestly shocking and there was no way to look away from it and from the resulting inequities and injustices we see today. The more I recognize my own White privilege, the more I see how my experiences and interactions are so different (easier, less stressful, bending toward health, educational and economic success) than those of people of color. And that level of "seeing" gives me a constant reminder that none of this is fair and I need to be vigilant about creating ways to counter that unearned privilege at every turn.

Question 6: What tools or strategies do you use in your work or personal life that strengthen your knowledge and behavior regarding equity (and anti-bias/anti-racism)?

Anthony Broughton: I read scholarship that focuses on critical race theory, African diasporic literacy, culturally relevant/sustaining pedagogies, and critical pedagogy. I also engage in self-reflection and self-discovery activities.

Michael Gonzalez: I use a lot of Jon Gordon books that inspire me to be positive and not let any negative energy consume me. The books never talk about race, but they do talk about how to not let negativity bring you down ("I *get* to be here today not *have* to") and think about things I am grateful for. With COVID-19, it was a loss of my job, but I was able to spend so much time with my family. We went on nature walks and spent so much time outdoors away from others. This is something that we would have never done without us being at home and on unemployment. They were great times.

Jillian Herink: I commit to listen and seek to understand. I have also taken several trainings (and continue to) so that I can improve my own actions and make the organization more inclusive and supportive. I am currently working to embed reflective practices for myself, my staff, and my board. We are examining and strengthening our knowledge and behaviors regarding diversity, equity, and inclusion. We are looking to improve our policies and practices in continuous pursuit of our goal to become a high-performing, inclusive organization (HPIO).

Steven Hicks: I think I get most of my strength from my husband. We are aligned in our understanding of anti-bias/anti-racism but are able to challenge and hold each other accountable. My family, too, is my touchstone. We are 30 strong, and these issues are part of our weekly Sunday calls, our daily WhatsApp texts, and the books we share, like *How to Be an Antiracist*. At work, I decided six months in that we needed to build a common understanding around race and equity. For eight months, 45 members of my 220-person staff went on a journey together under the guidance of the Mid-Atlantic Equity Consortia to build a common understanding amongst ourselves so we could then expand it to the rest of our staff, dig deeper, and integrate that understanding into our work with families and providers. Our family engagement summits in Maryland for early childhood teachers and administrators have been focused for the last two years on implicit bias and equity. We have also integrated the NAEYC's position statement on advancing equity into our grant making.

Tamara Johnson: Self-reflection. I am also a very curious person and I take time to read and learn things that I don't know or feel like I/everyone should know and understand.

Jen Neitzel: I read all of the time. I make sure that I am reading mostly Black authors. I watch documentaries (e.g., *13th, Toni Morrison: The Pieces I Am*). I watch movies and television (e.g., *32, Selma, When They See Us*). I engage in a near-constant state of self-reflection. Most importantly, I make sure that I am proximate to the individuals who are most affected by inequitable policies and practices. I volunteer in high-poverty, mostly Black schools. I work with community advocates and activists who are working toward change in mostly Black, high-poverty neighborhoods. We cannot understand the problems or the solutions unless we get proximate. Otherwise, the children and families we are trying to help are just statistics.

Karen Nemeth: I have actively sought out work in areas that help me learn all the ways that young children and families and early childhood educators experience early learning. I have worked with migrant Head Start programs, programs that serve refugee families, rural programs, high-risk urban programs, and in other countries.

I pay attention to a lot of data and demographic reports to keep in mind and to share the complexities of working with children, families, and staff that speak different languages. This helps to elevate the discussions to understand people who speak Spanish, for example, are not all the same. People have experiences with trauma, uncertainty, physical and mental health, and prejudice in addition to their language differences. I regularly rewatch Chimamanda Ngozi Adichie's TED Talk on the dangers of one story. I work hard on getting past the practice of lumping all children who are DLLs into one group that can be addressed with one set of strategies. For myself and for my audience, I highlight the importance of building a respectful, mutual relationship with each child and with each family. I believe that early childhood education must start not with a curriculum for all but with a relationship with each child and family, then adapting and using a flexible and responsive curriculum to give every child access to what they need.

Nicol Russell: I read a lot by Indigenous and Black authors, and I think even more about what I read. I follow Indigenous, Black, Latino/a, and Asian educators, researchers, leaders on social media. I engage in conversations with these folks because I believe you cannot talk about anti-bias and anti-racism without hearing straight from those most affected by bias and racism. As people intensify the talk about principles and behaviors, I never want to lose sight of the people.

Shannon Wanless: I have been lucky to be able to bring a social justice and equity learning agenda to my office, including monthly trainings, a shared resource library, and one-on-one consultation with outside experts. This initiative creates constant opportunities to learn on a regular basis, generates a community of learners so we can grapple together, and holds me accountable for staying focused on my own learning so that I can share

with others. Personally, I have also joined a number of listservs, social media sites, and other subscription services that are generated by people of color to ensure that there are constant reminders in my inbox to learn from people with perspectives different from my own.

Question 7: What, if anything, do you do to strengthen equity and counter anti-bias/anti-racism in your work?

Anthony Broughton: I embrace intersectionality because it helps others and me identify connections between phenomena, concepts, and experiences. Additionally, engaging in courageous conversations with others helps me to name my realities and to work through them while learning from other perspectives. I am able to resist oppressive and deficit frameworks by having the courage to speak out against them.

Michael Gonzalez: Lately it has been to sit down with colleagues and just talk about random topics related to racism. We begin with an understanding that we are in a safe space and no matter what is discussed in this space, it's to educate ourselves. For example, we discussed the question, *How do you feel about football players kneeling during the anthem?* We learned that some took offense because they have family in the military while others agreed with it because it is recognized as a freedom, and we still have work to do. We understand the situation better.

Jillian Herink: I have changed the type of speaker we engage with for our events and diversified the topics. I have promoted board-supported equity statements, and we are reviewing both policies and practices. In April 2018, we held the Iowa AEYC Spring Leadership Institute, which focused on equity, diversity, and inclusion with several groups, including speakers representing the aging population, members of the LGBTQIA+ community, people with disabilities, and a business leader who was also an immigrant. The keynote that began our day included an overview of equity, diversity, and systematic racism. I have scheduled—and we have now started—staff and board equity training so that we all have some baseline knowledge, and we will be assessing policies for equitable and inclusive practices.

Steven Hicks: We have recently completed our five-year strategic plan, *Maryland Ready: A Path to School Readiness and Success*, and are now developing equity-based metrics to hold us accountable for the work we do with families, children, and providers.

Tamara Johnson: First and foremost, I speak up. I also am okay with making unpopular, innovative, and/or courageous decisions.

Jen Neitzel: In my work, I do a lot of trainings on implicit bias and structural racism. I think the biggest issue is helping people move from viewing racism as just individual to structural. A focus on individual racism allows White people to deflect and deny racism's existence. I like to walk workshop participants through the timeline of the educational system so that they can see the roots of the inequities and understand how racism has morphed over time, which makes it really easy to pretend that it does not exist. In my actual workspaces, I work to ensure that I am one of the only White people in the room. I think that true equity work will only occur when White people step aside and let those who are and have been most affected by racism lead the way.

Karen Nemeth: One thing I did to counteract inequities is that I asked for the opportunity to write DLL adaptations for every issue of *Teaching Young Children*. I did this first as a volunteer and later as a paid author. This meant that every issue of this magazine made it clear that teachers need intentional alternatives to traditional guidance and strategies. I have taken on bestselling authors and Harvard professors as well. When they write about best practices for young children and say nothing about DLLs, I call them out on it. And when they reply that they "were just writing about children in general" or they "didn't have enough space to cover everything," I say that's not good enough because we can't afford to ignore equitable access to learning for fully one-third of our population of young children!

Nicol Russell: I stay open to having my thinking and perspective challenged. I recently had a colleague ask me if I'm just talking the talk or am I willing to walk the walk. That kind of feedback pushes me to be action-oriented and to be mindful of paying lip service.

Shannon Wanless: I recently transitioned into my role as director and have taken time to learn about what it would mean to have an equitable and anti-racist workplace. This has meant (1) looking carefully at staff salaries, promotions, resource allocations, and performance appraisals, by race; (2) identifying other offices as examples of anti-racist policies and mission/vision statements; and (3) seeking outside consultants and resources that help our leadership team become more aware of how to cultivate equity in each of their divisions.

I also continue to work as a professor and researcher in the School of Education. It has taken some time to think about how to integrate racial equity and anti-racism into my teaching and scholarship because it was hard to see what my role as a White woman was in this work. Over time, it is becoming clearer, and I am shifting my syllabus and research agenda to have a major focus on racial equity. My immediate reaction to learning about racism was to figure out how to help Black children who were struggling to survive discrimination and prejudice. Now, however, I have shifted my thinking to consider how I can shift resources and support to lift up Black leaders who work with Black children, and how I can more visibly work with White women (my own identity) to develop their capacity to see and act against racism.

Question 8: Are there tools, strategies, workshops, or readings that you would suggest to early childhood professionals to strengthen their knowledge and skills in this area?

Anthony Broughton: The following represents a small sample of works I reference when I conduct workshops on Culturally Relevant Pedagogy in Early Childhood: *The Dreamkeepers: Successful Teachers of African American Children*, by Gloria Ladson-Billings (Jossey-Bass, 1994); *Educating African American Students: And How Are the Children?* by Gloria Swindler Boutte (Routledge, 2015); *Evidence-Based Approaches to Becoming a Culturally Responsive Educator: Emerging Research and Opportunities*, by Anthony Broughton (IGI Global, 2019); *We Want to Do More than Survive: Abolitionist Teaching and the Pursuit of Educational Freedom*, by Bettina L. Love (Beacon Press, 2020); *The Mis-Education of the Negro*, by Carter G. Woodson (The Associated Publishers, 1933); *The Brilliance of Black Boys: Cultivating School Success in the Early Grades*, by Brian L. Wright, with Shelly L. Counsell (Teachers College Press, 2018); *Critical Pedagogy Primer*, by Joe L. Kincheloe (Peter Lang, 2004); and works by Christopher Emdin, who inspired my work.

Michael Gonzalez: I would recommend Risha Grant. She attended the American Society of Association Executives conference this year, and in just 25 minutes put it all out there for people to have a conversation afterwards. She starts the conversation, and the group finishes it. It wasn't just about Black Lives Matter, but more about education for all. What in your life caused you to be judgmental? Was it your parents or an incident? Whatever it is, learn how and why and gain an understanding about yourselves.

Jillian Herink: I am no expert, and I am always looking for strategies myself, but I feel like an organization needs to branch out beyond typical partnerships and work with refugee and minority-based organizations to work and collaborate with. I think staff should take their own implicit bias assessments, like the Harvard ones, to see where they are at and go through some training. I think the Doll Test is good for people to see or read about as well as information about bias in preschoolers and expulsion information. I believe that for many people, book studies are a great tool for strengthening skills and participating in discussion. A book I recommend is *You Can't Celebrate That! Navigating the Deep Waters of Social Justice Teaching*, by Nadia Jaboneta (Redleaf Press, 2019). I also believe that much of this learning is personal and that there needs to be options for people. As an agency, we are taking part of localized efforts, which I also recommend. Here is an example of one such effort: www.eddiemoorejr.com/21daychallenge. My largest recommendation for any strategy is that whatever is done is ongoing and embedded in agency/program practice.

Steven Hicks:

> *Anti-Bias Education for Young Children and Ourselves*, Second Edition, by Louise Derman-Sparks and Julie Olsen Edwards, with Catherine M. Goins (NAEYC, 2020)

> Guide for Selecting Anti-Bias Children's Books: www.teachingforchange.org/selecting-anti-bias-books

> *Other People's Children: Cultural Conflict in the Classroom*, by Lisa Delpit (The New Press, 2006)

> *How to Be an Antiracist*, by Ibram X. Kendi (One World, 2019)

> *Each and Every Child: Teaching Preschool with an Equity Lens*, edited by Susan Friedman and Alissa Mwenelupembe (NAEYC, 2020)

Tamara Johnson: Dr. Sharroky Hollie's workshops, or anything he facilitates. Also the books *For White Folks Who Teach in the Hood . . . and the Rest of Y'all Too: Reality Pedagogy and Urban Education*, by Christopher Emdin (Beacon Press, 2017) and *White Fragility: Why It's So Hard for White People to Talk About Racism*, by Robin DiAngelo (Beacon Press, 2018).

Jen Neitzel: These are some of the resources that I reference for my work, self-reflection, motivation, and approach:

> "Becoming a Culturally Responsive Early Childhood Educator: A Tool for Support Reflection by Teachers Embarking on the Anti-Bias Journey," by Dora W. Chen, John Nimmo, and Heather Fraser (*Multicultural Perspectives* Vol. 11, No. 2, 2009)

> *How to Teach Students Who Don't Look Like You: Culturally Relevant Teaching Strategies*, by Bonnie M. Davis (Corwin Press, 2007)

> *Anti-Bias Education for Young Children and Ourselves*, Second Edition, by Louise Derman-Sparks and Julie Olsen Edwards, with Catherine M. Goins (NAEYC, 2020)

> *Culturally Responsive Teaching: Theory, Research, and Practice*, by Geneva Gay (Teachers College Press, 2000)

> *Raising White Kids: Bringing Up Children in a Racially Unjust America*, by Jennifer Harvey (United Methodist Publishing House, 2017)

> "Becoming Culturally Responsive Educators: Rethinking Teacher Education Pedagogy," by Cathy Kea, Gloia D. Campbell-Whatley, and Heraldo V. Richards (National Center for Culturally Responsive Educational Systems, 2006)

> *The Dreamkeepers: Successful Teachers of African American Children*, by Gloria Ladson-Billings (Jossey-Bass, 1994)

> *Roots and Wings: Affirming Culture and Preventing Bias in Early Childhood*, by Stacey York (Redleaf Press, 2016)

Karen Nemeth: There are many tools, strategies, and readings to strengthen knowledge and skill in the area of equitable early childhood education for children who are DLLs. I have created a lot of these resources and posted many on my website (www.languagecastle.com). Some of the best data and demographic reports come from Migration Policy Institute. Two helpful websites are www.colorincolorado.org and https://eclkc.ohs.acf.hhs.gov. I recommend the following critical teaching strategies:

> Reduce or eliminate whole group instruction. It is not often possible to respond to the needs or ensure comprehension for children who are DLLs in large groups. Replace these with small group or individual interactions.

> Support home languages in meaningful ways that help children understand the content and vocabulary of what is to be learned.

> Reduce teacher talk and give children more opportunities to do the talking during meaningful conversations with adults and peers in any of their languages.

> Update the displays and learning materials available to make sure they are actively used to build each child's sense of belonging and relevance and to support linguistically responsive and developmentally appropriate learning.

Nicol Russell:

> *Stamped: Racism, Antiracism, and You*, by Jason Reynolds and Ibram X. Kendi (Little, Brown and Company, 2020)

> *Bury My Heart at Wounded Knee: An Indian History of the American West*, by Dee Brown (Holt, Rinehart and Winston, 1970)

> *An Indigenous Peoples' History of the United States*, by Roxanne Dunbar-Ortiz (Beacon Press, 2015)

> *Decolonizing Methodologies: Research and Indigenous Peoples*, by Linda Tuhiwai Smith (Zed Books, 2012)

> *Kanaka ʻŌiwi Methodologies*, edited by Katrina-Ann R. Kapāʻanaokalāokeola Nākoa Oliveira and Erin Kahunawaikaʻala Wright

> Critical Practices for Anti-Bias Education: Teacher Leadership: www.tolerance.org /professional-development/critical-practices -for-antibias-education-teacher-leadership

> "Do Early Educators' Implicit Biases Regarding Sex and Race Relate to Behavior Expectations and Recommendations of Preschool Expulsions and Suspensions?" by Walter S. Gilliam, Angela N. Maipin, Chin R. Reyes, Maria Accavitti, and Frederick Shic (Yale University Child Study Center, 2016)

Shannon Wanless: Erin Winkler's article, "Children Are Not Colorblind: How Young Children Learn Race," is a clear and concise description of how young children understand and experience their lives in a highly racialized society.

I have not found any one resource to be "the one" that really helped me more than others. Instead, it seems to be the constant search for new resources and engaging with many different kinds of tools over time, that has been important for learning about racism from a lot of different angles (e.g., history, research, personal stories). For example, during a long drive home from a work trip, I binged episodes of the podcasts "Code Switch" and "In My Skin" in the car. The next day, at work, my colleague caught me up on a recent webinar held by EmbraceRace, and my Facebook page was filled with local stories of an incident of race-based police brutality and news from PushBlack.

When I do have some time for myself, I usually keep three types of books going at the same time: (1) A heavier history book (right now that is *Stamped from the Beginning: The Definitive History of Racist Ideas in America*, by Ibram X. Kendi [Nation Books, 2016]); (2) a book that leads me to self-reflecting (right now that is *What Does Not Kill You Makes You Blacker: A Memoir in Essays*, by Damon Young [Ecco, 2019]); and (3) a fiction book from the perspective of a Black lead character (right now that is *An American Marriage*, by Tayari Jones [Algonquin Books, 2018]) to help me build my perspective-taking.

Although there is a constant flow of new books and resources that I am discovering and reading, I also need to point out that it is really important to keep some options around that are not about race at all. It is emotionally exhausting to work hard at learning about race and thinking about how to end racism all of the time. Even though the work is urgent, and even though it is a privilege to be able to put it on the shelf and walk away sometimes, I find that I have to allow myself a break sometimes. The ultimate goal is to stay engaged with as much presence as possible to make big change in my spheres of influence. And that will likely require taking some self-care breaks so that I don't burnout.

Conclusion

These self-reflections from the field indicate that everyone's journey is different but that everyone has a journey. They are motivated by different lived experiences that have made them who they are today. The outcomes are about all children having the opportunity to thrive and be their best in a society that doesn't always value who they are or what they bring to the table.

These reflections indicate that it is not one incident that begins the journey, but might be a small indiscernible pebble that creates the wave and begins the journey. While everyone has a definition of what equity is, there is commonality in understanding that equity is about providing equitable opportunities to those who have historically or are currently being marginalized from experiencing high-quality early learning, such as dual language learners or Black children. There is also a recognition that it is not about fixing a child or family but about strengthening the system to do better and better. This means recognizing the current gaps of the system and addressing them. It also means recognizing the role that each individual plays in either maintaining an inequitable system through their privilege or seeking to better it through their work. To do this well, these early childhood professionals remind us that it is critical that we continue to read and learn through diverse media from conversations to readings to seminars. It is paramount to read literature beyond the early childhood field, including popular literature, to inform oneself about the experiences of the "others." If you are not in the skin of the "other," one way to expand one's knowledge base and experience is through this different media (e.g., movies, books, art, lectures, conferences, reports, data). If we are not going through a continuous quality improvement of our perspectives and work, how can we expect it of others, including programs?

Reference

NAEYC. 2019. "Advancing Equity in Early Childhood Education." Position statement. Washington, DC: NAEYC. www.naeyc.org /resources/position-statements/equity.

This chapter supports recommendations from the NAEYC position statement:

Recommendations for Everyone

Item 1: Build awareness and understanding of your culture, personal beliefs, values, and biases.

Item 2: Recognize the power and benefits of diversity and inclusivity.

Item 5: View your commitment to cultural responsiveness as an ongoing process.

Reflections on Our Profession

CHAPTER 2
Why History?
Educating the Early Childhood Workforce for Equity

Barbara T. Bowman

> There is growing awareness of the limitations of child development theories and research based primarily on a normative perspective of White, middle-class children. . . .
>
> [It] requires understanding this broader societal context, the ways that historical and current inequities have shaped the profession, as they have shaped our nation.
>
> —NAEYC, "Advancing Equity in Early Childhood Education"

Early childhood professionals usually spend little time thinking about the history of identity groups and its role in understanding family dynamics and children's development. Our focus is usually on an individual's direct experience, the here and now. Yet all of us belong to communities whose past experiences play a critical role in how we as individuals think and act. When we fail to consider history, we lose a valuable source of information about why people behave the way they do. This chapter focuses on people of African descent and speaks to how and why knowing their history can shed light on their current practices and help us design more responsive programs. Many aspects of this chapter may also speak to other marginalized groups because understanding the historical context of racism and the Black response is relevant to all communities of color in the United States.

Those of us in the human services recognize how a family's history gives us insight into the present. We see a connection between past stresses and resources and the way people live their lives today. For example, divorce often causes interpersonal tensions that result in ruptured relationships between parents and children. The effects of this change may persist long after the divorce is finalized.

However, when we know about the divorce, we can plan interventions specific to the family, such as attention to separation and abandonment issues.

The same process applies to communities. The past continues to influence its members. Cultures, like people, are not static, but the effect of prior experiences lingers as new experiences are viewed through the lens of the community's history.

Some teachers know that Black children and families are different but believe such differences are superficial. For example, they may think whether you eat cornbread or bagels for breakfast or broccoli or collards for supper are meaningless variations easily changed. While many food differences do reflect unimportant personal choices, others are important symbols. They relate to a person's identity and help define who they are. For many Black Americans, cornbread and collards are not just nutrition, they are meaningful aspects of their community and its traditions. Changing recipes is not a minor adjustment, but one that requires changes in taste and enjoyment, which some Black families may resist.

Unfortunately, some teachers think differences in Black children and families are indications of incompetence or deficits. They do not connect the history—the past experiences—of the Black American community to how Black children and families think, feel, and act today. Because a teacher's own culture is so intuitive and natural, they may feel theirs is the only right way to think and behave and anything different is abnormal; they expect everyone to share their truths. This assumption causes them to misunderstand the normalcy of Black children and families.

Differences are not caused by the Black Americans' perversity or stupidity; they are caused by the differences in their experiences, past and present, from those of White Americans. Slavery, Jim Crow (legal segregation), and continuing oppression has had a pervasive influence on Black culture and, therefore, on community and family interactions. For example, some teachers see the discipline of Black American parents as harsh and authoritarian. However, when you understand the long history of White harassment and violence (even against children), the effects of segregation and community disinvestment, and the continuing unjust justice system, it is easy to understand the urgency of their discipline. There is no space for Black children to make a mistake and Black parents recognize the danger; they believe that early and sharp discipline will help keep their children safe. Therefore, efforts to change the style of discipline in Black families without focusing on the causes are unlikely to be successful.

Teachers also are concerned about the disparities in achievement of children of color who lag behind their White peers. They ask, "Why don't these children learn in school?" Most often, they only look for personal reasons for school failure—genes, family relationships, poor teachers, or curriculum. They don't ask, "What are the structural inequities that affect the quality of Black children's school experience?" When we ask this question, one of the things we find is inequity in the school funding formulas in many states (EdBuild 2019). These formulas do not resource programs as adequately for students from families with low income (who need it most) as they do for students from families with higher income (who need it less). Children of color are often the poorest, and therefore, suffer the most from regressive fiscal policies (Baker, Di Carlo, & Weber 2019). This is one example of systemic racism that leads to underfunded schools. Similar policy decisions result in white supremacist curricula, Euro-American centric pedagogy, color-blind practices, and disproportional rates of disciplinary action (Derman-Sparks & Edwards with Goins 2020; Gilliam et al. 2016; Howard 2010). These historical racist policies and practices make underachievement for children of color the most likely outcome.

Many cultural patterns cannot be fully understood without knowing their evolution. This chapter gives two examples that are rooted in slavery and affect ideas and practices today. These examples also illustrate how groups adapt as their experiences change. Finally, I suggest five things that early childhood professionals can do to promote equity using their understanding of community experience, actions that make us part of the solution rather than the problem.

Example 1: African American English Vernacular, Black English, or Ebonics

Many people consider African American English Vernacular (AAEV) to be an incorrect form of Standard English that indicates the ignorance of the speakers. In fact, Black people developed this language in what is now the United States during slavery because they came from different tribes with different languages and had to create a lingua franca to communicate with each other and their slave owners. They designed a language that contained elements of many of their home languages and English but combined them in a logical and linguistically consistent way. Instead of being a misuse of English, AAEV was (and is) an intellectual equivalent language to English (Labov 1970). During its development, AAEV reflected the separation of Blacks slaves from White owners; its continued use reflects segregation today—in housing, employment, education, religion, and many of the social amenities.

Jim Crow was codified in *Plessy v. Ferguson* in 1896 and remained in force until the Civil Rights Act of 1964 was enacted. During the great migration (1916–1970), Black Americans moved out of the South to northern cities where employment opportunities were greater. One might have expected them to begin speaking Standard English as they gained a foothold in the North; however even there, where segregation was not legally required, it was widespread and pervasive. Black people were almost as rigidly segregated in employment, residence, and schools in Los Angeles, Detroit, and Cleveland as they had been in the South. The community language persevered; Black Americans took the basic structure of AAEV with them. In northern ghettos, you could hear the community's unique use of the verb *to be*: "I's here" and "She be's here." As Black people continued to live segregated lives, they continued to use their language for social interaction (NPR 2017).

Unlike other ethnic groups, many economically advantaged Black Americans live in segregated Black neighborhoods, where the residents are poorer, less well educated, attend schools of lower quality, and use features of AAEV in their speech. What is it about their experiences that accounts for why they live in such communities? Two factors are important. One, Black Americans are likely to feel safer and more valued in Black communities. Most Black Americans regularly receive direct and indirect racial insult at their jobs, in the street, in public facilities, and in the legal system. Generally, Black people have more difficult lives than White people with the same or similar background (Denby 2017). Their physical safety as well as their self-esteem are regularly compromised. Comradery and the support of the community, including via a shared language, become important antidotes for both the depression and rage that this treatment elicits.

Two, racial segregation is determined by White people. It is responsive to the decisions made by banks, realtors, insurance companies, city governments, judges, and law enforcement (Nodjimbadem 2017). These decisions, though ostensibly made for economic reasons, are in reality often based on race and have a far-reaching effect on Black Americans. Legally and illegally, Black people are limited in their access to residences, employment, markets, insurance, and social opportunities outside of their own communities.

Today, Black speech is increasingly diverse as more opportunities open up outside of their communities and more Standard English is incorporated. Nevertheless, vestiges of AAEV have been retained in many communities, as red marks on student essays attest. Additional changes are inevitable as new experiences create new challenges (media, computers), but some forms will undoubtedly continue to be used as long as so many communities remain segregated. Interestingly, just as AAEV has changed in the last 50 years as interrace contact has increased, so too has Black slang spread outward to the general public, where it is now part of everyday speech for many Americans.

Example 2: Color and Colorism

We speak of *people of color* in the United States because of their common experiences with European and American prejudice and discrimination. The different meanings of skin color, however, is an illustration of how knowing history provides insight into different attitudes and different assimilation behavior among groups with African heritage.

Differences Within Groups

During slavery, children of mixed-race African slaves often lived in the homes of their White owners, thereby enjoying a more advantaged lifestyle. Skin color operated as a benefit, as the whiter the slave, the greater economic and social opportunity; however, Black people with White-like complexions and hair were still considered Black. The adage "One drop of African blood makes you Black" was originally designed to keep mixed-race people enslaved. Post-slavery, it has meant that no amount of White ancestry could overcome the stigma of African heritage.

With emancipation, the privilege of "house slaves" translated more easily into jobs and further education, so light-skinned Black people enjoyed privileges not always available to darker-skinned peers. Skin color conferred benefits in the White world and became a mark of beauty among Black Americans; "whiter skin" was deemed more attractive and often carried more benefits than darker coloring. After the civil rights era and the recognition that "Black is beautiful," this preference became less important; however, skin color can still evoke ambivalent feelings within Black American communities.

Differences Between Groups

Color had a different history in Caribbean and Central and South American countries than in the United States. In these areas, just as in the United States, during and after slavery, mixed-race people enjoyed a more privileged lifestyle than their darker peers. However, unlike the United States, there was no legal Jim Crow and the doctrine of "one drop" was not used as the criteria of who was Black. Unlike in the United States where race was fixed, people from these areas had different ideas about color, interracial mixing, and assimilation. Without anti-miscegenation laws, racial mixing did not have legal consequences, and many of these countries developed multiple racial divisions. The Caribbean nations for example, were heavily dependent on Black slavery, but emancipation did not elicit legal Jim Crow as it did in the United States and racial mixing was more prevalent.

The African experience was also different. Although Africans experienced the oppression of colonialism, they come from majority-Black countries, where Blackness is ubiquitous. In most of those countries, freedom from European direct domination is several generations old. In addition, as Ogbu and Simons (1998) point out, immigrants, like those of African and Caribbean descent, have come to the United States voluntarily and are more willing to adopt new customs. All Black groups are likely to face prejudice and discrimination in the United States, yet these seem to be less of a hindrance for Black immigrants. The Pew Foundation reports that on every measure of success—annual income, home ownership, education—African and Caribbean immigrants' achievement exceeds that of native-born Black Americans (Anderson 2015; Valentine 2012). It suggests that voluntary Black immigrants, without the onus of colorism, are more able to cope with American barriers to achievement.

These examples show that history affects communities, but also that communities adapt to different experiences. They also show that if we want different outcomes for our democracy, we must change the experiences of communities as well as those of individuals.

Intervention: Early Childhood Programs

We are rightly quite pleased that early childhood programs can help alleviate some of the effects of inequitable education practices experienced by communities of color. However, it is essential for early childhood educators to recognize their limits as well. This was brought home to me during a visit to a Head Start center (an anti-poverty program), where the teacher and a grandparent proudly told me that the grandchild was the third generation in the program. A quick review of research on the intergenerational cycle of poverty shows that this was the expected outcome, not an unusual one.

Programs such as Head Start have shown positive educational and social results for poor children and their families (Barr & Gibbs 2017; Deming 2009); however, often those benefits do not persist or foster class mobility. The effects of early childhood programs may be curtailed by the quality of the preschool program or the inadequacy of the K–12 schools that the children subsequently attend. Or alternatively, change may be limited by the racism that members of the community encounter every day, which dooms children's outlook and expectations for the future. This suggests that rather than focusing exclusively on the personal issues common to all families, anti-poverty programs for Black children must look at the broad range of factors that undermine communities, such as unsafe housing, job discrimination, bank and insurance policies, air and water expenditures, and tax allocations.

NAEYC's "Advancing Equity in Early Childhood Education" position statement notes that focusing solely on an individual's direct experiences should not prevent us from examining the sociocultural and historical influences on the Black American community and other marginalized groups. Instead, we must be as active combatting the systemic forces of poverty and racism that imperil the community as we are in treating individuals for their effects.

How Should the Early Childhood Profession Respond?

1. The early childhood system has the obligation to deliver exemplary services in an equitable way. This means advocating for public policies that pay attention to quality and access for all. It also means making sure that current policies and practices consider cultural and linguistic differences as they plan for children and families.

2. Early childhood professionals have an obligation to teach children about each other in a positive and respectful way. This is more than scheduling a food-tasting lunch or reading a book or two about Indigenous peoples. It requires thoughtful attention to communities, families, and materials so that what children learn is authentic and accurate.

3. The early childhood professional should also be prepared to study the cultural patterns and history of the various groups in their programs to learn about their past and current experience. This is particularly important when groups have experienced generations of oppression, with inequalities in resources and justice. Most important, educators must understand the difference between knowing about the cultures of others and stereotyping them.

4. While we focus on helping families deal with the stresses in their lives, we also need to work to change the systems that keep children of color from enjoying the benefits of full citizenship. Early childhood professionals, well versed in child development, have an obligation to advocate for policies and practices that support young children and their families. But educators need to be aware of how current systems continue to undermine competence and agency in Black communities. There are many sources—parents, books, the internet, classes, and knowledgeable community members—that can provide this information.

5. Clearly, history cannot be changed, but cultures are not set in stone. New challenges and opportunities demand changes in beliefs and practices. This means that our responsibility to sponsor equity does not end with quality and access or knowledge of history. It includes the responsibility to take an active role in advocating corrective policy. This means bringing all voices to the table to share public policy debates. It means advocating for equity both as a member of professional organizations and a citizen in our society.

> **Key Points**
>
> › Early childhood teachers need to learn about the social and economic forces that have shaped the community where they work.
>
> › To understand the relationship between a community's history and current attitudes, beliefs, and behaviors, early childhood educators need multiple sources of information: books, media, consultants—and most important—community members.
>
> › Early childhood programs need to respect community views and actions and, at the same time, offer opportunities for change.

References

Anderson, M. 2015. *A Rising Share of the U.S. Black Population Is Foreign Born; 9 Percent Are Immigrants; and While Most Are from the Caribbean, Africans Drive Recent Growth*. Report. Washington, DC: Pew Research Center. www.pewsocialtrends .org/2015/04/09/a-rising-share-of-the-u-s-black-population -is-foreign-born.

Baker, B.D., M. Di Carlo, & M. Weber. 2019. *The Adequacy and Fairness of State School Finance Systems*. Report. Washington, DC: Albert Shaker Institute; New Brunswick, NJ: Rutgers Graduate School of Education. www.shankerinstitute.org /resource/adequacy-and-fairness-state-school-finance-systems.

Barr, A., & C.R. Gibbs. 2017. "Breaking the Cycle? Intergenerational Effects of an Anti-Poverty Program in Early Childhood." EdPolicyWorks Working Papers Series No. 61. University of Virginia.

Deming, D. 2009. "Early Childhood Intervention and Life-Cycle Skill Development: Evidence from Head Start." *American Economic Journal: Applied Economics* 1 (3): 111–134.

Denby, G. 2017. "How Black Americans See Discrimination." *NPR*, October 25. www.npr.org/sections/codeswitch/2017/10/25 /559015355/how-black-americans-see-discrimination.

Derman-Sparks, L., & J.O. Edwards. With C.M. Goins. 2020. *Anti-Bias Education for Young Children and Ourselves*. 2nd ed. Washington, DC: NAEYC.

EdBuild. 2019. *23 Billion*. Report. Jersey City, NJ: EdBuild. www .edbuild.org/content/23-billion.

Gilliam, W.S., A.N. Maupin, C.R. Reyes, M. Accavitti, & F. Shic. 2016. "Do Early Educators' Implicit Biases Regarding Sex and Race Relate to Behavior Expectations and Recommendations of Preschool Expulsions and Suspensions?" Research brief. New Haven, CT: Yale University Child Study Center.

Howard, T.C. 2010. *Why Race and Culture Matter in Schools: Closing the Achievement Gap in America's Classrooms*. New York: Teachers College Press.

Labov, W. 1970. "The Logic of Non-Standard English" In *Language and Poverty*, ed. F. Williams. Chicago: Markham Press.

Nodjimbadem, K. 2017. "The Racial Segregation of American Cities Was Anything But Accidental." *Smithsonian Magazine*, May 30. www.smithsonianmag.com/history/how-federal -government-intentionally-racially-segregated-american-cities.

Ogbu, J.U., & H.D. Simons. 1998. "Voluntary and Involuntary Minorities: A Cultural-Ecological Theory of School Performance with Some Implications for Education." *Anthropology Education Quarterly* 29 (2): 155–188.

Valentine, C. 2012. "Rethinking the Achievement Gap: Lessons from the African Diaspora." *The Washington Post*, September 4. www.washingtonpost.com/blogs/therootdc /post/rethinking-the-achievement-gap-lessons-from-the -african-diaspora/2012/09/04/eebc5214-f362-11e1-a612 -3cfc842a6d89_blog.html?noredirect=on&utm_term= .9ccacd763ff1.

This chapter supports recommendations from the NAEYC position statement:

Recommendations for Everyone

Item 6: Recognize that the professional knowledge base is changing.

Recommendations for Early Childhood Educators

Advocate on Behalf of Young Children, Families, and the Early Childhood Profession

Item 1: Speak out against unfair policies or practices and challenge biased perspectives.

Item 2: Look for ways to work collectively with others who are committed to equity.

Quality Includes Removing Bias from Early Childhood Education Environments

Felicia L. DeHaney, Carla Thompson Payton, and Alandra Washington

The year 2019 marked the 65th anniversary of *Brown v. Board of Education*, the US Supreme Court case which declared racial segregation in public schools unconstitutional. *Brown v. Board of Education* was critical in establishing that "equal" access, funding, and quality of resources were not provided to all students, specifically Black children. More than six decades later, efforts toward embracing, advancing, and achieving equity in educational systems continue. As the field of education embraces the change in demographics across the country, it must also acknowledge and understand the systemic institutional practices that are still in place throughout our educational system. These include inequitable levels of educational access and advancement, barriers to resources and funding, and marginal actions toward culturally relevant practices and policies. This chapter examines efforts made toward removing racial and ethnic biases, addresses our current state as a field, and asserts how the field of early childhood education must be committed to advance equity with the assets of children, families, and communities front and center.

Relatedly, within the last decade, and for the first time since the public education system was established in the United States, the majority of students are children of color. According to a *Public School Review* article (citing a report published by the Pew Research Center), "in 1997, over 63 percent of 46.1 million US public school students were White. Today, White students comprise 49.7 percent of the 50 million students enrolled" (Chen 2019). In 2018, *Public School Review* reported that 52 percent of public school students were children of color, and 48 percent were White (Chen 2019).

Yet even after a half-century of desegregation, the majority of America's school children still attend racially homogenous schools (EdBuild 2019). Our public education system is legally separate and de facto discriminatory. Recently Gary Orfield, a professor at UCLA and the cofounder of The Civil Rights Project, reported that the average White student attends schools that are 69 percent White; the average Latino/a student attends schools that are 55 percent Latino/a or that have a 66 percent mix of Black and Latino/a students; the average Black student attends schools that are 47 percent Black or that have a 67 percent mix of Black and Latino/a students; and the average Asian American student attends schools that are 24 percent Asian American (Tilghman 2013). These asymmetries reveal how systemic racism and intentional segregation continues to shape public education in America.

Moreover, research shows that schools that serve predominantly Black and Latino/a children receive fewer dollars than schools that serve predominantly White children. For example, a recent EdBuild (2019) report revealed that non-White school districts receive 23 billion dollars less than White school districts, despite serving a similar number of children. Of the 35 states in the country that are racially diverse enough to support an equity-based analysis of their school funding structures, more than half use funding mechanisms that create disparities (EdBuild 2019). More than 10 million students are enrolled in districts that are funded at lower levels than their state counterparts (EdBuild 2019).

Funding for, and access to, early childhood education has also been shaped by systemic racism and intentional segregation. As such, some view *Abbott v. Burke* as the most significant legal case regarding the rights of poor and minority school children since *Brown v. Board of Education*. In 1985, the New Jersey Supreme Court ruled that the education provided to school children in poor communities in the state was inadequate and unconstitutional, and ordered that state funding in these districts should equal what was spent in the state's wealthiest districts (ELC, n.d.). At the time, the court's mandate in *Abbott v. Burke* broke new ground in school finance and education policy. New Jersey became the first state to mandate early education for children "placed at risk" of entering kindergarten or primary school behind their more advantaged peers, starting at age 3.

While *Abbott v. Burke*'s legacies are still evolving—much like *Brown v. Board of Education*'s—there is clear and reliable data about nationwide early childhood education enrollment, which mirrors in many ways the changed student population in public schools. In their recent data report, Child Trends Databank (2019) found that "non-Hispanic Black children were more likely to be enrolled in full-day preschool programs (42 percent) than their non-Hispanic White and Hispanic peers (29 and 23 percent, respectively), while non-Hispanic White children were the most likely to be enrolled in a part-day program (27 percent), compared to Hispanic and non-Hispanic Black children (23 and 14 percent, respectively)." (See Figures 3.1 and 3.2.)

As we know, high-quality early childhood education supports the rapid development that happens in the first years of a child's life and has long-lasting benefits well into adulthood. Yet barriers to access persist. For example, a recent report from the Education Trust (2019) reveals that of the 26 states in their study, none of the states provides high-quality and high-access state-funded preschool for Black and Latino/a 3- and 4-year-olds. The study reported that only 1 percent of Latino/a children and 4 percent of Black children in 26 states were enrolled in high-quality, state-funded early learning programs (The Education Trust 2019). "Systemic racism causes opportunity gaps for Black and Latino children that begin early—even prenatally, which makes it crucial for these

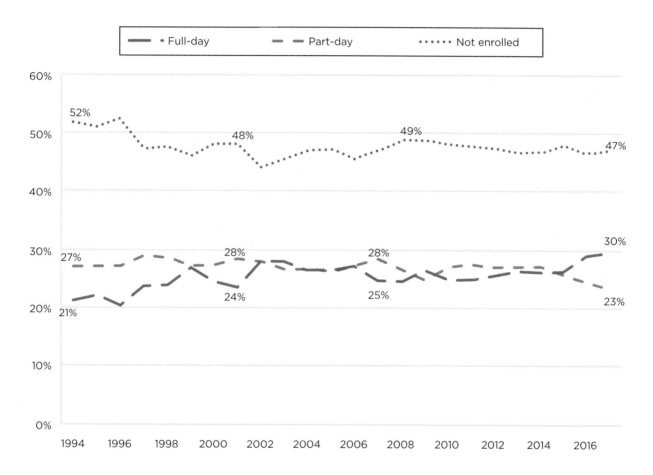

Figure 3.1. Percentage of Children Ages 3 to 5 (Not in Kindergarten or Elementary School) Enrolled in Prekindergarten or Preschool Programs: 1994–2017

Note: This indicator includes children ages 3 to 5 whose parents answered nursery school (prekindergarten or preschool) when asked what grade their children were attending. Parents were then asked to specify whether their children were attending a full-day or part-day program. Because of the way in which the question was phrased, parents may have included a wide variety of childcare options when responding that their child participated in "nursery school." Children ages 3 to 5 who were enrolled in kindergarten or higher grades were excluded from these estimates.

Source: Child Trends' original analysis of data from the Current Population Survey, October Supplement, 1994–2017.

Reprinted, with permission, from Child Trends Databank, *Preschool and Prekindergarten* (Bethesda, MD: Child Trends, 2019).

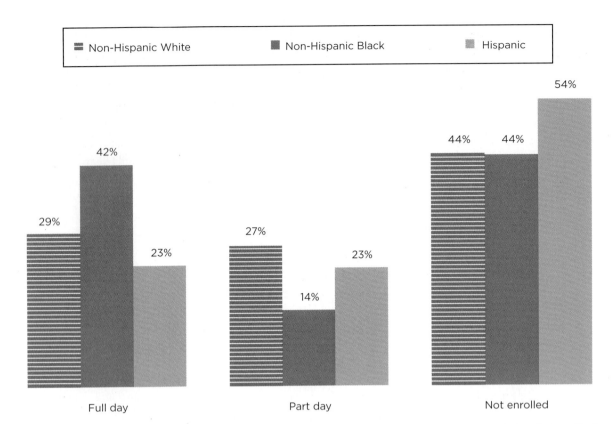

Figure 3.2. Percentage of Children Ages 3 to 5 (Not in Kindergarten or Elementary School) Enrolled in Full-Day Prekindergarten or Preschool Programs, by Race and Hispanic Origin: 2017

Note: This indicator includes children ages 3 to 5 whose parents answered nursery school (prekindergarten or preschool) when asked what grade their children were attending. Parents were then asked to specify whether their children were attending a full-day or part-day program. Because of the way in which the question was phrased, parents may have included a wide variety of childcare options when responding that their child participated in "nursery school." Children ages 3 to 5 who were enrolled in kindergarten or higher grades were excluded from these estimates.

Reprinted, with permission, from Child Trends Databank, *Preschool and Prekindergarten* (Bethesda, MD: Child Trends, 2019).

families to have access to high-quality [early childhood education] opportunities as a pathway to success into their K–12 education" (The Education Trust 2019, 3). The report continues to state that of the 26 states analyzed, 13 enrolled fewer than 25 percent of their Latino/a children in state-funded preschool programs, and 10 enrolled fewer than 25 percent of their Black children (The Education Trust 2019).

The Importance of Racial Equity in Early Childhood Education Settings

NAEYC's "Advancing Equity in Early Childhood Education" position statement advances the rights of all children to achieve their full potential as engaged learners and valued members of society, and the necessity of equitable learning opportunities. The organization requires accountability from all stakeholders—including early childhood educators, administrators, and policymakers—to actively acknowledge and address patterns of inequity. NAEYC also asserts that society benefits when children and families from resource-denied and marginalized communities are equitably served (NAEYC 2019).

Indeed, years of research, study, and evaluation provide overwhelming evidence that investing in high-quality early childhood programs sets children on an upward trajectory in school and in life. Conversely, we also see that children who enter kindergarten behind their peers are more likely to remain behind. While some states have made great efforts to ensure that early investments prepare children for kindergarten, depending on the state, zip code, and school zoning area, access to and opportunities for high-quality education are limited.

Advancing Equity and Embracing Diversity in Early Childhood Education

As LaRue Allen, chair of the National Academies of Sciences, Engineering, and Medicine Committee on Transforming the Workforce, states

> While high-quality early care and education for children from birth to kindergarten entry is critical to child development and has the potential to generate significant economic returns in the long run, it has been financed in such a way that makes early education available only to a fraction of the families needing and desiring care, and does little to further develop the early care and education workforce. (NASEM 2018)

Moreover, there is an underlying racialized, structural barrier that prevents children of color from receiving quality and equitable early childhood education: implicit bias. Implicit bias makes it more difficult for young children of color to have healthy, successful starts in life. Evidence for the prevalence and impact of implicit bias may be found in preschool systems across the country, where suspension and expulsion rates have been increasing among children of color. In 2005, a national study of state-funded prekindergarten systems operating in 40 states across the country found that prekindergartners are expelled at a rate that is more than three times that of their older peers in grades K–12: 6.67 per 1,000 preschoolers to 2.09 per 1,000 K–12 students (Gilliam 2005). The study also found that rates were higher for older preschoolers and that Black preschoolers were twice as likely to be expelled as White preschoolers.

That trend has continued. The US Department of Education Office of Civil Rights found that while Black preschoolers comprise 19 percent of overall preschool enrollment, they account for 47 percent of the suspension rates (OCR 2014). As a result of increased time spent away from their class and classmates, some researchers link these inequitable disciplinary practices to a reduction of educational opportunities for young Black students (Henneman 2014; Keane & Calkins 2004). Finally, recent research of student discipline records from over 1,800 schools serving more than one million students found that discipline disproportionality is largely attributable to racial disparities (McIntosh et al. 2018).

The Impact of Implicit Bias

Implicit bias is not a new concept. The earliest definitions emerged in the early 1920s; it was suggested that people filtered information through preconceived notions or stereotypes that reflected subjective perceptions (Eberhardt 2019). And more than 20 years ago, in their book *Blindspot: Hidden Biases of Good People*, psychologists Mahzarin Banaji and Anthony Greenwald (2016) noted that implicit bias occurs when forces we are unaware of guide our impulses and decisions. They defined implicit bias as attitudes and stereotypes that affect our understanding, actions, and decisions in an unconscious manner (Banaji & Greenwald 2016).

Research on human cognitive functioning offers insights into conscious and unconscious cognition and how implicit bias works. Unconscious cognition, where most of our cognition occurs, is associated with implicit bias (Staats 2016). Unconscious stereotypes drive how people behave, as well as how they make judgments and decisions (Staats 2016). When implicit bias informs how people view identities—including race, language, economic status, gender, ability, and religious affiliation—it creates structural barriers, inequitable outcomes, and disparities. While explicit prejudice has been correlated with deliberate acts of discrimination, implicit bias is predictive of spontaneous, nonverbal behaviors (Dovidio, Kawakami, & Gaertner 2002; McConnell & Leibold 2001). It also shows up across our social, cultural, political, and educational system and causes harm without overt intent. While some prejudice is explicit, implicit biases outside of an individual's awareness can be even more complicated and difficult to apprehend.

Yet addressing this issue is even more critical, given the racial differences between the teaching and student population. The National Center for Education Statistics reported that students of color made up 45 percent of the public school population (prekindergarten through high school), but only 17.5 percent of educators in the workforce were faculty of color (Nganga 2015). The vast demographic differences between students and the teaching corps have had devastating impacts. In 2018, the US Government Accountability Office report on the US Department of Education's suspension and expulsion data reported that Black students are suspended more than any other racial group, with this trend beginning in preschool. (See Figure 3.3.)

Given what we know about systemic racism and the acute underrepresentation of Black educators in the teaching profession, this upward trend of suspensions and expulsions is likely driven by implicit bias, which in turn, is fed by powerful and widely circulated negative stereotypes associated with Black people. For example, behaviors exhibited by many boys and young men, such as high levels of assertiveness, energy, and physicality, are seen as negative when attributed to Black boys and young men. These negative associations—and resulting experiences of

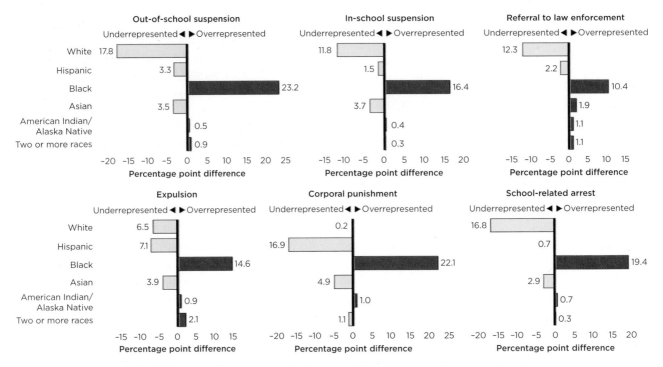

Figure 3.3. Representation of Students Who Received Disciplinary Actions Compared to Overall Student Population, by Student Race or Ethnicity, School Year 2013–2014

This chart shows whether each race or ethnicity was underrepresented or overrepresented among students who received six types of discipline. For example, White students were underrepresented among students suspended out of school by approximately 18 percentage points, as shown in the chart, because they made up about 50% of the overall K–12 student population, but 32% of the students suspended out of school.

Source: GAO analysis of Department of Education, Civil Rights Data Collection. I GAO-18-258.

Reprinted from US Government Accountability Office (GAO), *Discipline Disparities for Black Students, Boys, and Students with Disabilities* (Washington, DC: GAO, 2018), 14.

bias and discrimination—lead to behavioral, psychological, and academic trauma (Harper & Associates 2013).

Approaches for Countering the Impact of Implicit Bias

Even at very young ages, school-based trauma often leads to negative self-image, the internalization of these labels, and the erosion of the very qualities and characteristics that make these children unique and special. Yet it is possible to positively and effectively address high rates of suspensions and expulsions from preschool programs. Research tells us that there are at least three approaches to counter this alarming trend and significantly reduce the occurrences.

Increase Hiring and Retention of Teachers of Color

Research suggests that hiring and retaining more teachers of color may reduce the influence of implicit

bias (Milton-Williams & Bryan 2016). Similarly, hiring bilingual teachers in schools with linguistically diverse children will lead to equitable practices. Bristol (2014) suggests that Black male teachers provide better support to the academic and social needs of Black boys due to their heightened ability to connect, bridge cultural understanding, and increase accountability grounded in realistic expectations.

Currently however, Black men comprise only 1 percent of all teachers in all grade levels. Given this very low rate of representation, investing in programs like Call Me MISTER, an initiative funded by W.K. Kellogg Foundation, is an urgent, essential intervention. Since its inception in 2000, the program has graduated 150 MISTERs (Mentors Instructing Students Toward Effective Role Models), who have been fully certified and secured teaching positions. To date, all program graduates remain teachers, and some have even moved up to principal or program director positions. All MISTERs have met or exceeded their commitment to give back to their public schools and communities.

Build Empathy and Cultural Competence to Reduce Bias in the Classroom

For 90 years, the W.K. Kellogg Foundation has been at the forefront of directly addressing racial equity and systemic racism in education systems. Embedded within all we do are commitments to advance racial equity and racial healing, to develop leaders, and to engage communities in solving their own problems. In the education domain—and more specifically, within the field of early childhood education—implicit bias can be a harmful and enduring obstacle to early success and achievement. Because these assumptions, beliefs, and stereotypes are held by all individuals, including well-intentioned education professionals and teachers, early childhood educators and leaders must be absolutely committed to creating and maintaining equitable learning environments (Valbrun 2017).

Indeed, increased self-awareness of how bias impacts interactions in educational settings is a prevailing theme in the research (Durden, Escalante, & Blitch 2015). Teachers' expectations and interpretations of student behavior is a function of racial, linguistic, or ethnic match; more specifically, White teachers tend to misinterpret the behavior of children of color across the K–12 spectrum (Bates & Glick 2013; Gregory, Skiba, & Noguera 2010). Part of this awareness stems from using reflective practices to create a pattern that allows them to find themselves within each child, and then seeking and finding positive attributes for each child (Bryan 2017).

NAEYC's position statement on advancing equity addresses this through the charge to recognize each child's unique strengths and support the inclusion of all children—helping children recognize and support each other as valued members of the community—so that no one feels invisible or unnoticed. The ability to see themselves and the children in their classrooms as unique and with much to offer fundamentally changes in-class interactions and the attributions associated with each interaction. The ability to use cultural differences as connectors, instead of dividers, can help teachers become aware of their biases and false or low expectations, as well as allow for innovative teaching practices that are nuanced and agile.

Teachers should be prepared in culturally and linguistically responsive and sustaining teaching practices (e.g., classroom management, family engagement), draw from culturally and linguistically relevant materials, and use their cultural competence and sociopolitical awareness to support the academic success of all children

(Ladson-Billings 2009; Milner 2016). These efforts include matching instruction to the learning styles of students, devising curricula that engage students and reflect their daily lives, and using learning resources informed by students' communities and experiences.

For instance, a pre- and post-test study of a small teacher education program in a rural state in the Rocky Mountain region, where the population of people of color grew by 17 percent between 2010 and 2013, revealed that the majority of pre-service teachers' responses reflected critical misconceptions about anti-bias curriculum (Nganga 2015). Additionally, research conducted by the US Department of Education Office for Civil Rights (OCR 2014) found that most schools lacked resources and offered deficient education and training, specifically in self-reflective strategies that may aid in identifying and rectifying potential biases in teacher perceptions and classroom practices.

Findings from the 2019 study "Empathy Intervention to Reduce Implicit Bias in Pre-Service Teachers" indicated that empathy interventions within teacher education training programs may provide a foundation for educators to be more aware of their own implicit bias, and provide strategies for countering it. The results indicate that this type of teacher training holds promise for promoting empathy. Even brief interventions, which incorporated evidence-based effective methods (that is, short story point of view and writing exercises with reflection and point of view) significantly reduced bias (Whitford & Emerson 2019).

This type of professional development provides opportunities for future educators to acquire knowledge and dispositions that will help them meet the needs of all learners (Nganga 2015). These practices are further reinforced as biases are eliminated from all assessments and strengths-based pedagogical approaches are employed. In these ways, we honor the unique contributions each student and family brings to the school setting.

Promote Positive School–Family Interactions and Effective Family Engagement

Schools are often seen as the hubs of communities. Early childhood education programs, in particular, are commonly used as "training grounds," where parents and caregivers come to understand what to expect as children move through their academic experiences. Yet often, parents and caretakers are valuable resources that are overlooked and underappreciated by early childhood programs (Flaugher 2006). When there is a breakdown between staff-designed family engagement activities, based on staff needs, beliefs, and experiences, rather than those of the families and community, a vicious cycle can be created (Moule 2009). Nonalignment, poor communication between staff and families, and implicit bias create unhealthy learning environments.

NAEYC (2019) challenges us to reexamine the way we interact in our work with families and communities of color. Taking the time to learn about the families with whom we work while establishing reciprocal relationships is critical to authentic and effective family engagement. We must embrace the primary role of families in children's development and learning while upholding every family's right to make decisions for and with their children. Traditional parent engagement models across early childhood education systems—such as parent-teacher associations and volunteer day activities—may seem inflexible to some family members. For example, many family engagement program designs create participation barriers that limit accessibility because of child care difficulties, transportation challenges, and/or work schedule conflicts (Berthelsen et al. 2012; Mendez et al. 2009). Consequently, family members may perceive early childhood education staff as insensitive to their time, financial, or personal limitations.

Effective family engagement is supported by ongoing, reciprocal, strengths-based partnerships between families and their children's teachers and schools (Halgunseth et al. 2009). It is a critical marker of quality within early childhood education programs. It's also essential for enhancing children's learning and families' well-being. The practice of understanding and respecting differences, while seeing the unique skills each child and family brings, can also radically reduce bias in classroom interactions. In 2019, the W.K. Kellogg Foundation released a report, *Cultivating a Community of Champions for Children Through Transformative Family Engagement*, highlighting the findings of their family engagement grant work and presented a few considerations for ways to develop and improve teacher-family-community relationships. The report suggests eight strategies to strengthen ties (W.K. Kellogg Foundation 2019):

1. Recognize families as assets, valued partners, and experts about their children.

2. Identify goals and resources in partnership with families.

3. Integrate family and community culture into the early learning system.

4. Develop continuous two-way communication.

5. Commit to co-governance and shared leadership.

6. Institutionalize structures and processes that strengthen families and organization.

7. Build strong networks among families and communities.

8. Support families to develop and assert their role as leaders and agents of change.

Children, their families, and communities have the potential to reveal and share the unique perspectives each family brings and co-create opportunities that increase programmatic change and academic advancement by focusing on changing negative narratives and establishing practices that share leadership and responsibility.

While there are not many studies assessing strategies that mitigate implicit bias in early childhood education settings, some research advances specific strategies ranging across different areas, including school policy setting, teacher professional development, and school discipline.

Conclusion

At the W.K. Kellogg Foundation, we know that children are part of families and do not show up to schools independent of their family and community context. We approach equity toward school readiness and school success as a collective effort.

Culturally and linguistically relevant strategies must be developed with an equity lens to transform outcomes for children. Educators are influential partners in this collective effort. They must embrace a commitment to examining their own biases and cultural beliefs, as well as the practices they use with the children and families they serve.

Early childhood educators must also be fairly compensated toward these efforts. Early childhood educators and early care and education programs must focus on high-quality standards and competencies and implement effective strategies to support equitable access to high-quality school readiness and early school success.

Key Points

> Child Trends Databank (2019) found that "non-Hispanic Black children were more likely to be enrolled in full-day preschool programs (42 percent) than their non-Hispanic White and Hispanic peers (29 and 23 percent, respectively), while non-Hispanic White children were the most likely to be enrolled in a part-day program (27 percent), compared to Hispanic and non-Hispanic Black children (23 and 14 percent, respectively)."

> School-based trauma often leads to negative self-image, the internalization of these labels, and the erosion of the very qualities and characteristics that make these children unique and special.

> Traditional parent engagement models across early childhood education systems—such as parent-teacher associations and volunteer day activities—may seem inflexible to some family members.

> Children, their families, and communities have the potential to reveal and share the unique perspectives each family brings and co-create opportunities that increase programmatic change and academic advancement by focusing on changing negative narratives and establishing practices that share leadership and responsibility.

References

Bates, L.A., & J.E. Glick. 2013. "Does It Matter if Teachers and Schools Match the Student? Racial and Ethnic Disparities in Problem Behaviors." *Social Science Research* 42 (5): 1180–1190.

Banaji, M.R., & A.G. Greenwald. 2016. *Blindspot: Hidden Biases of Good People*. New York: Bantam Books.

Berthelsen, D., K. Williams, V. Abad, L. Vogel, & J. Nicholson. 2012. *The Parents at Playgroup Research Report: Engaging Families in Supported Playgroups*. Research report. Brisbane, Australia: Queensland University of Technology. http://eprints.qut.edu.au/50875/1/Parents_at_Playgroup_Final_Report.pdf.

Bristol, T. 2014. "Teaching Boys: Towards a Theory of Gender-Relevant Pedagogy." *Gender and Education* 27 (1): 53–68.

Bryan, N. 2017. "White Teachers' Role in Sustaining the School-to-Prison Pipeline: Recommendations for Teacher Education." *Urban Review* 49 (2): 326–345.

Chen, G. 2019. "White Students Are Now the Minority in US Public Schools." *Public School Review*, October 14. www.publicschoolreview.com/blog/White-students-are-now-the-minority-in-u-s-public-schools.

Child Trends Databank. 2019. *Preschool and Prekindergarten*. Report. Bethesda, MD: Child Trends.

Dovidio, J.F., K. Kawakami, & S.L. Gaertner. 2002. "Implicit and Explicit Prejudice and Interracial Interaction." *Journal of Personality and Social Psychology* 82 (1): 62–68.

Durden, T., E. Escalante, & K. Blitch. 2015. "Start with Us! Culturally Relevant Pedagogy in the Preschool Classroom." *Early Childhood Education Journal* 43 (3): 223–232.

Eberhardt, J.L. 2019. *Biased: Uncovering the Hidden Prejudice That Shapes What We See, Think, and Do*. New York: Viking.

EdBuild. 2019. *23 Billion*. Report. Jersey City, NJ: EdBuild. www.edbuild.org/content/23-billion.

The Education Trust. 2019. *Young Learners, Missed Opportunities: Ensuring That Black and Latino Children Have Access to High-Quality State-Funded Preschool*. Report. Washington, DC: The Education Trust. https://s3-us-east-2.amazonaws.com/edtrustmain/wp-content/uploads/2014/09/05162154/Young-Learners-Missed-Opportunities.pdf.

ELC (Education Law Center). n.d. "The History of Abbott v. Burke." Accessed October 14, 2020. www.edlawcenter.org/litigation/abbott-v-burke/abbott-history.html.

Flaugher, P. 2006. "Two Dimensions of Parent Participation in an Inner School District." *Education and Urban Society* 38 (2): 248–261.

GAO (US Government Accountability Office). 2018. *Discipline Disparities for Black Students, Boys, and Students with Disabilities* (GAO-18-258). Report. Washington, DC: GAO. www.gao.gov/assets/700/690828.pdf.

Gilliam, W.S. 2005. "Prekindergartners Left Behind: Expulsion Rates in State Prekindergarten Systems." Policy brief. New York: Foundation for Child Development.

Gregory, A., R.J. Skiba, & P.A. Noguera. 2010. "The Achievement Gap and the Discipline Gap: Two Sides of the Same Coin?" *Educational Researcher* 39 (1): 59–68.

Halgunseth, L.C., A. Peterson, D.R. Stark, & S. Moodie. 2009. *Family Engagement, Diverse Families, and Early Childhood Education Programs: An Integrated Review of the Literature*. Report. Washington, DC: NAEYC and Pew Charitable Trusts.

Harper, S.R., & Associates. 2013. *Succeeding in the City: A Report from the New York City Black and Latino Male High School Achievement Study*. Report. Philadelphia: University of Pennsylvania, Center for the Study of Race and Equity in Education.

Henneman, T.K. 2014. "Preschool Expulsions: Parental Experiences of Black Boys Who Were Pushed Out or Left Behind." Unpublished doctoral dissertation. Oakland, CA: Mills College.

Keane, S.P., & S.D. Calkins. 2004. "Predicting Kindergarten Peer Social Status from Toddler and Preschool Problem Behavior." *Journal of Abnormal Child Psychology* 32: 409–423.

Ladson-Billings, G. 2009. *The Dreamkeepers: Successful Teachers of African American Children.* San Francisco: Jossey-Bass.

McConnell, A.R., & J.M. Leibold. 2001. "Relations Among the Implicit Association Test, Discriminatory Behavior, and Explicit Measures of Racial Attitudes." *Journal of Experimental Social Psychology* 37 (5): 435–442.

McIntosh, K., K. Ellwood, L. McCall, & E.J. Girvan. 2018. "Using Discipline Data to Enhance Equity in School Discipline." *Intervention in School and Clinic* 53 (3): 146–152.

Mendez, J.L., J.L. Carpenter, D.R. LaForett, & J.S. Cohen. 2009. "Parental Engagement and Barriers to Participation in a Community-Based Preventive Intervention." *American Journal of Community Psychology* 44 (1/2): 1–14.

Milner, H.R. 2016. "A Black Male Teacher's Culturally Responsive Practices." *The Journal of Negro Education* 85 (4): 417–432.

Milton-Williams, T., & N. Bryan. 2016. "Respecting a Cultural Continuum of Black Male Pedagogy: Exploring the Life History of a Black Male Middle School Teacher." *Urban Education.* doi:10.1177/0042085916677346.

Moule, J. 2009. "Understanding Unconscious Bias and Unintentional Racism." *Phi Delta Kappan* 90 (5): 320–326.

NAEYC. 2019. "Advancing Equity in Early Childhood Education." Position statement. Washington, DC: NAEYC. www.naeyc.org /resources/position-statements/equity.

NASEM (National Academies of Sciences, Engineering, and Medicine). 2018. "Financial Structure of Early Childhood Education Requires Overhaul to Make It Accessible and Affordable for All Families and to Strengthen the Workforce in This Field." News release. www.nationalacademies.org/news /2018/02/financial-structure-of-early-childhood-education -requires-overhaul-to-make-it-accessible-and-affordable -for-all-families-and-to-strengthen-the-workforce-in-this-field.

Nganga, L. 2015. "Culturally Responsive and Anti-Biased Teaching Benefits Early Childhood Pre-Service Teachers." *Journal of Curriculum and Teaching* 4 (2): e1–e16.

OCR (US Department of Education Office of Civil Rights). 2014. *Snapshot: School Discipline* (Issue Brief No. 1). Civil Rights Data Collection. www2.ed.gov/about/offices/list/ocr/docs /crdc-discipline-snapshot.pdf.

Staats, C. 2016. "Understanding Implicit Bias: What Educators Should Know." *American Educator* 39 (4): 29–43.

Tilghman, S. 2013. "Episode 3: Still Segregated." *The March @50.* PBS. www.pbs.org/black-culture/explore/march-on -washington/web-series/episode-3-equality-in-education.

Whitford, D. K., & A.M. Emerson. 2019. "Empathy Intervention to Reduce Implicit Bias in Pre-Service Teachers." *Psychological Reports* 122 (2): 670–688.

W.K. Kellogg Foundation. 2019. *Cultivating a Community of Champions for Children Through Transformative Family Engagement.* Report. East Battle Creek, MI: W.K. Kellogg Foundation. www.wkkf.org/resource-directory /resources/2019/07/cultivating-a-community-of-champions -for-children–through-transformative-family-engagement.

Valbrun, V. 2017. "Equity vs. Equality: Eliminating Opportunity Gaps in Education." *The Inclusion Solution*, August 10. www.theinclusionsolution.me/equity-vs-equality-eliminating -opportunity-gaps-education.

This chapter supports recommendations from the NAEYC position statement:

Recommendations for Everyone

Item 4: Acknowledge and seek to understand structural inequities and their impact over time.

Recommendations for Early Childhood Educators

Advocate on Behalf of Young Children, Families, and the Early Childhood Profession

Item 1: Speak out against unfair policies or practices and challenge biased perspectives.

Recommendations for Administrators of Schools, Centers, Family Child Care Homes, and Other Early Childhood Education Settings

Item 1: Provide high-quality early learning services that demonstrate a commitment to equitable outcomes for all children.

Item 9: Create meaningful, ongoing opportunities for multiple voices with diverse perspectives to engage in leadership and decision making.

CHAPTER 4
Being an Equity Leader

John Nimmo, Debbie LeeKeenan, and Louise Derman-Sparks

> When the best leaders' work is done, the people say, "We did it ourselves."
>
> —Lao Tzu, *Tao Te Ching*

Integrating an equity approach to diversity into early childhood education (ECE) programs calls for both *visionary* and *strategic* leadership. It requires critical assessment and change in all parts of an ECE program and engagement of the various members of the program—teachers, staff, families, and children. While the ideals of equity may feel right and good, changing the way things are to the way they ought to be in relation to equity and diversity brings challenges as well as rewards. In this chapter, we describe the key concepts and strategies for leading change toward equity and diversity in ECE programs. We use the term *leader* to name the role of directing or administering ECE programs.

A Framework for Change
Critical Awareness

Building a program that reflects equity principles requires leaders who seek out a critical awareness of their own history and identities, develop an understanding of the dynamics of institutional oppression within schools and society, and have a clear commitment to social justice (Khalifa 2018; Khalifa, Gooden, & Davis 2016). This learning occurs simultaneously with leaders taking action in the daily life of the program. As both advocate and activist, an equity leader is willing to take risks when faced with obstacles and resistance (Long, Souto-Manning, & Vasquez 2015). The leader's knowledge of how inequities are both perpetuated and challenged, along with a clear understanding of the context of their program, forms the basis for supporting teacher professional development. As with all learning curves, leaders deepen their knowledge and skills over time from experience in their programs, critical self-reflection on these experiences, and study.

Intentional, Facilitative, and Strategic Leadership

Every decision an equity program leader makes needs to keep the long-term social justice vision and mission in the foreground while managing the day-to-day immediate issues. Program leaders plan and implement a long-term strategy for shifting the culture of the school to one that reflects the values and principles of NAEYC's "Advancing Equity in Early Childhood Education" position statement (2019).

They make decisions about both short- and long-term goals, set priorities, determine the most effective route to meet goals, muster resources, and manage the speed at which to proceed to ensure sustainability. Through observation, listening, and focused conversations with staff, families, and community members, equity leaders gather and analyze information about the context, history, culture, stakeholders, and resources in their programs. They also identify the challenges, strengths, allies, and gatekeepers that shape the opportunities and obstacles facing their work. This data gathering informs the leader's priorities, goals, and the road map of strategies needed for the shift toward greater equity (Derman-Sparks, LeeKeenan, & Nimmo 2015).

Facilitative leadership involves all the stakeholders sharing in the power and responsibility to meet an organization's goals (Forester 2013). The leader develops collaborative partnerships with staff and families so that there is a collective voice in the planning, decision-making, and implementation of the equity mission. However, when sharing power, there are decisions that are ultimately the administrator's responsibility, such as budget and staffing. Before making such decisions, effective leaders authentically gather input from staff and families (LeeKeenan & Ponte 2018).

Creating a Culture for Creativity, Risk-Taking, and Co-Learning

Building programs where diversity and equity can live, and that effectively solve the challenges this process involves, rests on a school culture that nurtures creativity, risk-taking, and co-learning. The goal is to create a space where everyone feels they can offer their perspectives, take risks, make mistakes, and contribute at their own pace. This requires everyone learning from and with each other.

Equity leaders make it possible for staff and families to develop connections and build trusting relationships with each other. They encourage the various stakeholders to expand their perspective beyond a focus on their own interests to being able to empathize with and see other points of view and the big picture of how one's actions intersect with those of others. The leader proposes ground rules for safe and courageous conversations and encourages a healthy embrace of dissonance and disagreement (Nicholsona et al. 2018).

Managing Conflict and Finding the Third Space

Conflict, disequilibrium, and tension are inevitable in the journey of equity and anti-bias efforts. Many conflicts come from dissonance between staff and families' cultural beliefs, practices, and histories. Others are rooted in differing beliefs about diversity that reflect learned stereotypes and prejudices. The leader has the authority and big-picture perspective to play a proactive role in seeking out a *third space*—an intellectual and emotional place where people in conflict move beyond either/or viewpoints and embrace a spectrum of possibilities (Barrera, Kramer, & Macpherson 2012). The objectives of third space conversations are to inform and understand each other, build on each other's ideas, and propose solutions that work for everyone. In seeking a third space, conflicts become opportunities for building collaborative relations, and inclusion. One approach to finding a more inclusive third space is the following three-step process:

1. *Acknowledge*. Listen deeply and name the difference in opinions, beliefs, or values that need to be addressed and analyzed.

2. *Ask*. Gather information from all parties to develop a more inclusive and empathetic understanding of the underlying issues. This step involves clarifying the priorities and being receptive to learning about others.

3. *Adapt*. Create alternatives for adapting policies and practices that are inclusive and reflect equity principles.

Third space solutions are new ways of looking at the issues, not simply a compromise. In a discussion of solutions, leaders identify non-negotiable practices and policies aligned with the equity mission (Derman-Sparks, LeeKeenan, & Nimmo 2015).

Strategies for Change

While the long-term goal is to distribute leadership broadly across program stakeholders, leaders with responsibility for policy, budgeting, supervision, and staff development can act immediately and decisively. They can use their power in ways that are both structural and wide-reaching to encourage and support a range of equity initiatives from teachers and families. These strategies are informed by the NAEYC's "Advancing Equity in Early Childhood Education" position statement (2019), which implores leaders to listen to diverse voices, foster learning communities with adults, and engage in reciprocal partnerships with families.

Program Leader Tasks

The following are suggestions of tasks a program leader can undertake to advance equity:

> **Engage teachers, staff, and yourself in reflection and education.** Effective change toward equity rests on people being reflective about their attitudes, knowledge, and practices, and continuing to expand their understanding of equity issues. Create the time, space, and support so everyone can take steps in their own equity and diversity journey.

> **Form an equity inclusion team.** Develop a team that oversees equity initiatives and that ensures commitment, accountability, and coordination with equity activities. The team should include stakeholder representatives (for example, staff, families, an advisory board, and others who have direct involvement in the program) who are committed to the equity mission and can act as conduits for these efforts into their various constituencies. Ensure that your team does not become diverted into "diversity" activities (e.g., multicultural dinners) that may be helpful community-builders but do not address the underlying inequities in the system (Gorski 2018).

> **Cultivate commitment through a mission statement.** Make your equity commitment transparent by explicitly making it a part of your program's mission statement. Engage program staff, teachers, and families in developing and regularly reviewing the mission statement to ensure shared accountability. Seek feedback from others directly invested in your program.

> **Budget for equity work.** Equity work must be an explicit priority in budget lines for materials, professional development, and recruitment. Identify specific fundraising projects related to your equity strategic plan; for example, ensuring that your children's book collection reflects all the backgrounds and languages spoken by the families within the community your program serves.

> **Create equitable policies in staff and family handbooks.** Policies and procedures will communicate the values and goals of your program; they should explicitly reflect your equity commitment. For example, program leaders can address the inequitable impact of disciplinary and exclusionary practices that affect children of color, particularly boys, by requiring positive alternatives and ongoing assessment of teachers' disciplinary and exclusionary practices.

> **Assess progress.** Ongoing program assessment includes progress toward explicit annual equity goals. Observation, documentation, surveys, and focus groups with staff, families, and other stakeholders reflect and influence your strategic planning.

> **Diversify.** Be intentional in your outreach to recruit teachers and staff who reflect the languages and communities of the children and families you serve and to increase diversity. Mentor leadership development to build diversity in administrative roles. Lead with your mission and values in arguing why having a diverse population is a key element of your program.

> **Be present in the community.** Leaders have a vantage point from which to learn about and be an active participant in the community surrounding their program (Khalifa, Gooden, & Davis 2016). Specifically, include outreach to community elders and advocacy organizations representing groups traditionally marginalized in our society and schools. Community engagement enables program leaders to leverage resources to support the equity mission. In turn, school leaders can join in community efforts for social justice and be a role model to families and staff.

Engaging Teachers and Staff

Even the most talented, committed teachers and staff require the active support of their program leaders to be effective in their equity efforts in and outside the classroom. This involves recruitment, retention, and professional development.

> **Recruit and retain staff committed to anti-bias education.** Make your commitment to equity work visible in all your recruiting and public relations materials (e.g., websites, flyers, position descriptions). Be strategic in advertising and doing outreach, whether formally or by word of mouth. Include questions about equity and anti-bias education in interview protocols when hiring. Implement retention strategies that ensure all staff feel included, visible, and engaged in decision-making.

> **Facilitate collaboration.** Arrange staff work schedules to facilitate relationship building and collaboration, through curriculum planning, team teaching, and common professional development experiences.

> **Engage staff in critical thinking.** Facilitate courageous conversations among teachers and staff about their social identities and about planning, implementation, and assessment of anti-bias materials, environments, and curricula experiences. These activities would include

- Discussing an anti-bias article

- Reviewing children's books for anti-bias issues using a tool such as Social Justice Books (https://socialjusticebooks.org/guide-for-selecting-anti-bias-childrens-books)

- Sharing teachers' documentation of current anti-bias dilemmas in their classrooms.

Use protocols to help facilitate the conversation between colleagues, such as can be found through the School Reform Initiative (www.schoolreforminitiative.org).

> **Integrate anti-bias education into staff meetings and professional development.** This includes focused experiences, such as exploring the linguistic and social identity development of children, institutional dynamics of oppression, and anti-bias curriculum. Professional development for equity also includes bringing an equity lens to all aspects of early childhood education. For instance, the program leader ensures

that staff professional development on STEM education includes exploring how the science curriculum can reflect families' diverse cultural contributions.

> **Provide curricula resources.** Proactively and intentionally ensure that teachers have the classroom materials in the languages they need to support anti-bias activities with children (e.g., persona dolls, books, block accessories, labels, and puzzles that represent families in the program, as well as give visibility to diversity in the children's larger community).

> **Supervise and coach staff in anti-bias work.** As part of their annual individual professional development goals, teachers and staff should identify specific anti-bias education goals and be accountable for meeting equity expectations. Use a tool like a self-study guide to help staff identify their strengths and challenges (Chen, Nimmo, & Fraser 2009). Equity leaders aim to hire and develop staff who are committed to equity principles and want to contribute and expand their skills. At the same time, creating equity is a required competency in the work of staff, just like developing children's literacy or supporting social-emotional development. Leaders should have supervision strategies for working with staff who are not showing improvement or are resistant to the equity mission.

> **Distribute leadership.** Empower emerging equity leaders within the staff and families to take on responsibility for developing and implementing specific social justice projects. For example, taking the lead in creating an anti-bias library for the school or developing a professional development experience.

Including Families

While classroom teachers typically have the most direct and intense relationships with families, the program leader has important responsibilities in ensuring the inclusion of all families in a program's equity mission and implementation.

> **Set the program climate.** Provide opportunities for families (and staff) to socialize, dialogue, and learn together, in ways that give everyone a voice. Be sensitive and responsive to negotiating and adapting the differences among families around time, money, transportation, preferred communication, and language. Through your everyday interactions with families, model a *funds of knowledge* approach in which you learn from families about the strengths, knowledge, and expertise children bring to school from their families and communities (González, Moll, & Amanti 2005).

> **Communicate explicitly about anti-bias goals.** Provide opportunities for teachers and families to learn together about anti-bias education, such as teachers and families sharing their identity stories, favorite childhood memories, and creating an FAQ document for the family handbook about anti-bias education. Let families know about your program's anti-bias education with children, such as conversations with children, new children's books, activities happening in the classrooms, and ongoing professional development efforts (Derman-Sparks & Edwards with Goins 2020).

> **Reach out to families.** Take the initiative in reaching out to families, especially those who have traditionally been marginalized by school environments. Ensure that your program's environment, including hallways and offices, as well as classrooms, reflect cultural and linguistic diversity. Explicitly welcome and encourage families to visit in their native language. Take the time to meet with families in their community and in their homes, learning from and with them about the equity issues they confront each day and what program policies and practices need changing (Long, Souto-Manning, & Vasquez 2015).

Conclusion

Ultimately, leading change toward equity and diversity means firmly holding to the vision and mission, while inspiring, facilitating, and supporting step-by-step strategic action. This work takes time—change is a process, not an event or two. Developing a network of supportive colleagues with whom to learn, doing critical assessment, and celebrating small changes makes the complex job of equity leaders doable!

References

Barrera, I., L. Kramer, & T.D. Macpherson. 2012. *Skilled Dialogue: Strategies for Responding to Cultural Diversity in Early Childhood.* 2nd ed. Baltimore: Brookes Publishing.

Chen, D.W., J. Nimmo, & H. Fraser. 2009. "Becoming a Culturally Responsive Early Childhood Educator: A Tool to Support Reflection by Teachers Embarking on the Anti-Bias Journey." *Multicultural Perspectives* 11 (2): 101–106.

Derman-Sparks, L., D. LeeKeenan, & J. Nimmo. 2015. *Leading Anti-Bias Early Childhood Programs: A Guide for Change.* New York: Teachers College Press; Washington, DC: NAEYC.

Derman-Sparks, L., & J.O. Edwards. With C.M. Goins. 2020. *Anti-Bias Education for Young Children and Ourselves.* 2nd ed. Washington, DC: NAEYC.

Forester, J. 2013. *Planning in the Face of Conflict: The Surprising Possibilities of Facilitative Leadership.* Chicago: Planners Press.

González, N., L.C. Moll, & C. Amanti, eds. 2005. *Funds of Knowledge: Theorizing Practices in Households, Communities, and Classroom.* Mahwah, NJ: Lawrence Erlbaum.

Gorski, P. 2018. *Reaching and Teaching Students in Poverty: Strategies for Erasing the Opportunity Gap.* 2nd ed. New York: Teachers College Press.

Khalifa, M. 2018. *Culturally Responsive School Leadership.* Cambridge: Harvard Education Press.

Khalifa, M.A., M.A. Gooden, & J.E. Davis. 2016. "Culturally Responsive School Leadership: A Synthesis of the Literature." *Review of Educational Research* 86 (4): 1272–1311. doi:10.3102/0034654316630383.

LeeKeenan, D., & I.C. Ponte. 2018. *From Survive to Thrive: A Director's Guide for Leading an Early Childhood Program.* Washington, DC: NAEYC.

Long, S., M. Souto-Manning, & V.M. Vasquez, eds. 2015. *Courageous Leadership in Early Childhood Education: Taking a Stand for Social Justice.* New York: Teachers College Press.

NAEYC. 2019. "Advancing Equity in Early Childhood Education." Position statement. Washington, DC: NAEYC. www.naeyc.org /resources/position-statements/equity.

Nicholsona, J., K. Kuhlb, H. Maniatesc, B. Lina, & S. Bonetti. 2018. "A Review of the Literature on Leadership in Early Childhood: Examining Epistemological Foundations and Considerations of Social Justice." *Early Child Development and Care* 190 (2): 91–122. doi:10.1080/03004430.2018.1455036.

naeyc

This chapter supports recommendations from the NAEYC position statement:

Recommendations for Everyone

Item 5: View your commitment to cultural responsiveness as an ongoing process.

Recommendations for Administrators of Schools, Centers, Family Child Care Homes, and Other Early Childhood Education Settings

Item 2: Take proactive steps with measurable goals to recruit and retain educators and leaders who reflect the diversity of children and families served and who meet professional expectations.

Item 9: Create meaningful, ongoing opportunities for multiple voices with diverse perspectives to engage in leadership and decision making.

CHAPTER 5

Recognizing Shortcomings of a Traditional Professional Knowledge Base

Tonia R. Durden and Stephanie M. Curenton

Known internationally for being an accomplished, mighty, and revered tribe in East Africa, the Maasai warriors have a traditional greeting for one another: *Kasserian Ingera*, which means "And how are the children?" The traditional response is "All the children are well," or that peace and safety prevail. Such a traditional greeting and response of the Maasai acknowledges the high value they place on children's well-being and how children's safety and peace determine the future health and prosperity of their whole tribe. Here in the United States, what value do we place on young children's well-being when it comes to early childhood education? How do we address inequitable educational and learning experiences that are pervasive within early childhood programs and the schools in which children matriculate?

The focus of this chapter is to recognize the role early childhood teacher preparation and education play in contributing to the mass miseducation of racially and linguistically minoritized children. Racially minoritized children are Black children, Latino/a children, Asian/ Pacific Islanders, and Native Americans who have been *minoritized* by the United States' intentional historical process of using geographic markers (e.g., nationality) and/or phenotypic characteristics to socially construct a caste system that is based on biologically artificial racial categories (Benitez 2010; Stewart 2013). It is important to explicitly define our focus on racially minoritized children because this chapter will examine shortcomings in teacher preparation, development, and knowledge base that leads to the perpetuation of society's hegemony within early childhood classrooms.

Key questions we will explore include

1. How do early childhood educators perpetuate inequity and racial bias through markers of what is knowledge and intelligence?

2. What are the cultural standards being used to gauge effectiveness and what is the evidence that it works for all children?

3. What are the limitations and racial biases of the current professional knowledge base and expectations within teacher education?

4. What professional knowledge base is essential for effective teaching of racially and linguistically minoritized children within early childhood education?

We will explore these questions by building upon over 30 years of empirical evidence and seminal research that identifies how educational systems and early childhood programs have historically and currently created culturally and linguistically inequitable learning experiences for racially and linguistically minoritized children. Within this context, we will then explore the need for and benefits of educational practices and experiences that are responsive to young children of color (that is, anti-bias education by Derman-Sparks & Edwards with Goins 2020), culturally and linguistically relevant education (García, Kleifgen, & Falchi 2008; Ladson-Billings 2014), and anti-racist education (Escayg 2018). Lastly, we urge the reader to be willing to think critically about how our current professional learning experiences can be improved, not only to develop and create more high-quality, culturally responsive professionals and leaders, but also to advance educational equity efforts.

Professional Standards: Quality Redefined

Within early childhood education, there is a general consensus that quality programs provide young children with educationally rich and responsive environments that enhance their language and social and cognitive development, which is empirically linked to improving young children's social and cognitive outcomes (Burchinal & Cryer 2003; Minervino & One 2014). In education, we have used this consensus to identify professional standards and skills individuals within our workforce must develop in order to create quality learning environments for all children. If you were to crosswalk professional standards from the National Association for the Education of Young Children (NAEYC 2020), the Council for the Accreditation of Educator Preparation (CAEP 2013), the Council of Chief State School Officers (CCSSO 2011), and the National Board for Professional Teaching Standards (NBPTS 2012), you would find that they are similar in their focus on a set of foundational skills and knowledge that professionals should be expected to develop and master. For example, early childhood professionals across the teacher preparation spectrum are expected to develop, strengthen, and master competencies related to

> Understanding how young children learn and develop (child development)

> Implementing effective teaching practices (developmentally appropriate practice)

> Assessing children (observation and documentation)

> Engaging with families and communities (family/community partnerships)

> Adhering to professionalism standards (ethical practice and professional learning)

As we explore these standards more critically, however, we must ask whether they explicitly and intentionally require professionals to consider the complexity of dismantling racial inequity within early childhood education and teaching in a culturally responsive manner. Do we ask whether we are explicit in that to be developmentally appropriate and effective, best practices and assessment strategies must be culturally and linguistically responsive? Thereby, acknowledging and being intentional in our understanding and implementation of culturally and linguistically responsive education is not a separate or seasonal educational experience for some young children; rather, it is integral to the education of all children.

Professional Knowledge Base: Missing Links

The primary focus of professional development and initial teacher preparation is on establishing a foundational set of skills for educating young children (e.g., create hands-on learning experiences for children, use individual and group guidance techniques). We argue, however, that the missing component to this foundational set of

skills is providing an expectation of, and standards for, culturally and linguistically responsive teaching. Instead, we should prepare and train teachers who are expected to build upon the cultural identity and linguistic strengths children bring to the classroom and disrupt educational policies, instructional practices, and assessment measures that do not affirm children's cultural identity, language, and expectations of excellence. For example, traditionally we have promoted best practices such as preparing easily accessible and appropriate materials and designing child-centered, hands-on learning experiences for children. We are very diligent and thorough in providing examples of hands-on learning to teachers as well as opportunities for them to observe videos of children enthusiastically engaged in hands-on learning experiences. How often do we instead look outward to the cultural community of learners we teach for how to explore hands-on learning experiences? Hands-on learning in theory and practice (the what, why, and how) becomes culturally contextualized. For example, when educating Black children, teachers should be expected to develop knowledge and understanding of a Black ethos of teaching and learning. A Black ethos, also referred to as an African worldview, emphasizes experiences and ways of living that focus on spirituality, interdependence, harmony, movement, verve, affect, communalism, collective consciousness, expressive individualism, and oral tradition (Kambon 2004). Generally, Black children are exposed to home and community environments that encourage and support kinesthetic movement and high levels of motor activity (Hale 2001; Hilliard 1992; Kambon 2004).

Similarly, many children of color are also exposed to multiple literacies, such as oral storytelling, and engage in literacy experiences with multiple types of environmental print (e.g., music lyrics, recipes, magazines, digital print, newspaper, sales papers). As a result, students thrive in environments that use multimedia and multimodal teaching strategies (Hale 2001; Hilliard 1992). This stance of making culture and language the center of educational experience instead of a generic "developmentally appropriate practice" is a 180-degree shift from our current early childhood professional identity of "best practices." It is urgent that we question, *Best practices for whom? And at the cultural and linguistic exclusion of whom?*

Furthermore, in addition to making culture and language the foci of all instruction and assessment, we have to intentionally create opportunities within teacher education for professionals to explore how individuals, programs, and institutions create inequitable experiences for children of color, their families, and their communities. Unfortunately, within teacher preparation, the cultural "why" is a one-stop quick shop of courses and professional learning experiences that is not ongoing, rigorous, or helpful to professionals in deeply examining their own biases and prejudices and how those contribute to educational inequity (Boutte 2012; Carter 2008; Durden, Escalante, & Blitch 2015). There are few opportunities for professionals to develop a sociopolitical consciousness that leads to educational advocacy and equity reform (Hilliard 2000a; King 2015; Ladson-Billings 2014; Paris 2012). Professional learning that does focus on culturally and linguistically responsive teaching and efforts to dismantle educational equity are special features or optional. While the initial goal is to successfully implement culturally and linguistically responsive instruction (as it occurs at the classroom level), it also takes efforts at the program and institutional level (educational policies, teacher preparation, and professional learning) to achieve the goal of racial/ethnic educational equity. Until we set the same priority for mandating professional learning and standards focused on culturally and linguistically equitable teaching as we do with topics such as preventing challenging behaviors, infant/toddler responsive caregiving, or benefits of play, then we will continue to support an early childhood educational system that is not responsive or equitable to racially and linguistically minoritized (RLM) children. To move toward a trajectory of identifying a professional knowledge base that is inclusive of culturally and linguistically responsive principles and promotes educational equity, we must continue to critically ask ourselves, *How do early childhood educators perpetuate inequity and racial bias through markers of what is knowledge and intelligence?*

Professional Perspectives: One Size Only

Our early childhood professional system is driven by a set of core values, ideals, policies, and practices that represents the language of diversity but lacks an implementation of inclusion and equity. Recently, NAEYC issued a position statement specifically focused on advancing equity in early childhood education (NAEYC 2019). There are eight specific recommendations for teacher education and professional development that address teacher pedagogy (i.e., equity-centered NAEYC Professional Standards and Competencies for Early

Childhood Educators), teacher recruitment and retention (i.e., workforce diversity initiatives and supports), and teacher education and professional development systems of engagement (i.e., equitable access to professional development and postsecondary credentials) (NAEYC 2019). This is a momentous start to explicitly addressing how our professional standards and system should be first grounded within an equity and sociocultural context lens and then how educators, teacher educators, leaders, and policy officials can create equitable and inclusive spaces for RLM children, families, and adults. While this is a start, the "Advancing Equity in Early Childhood Education" position statement cannot be a standalone document without any action, accountability, or mobility in the successful implementation of the recommended actions we must take in our field. This position statement and the recommendations within it send the message that there is a need and expectation to implement equitable learning experiences for all children. As you reflect on our position in this chapter and those supported within NAEYC's position statement on equity, a valid question becomes, "Haven't we already highlighted through the NAEYC Code of Ethics and Core Values the expectation of recognizing 'that children are best understood and supported within the context of family, culture, community, and society' and respecting 'diversity in children, families, and colleagues' (NAEYC 2016, 4)?" The short answer is, in theory and print, yes; but in practice and according to the racially inequitable educational experiences that still exist for children of color, a resounding NO.

If we peel back the surface and critically explore our early childhood system and the practices we promote as *best* and *developmentally appropriate*, they almost exclusively align within a Eurocentric cultural framework. Take, for example, an individualist versus collectivist perspective, as explored by Zepeda and colleagues (2012). Table 5.1 compares several cultural priorities between these two contrasting value orientations. Also included in the table are indicator score descriptions from the *Infant/Toddler Environment Rating Scale*, Third Edition ([ITERS-3]; Harms et al. 2017), and the *Early Childhood Environment Rating Scale*, Third Edition ([ECERS-3]; Harms, Clifford, & Cryer 2014), one of the leading instruments used by early childhood systems to measure classroom quality.

When we examine these two different perspectives in relation to our professional and program standards, it is clear that the practices we promote are primarily centered on individualist principles. This is problematic

Table 5.1. Individualist and Collectivist Perspectives as Scored Using ITERS-3 and ECERS-3	
Individualist Perspective	**Collectivist Perspective**
Emphasis on **self-help** skills: "You zipped up your jacket by yourself, way to go!"	Child as member of a **group** with a focus on **group** esteem: "Look how awesome we are sitting criss-cross applesauce."
ITERS-3 indicator score:	
7.4 Staff actively teach **self-help skills** as children are ready (e.g., provide some finger foods for older babies; teach children to use spoon or fork, to wipe up spills, and clear table as ready).	
ECERS-3 indicator score:	
7.3 Staff actively teach **self-help skills** as children are ready (e.g., teach child to use napkin and spoon; teach 3s to use forks and give safe knives to older preschoolers to learn to cut).	
Learning is **child centered** and the child's role is as an explorer with **individual choice.**	Learning is **adult directed** and the child's role is as an observer.
ECERS-3 indicator score:	ITERS-3 indicator score:
7.1 Much teaching is **individualized**, with few if any exceptions.	1.2 The majority of staff-child interactions **occur with groups of children** and are staff initiated and directed (e.g., all the children are gathered together in a group for play activities such as music, art, or story time).
Playing with materials and objects is the priority in which children are expected to first learn how to be possessors of objects. Then they learn how to socially interact and share with others.	From the early beginnings of a child's life, sharing, relationships, and social interactions with others is more important than play with materials and objects.
	ECERS-3 indicator score:
	1.4 The majority of **interactions are with large group,** rather than with individual children or small groups.

Note: The range for ITERS-3 and ECERS-3 indicator scores is 1–7; 1 = inadequate and 7 = excellent.
Indicator scores from Harms, Clifford, & Cryer 2014 and Harms et al. 2017.

for two reasons. First, most RLM children are raised within collectivist perspective families. Therefore, there is often a cultural clash that occurs and is not often addressed between caregiving practices and educational goals and experiences at home and school. The second issue is that our benchmarks of quality center around creating environments, teacher–child interactions, and child outcomes that encourage independence, self-help skills, and individual achievement. While these skills are important, especially for one cultural group in our society, they exclude the focus and goals of cooperative engagement and the focus on group goals and accomplishments that is valued by another set of individuals and cultural groups. Furthermore, one of the leading environmental rating scales used by many early childhood state and regulatory systems is based on primarily individualistic perspectives. In other words, there are negative consequences and barriers (e.g., licensing requirement, a program's quality rating, teacher and program incentive) for programs and teachers who adhere to more collectivist perspectives

that are aligned with the cultural context of the children and families they teach and serve. As we examine more critically what we define as *quality* and how we measure program and teacher quality, we must ask ourselves, *What are the cultural standards being used to gauge effectiveness and what is the evidence that it works for all children?*

Professional Learning: Colonization Roots

It is critical to explicitly address how we are bringing forth the authentic voices, experiences, and strengths of culturally and linguistically diverse children, families, and communities. What currently exists is a system of educational experiences that values Eurocentric perspectives of learning and child development. It is important for us to begin with identifying how to decolonize early childhood education. Decolonization is a long-term process involving the cultural, linguistic, psychological, and bureaucratic divesting of colonial power or Eurocentric perspectives, beliefs, and experiences that permeates and dominates our educational and teacher education systems although other cultural perspectives and experiences exist (Hilliard 2000b; Nxumalo & Cedillo 2017). We must begin first with the rhetoric we use to describe children of color. We must stop labeling children by the circumstances within which adults and society place them (as disadvantaged, at risk) and shift our lexicon to one that acknowledges the cultural tools, languages, skills, and knowledge that children bring with them to school. Therefore, instead of labeling Karim as an "at-risk boy living in a single-parent home who can't focus and is always out of his seat," we view him as "an inquisitive, curious, and eager-to-learn 4-year-old who is a class leader." This reframes our view of Karim as a child who is always ready to be engaged in activities and with teachers and peers, and has a network and support system that extends to family, friends, the community, and the early childhood program where he attends and is valued.

Next in our efforts to decolonize early childhood education, we should acknowledge as a field how the educational theories we promote represent almost exclusively the voices and scholarship of White men (e.g., Piaget, Vygotsky, Bandura, Bronfenbrenner, Gardner). Our focus on these theorists not only perpetuates the dominant narrative of whose educational theory and scholarship is of value, but also silences and ignores the contributions of women and scholars of color who have made significant contributions to child development and early childhood education that benefit the learning and development of RLM children (e.g., Janice Hale, Louise Derman-Sparks, Gloria Ladson-Billings, Evelyn K. Moore, Janet Gonzalez-Mena, Gloria Boutte, Asa G. Hilliard III [also known as Nana Baffour Amankwatia II], Carolyn Brunson). Also, there is very little inclusion of theories such as critical theory or Latino/a critical theory when identifying practices and innovations within our field that benefit children, families, and educators of color.

Lastly, we must examine how the educational policies and practices we promote further suppress and silence the voices and cultural experiences of culturally and linguistically diverse communities. Take, for example, the widely known Safe to Sleep (formerly Back to Sleep) campaigns launched in the early 1990s that revolutionized state regulatory infant care practices, teacher education standards, and also parenting programs (Safe to Sleep, n.d.). In all states, there are similar safe sleep mandates

and professional learning criteria for early childhood programs and infant teachers. Recommendations to prevent Sudden Unexpected Infant Death (SUID) include promoting room sharing but not co-sleeping (AAP 2016). Co-sleeping is a widely used cultural practice in the United States and globally among many culturally and linguistically diverse families (Black, Latino/a, Filipino, Korean, Native American) and used less often within White families (Ball & Volpe 2013; Trawick-Smith & Smith 2014). While Native American/Alaska Native babies and non-Latino/a Black babies have the highest rates of SUID, it is important to question how safe sleep policies were developed and inclusive of the voices and experiences of families who have engaged historically and currently in co-sleeping practices (CDC 2020). As Ball and Volpe (2013) contend, the SUID reduction campaign and mandates' "failure to recognize the importance of infant sleep location to ethnic and sub-cultural identity has led to inappropriate and ineffective risk-reduction messages that are rejected by their target populations" (84). By not considering the cultural practices and asking what safe co-sleeping practices look like, this policy and practice undermines the sleep practices and experiences of many families and prevents opportunities to examine safe co-sleeping practices in the home and school. Culturally responsive and inclusive research on infant care and interventions that accommodate personal and cultural values are needed. As we consider other child development guidelines and practices we mandate, we must ask, *What are the limitations and racial biases of the current professional knowledge base and expectations within teacher education?*

Professional Expectations: To Be Qualified

There is much research and literature examining the educational, social, and developmental benefits of providing culturally and linguistically salient experiences for young children (Derman-Sparks & Edwards with Goins 2020; García 2008; Gay 2010). There is also an extensive body of research to suggest the need to train and prepare highly qualified teachers who are competent in meeting the unique needs of RLM children (García 2008; Gonzalez-Mena 2008; Hilliard [Baffour Amankwatia] 2006; Ladson-Billings 2014). In the next sections we both ask and answer the question, *What professional knowledge base is essential for effective teaching of racially and linguistically minoritized children within early childhood education?*

We explore what should be the expectations within teacher education, the ideology that governs our professional education system, and the practices that are expected of our professionals. We will also explore examples of measures that could be used to determine teacher effectiveness in promoting educational equity.

Adopting a Culturally and Linguistically Relevant, Anti-Bias Pedagogy

Scholars have articulated the ideological and pedagogical tenets of culturally relevant education (Ladson-Billings 1995), culturally responsive education (Gay 2010), bilingual education (García, Kleifgen, & Falchi 2008), anti-bias early childhood education (Derman-Sparks & Edwards with Goins 2020), and a culturally relevant anti-bias framework (Iruka, Curenton, & Eke 2014). These tenets contend that teaching should incorporate the cultural knowledge, languages, experiences, and learning and communication styles of children from diverse racial, ethnic, and linguistic backgrounds (Curenton & Iruka 2013). Combined, the tenets of these pedagogies/frameworks manifest in daily classroom interactions that characterize teacher-student and peer-to-peer exchanges that we will refer to as a *culturally and linguistically relevant, anti-bias framework* (CRAF). Instructional interactions should include academic, social, and emotional content, and scholars argue that there are interaction dynamics that might support (or deter) RLM children's academic and social-emotional outcomes, such as inequitable learning opportunities, discipline, English-only programs (deterrent) or teachers' use of culturally and linguistically relevant, anti-bias pedagogy (supportive). Because teachers bring many elements to the practice of teaching that influence the quality of their instruction (such as personal attitudes, racial bias, and even stereotypes) it is imperative to understand how these elements affect their classroom interactions with RLM children specifically to improve classroom practice and create positive learning environments for historically disenfranchised children (Sandilos, DiPerna, & The Family Life Project Key Investigators 2014).

We need to move beyond viewing classroom interactions as simply "high quality" and instead understand that interactions with students can *only* be "high quality" *if* they are also culturally and linguistically relevant and grounded in anti-bias principles. Traditional definition of *high quality* without consideration of cultural and linguistic relevance is insufficient to improve the educational opportunities, experiences, and outcomes of RLM children given the history of oppression and discrimination facing these ethnic/racial groups. Instead, it may be that RLM children need to be exposed to high-quality education that is *also* culturally and linguistically relevant and equitable (Humphries & Iruka 2017). If this is true, then the field needs a classroom measure that taps into aspects of quality as well as those cultural and equity constructs that are particularly relevant when educating RLM children.

Examining Classroom Quality Through an Equity Lens: Assessing Classroom Sociocultural Equity Scale

Some of the mostly widely used classroom observation measures in the early childhood field are the *Classroom Assessment Scoring System* ([CLASS]; Pianta, La Paro, & Hamre 2008), the *Early Childhood Environment Rating Scale*, Third Edition ([ECERS-3]; Harms, Clifford, & Cryer 2014), and the *Simple Interactions Tool* ([SIT]; Li 2014). All of these observational measures have various approaches to measuring *process quality* (that is, the back-and-forth classroom interactions between teachers and students that support children's learning and development). CLASS examines three domains: emotional support, classroom organization, and instructional support, which include 10 dimensions. ECERS-3 focuses on defining quality as it relates to learning opportunities, gross motor, teacher interactions, and math activities. Although ECERS-3 also contains items about the presence of photos and books featuring racial/ethnic or ability diversity in the classroom, the measure does not consider equity or anti-bias instruction during interactions. SIT is a very brief (four items) measure that assesses teachers' interactions with individual children in relation to connection, reciprocity, inclusion, and opportunity to grow. Although all of these measures are grounded in what NAEYC would consider to be the best standards of developmentally appropriate practice, none of these measures explicitly or intentionally address culturally relevant, anti-bias pedagogy.

The *Assessing Classroom Sociocultural Equity Scale* ([ACSES]; Curenton et al. 2020), pronounced "access," is unique from these prior measures in that regard. ACSES is an observation tool explicitly created to measure the process quality of equitable sociocultural interactions in early childhood classrooms (preschool to grade 3) with racially minoritized learners (RMLs). There are six aspects of the classroom that are observed when using the tool (Curenton et al. 2020):

1. Challenging Status Quo Knowledge

2. Equitable Learning Opportunities for RMLs

3. Equitable Discipline

4. Connections to Home Life

5. Personalized Learning Opportunities

6. RMLs' Participation and Engagement

The six aspects of the ACSES fit within a CRAF in several ways. For instance, for Challenging Status Quo Knowledge, the tool examines whether teachers encourage children to share their opinions and question whether or not information is "correct." Equitable Learning Opportunities measures whether RMLs are afforded the full chance to participate during classroom interactions, and Equitable Discipline measures whether or not RMLs are exposed to harsh discipline in the classroom. Connections to Home Life examines how teachers and children share personal experiences and stories about their lives outside of school. Personalized Learning Opportunities comprises those instructional practices that research has shown to be great for all types of learners, such as the use of multiple learning modalities (e.g., auditory, visual, tactile). Lastly, RMLs' Participation

and Engagement is based on the relationships among peers in the classroom, such as how well they get along and cooperate on learning activities. Curenton and colleagues (2020) have found that ACSES measures aspects of classroom interactions that are distinct from CLASS; therefore, this tool has the potential to make a unique contribution to the field by providing researchers, supervisors, and classroom coaches with a specific tool they can use to gauge the equity and cultural relevance of classroom interactions.

Conclusion

We began this chapter sharing how the Maasai warriors' traditional greeting focuses on the well-being of children and proceeded to detail how we must recognize our shortcomings within teacher education. We end the chapter with a call to action. We must move beyond the language of diversity to the practice of inclusion by decolonizing our professional standards, practices, and policies. Although not exhaustive, the following key points (formatted as questions and answers) highlight the main areas of focus in teacher education we must consider in order to enhance the cultural and educational excellence of young children, and questions we must continue to ask ourselves as early childhood professionals.

It is our hope that this chapter has placed an educational spotlight on recognizing how we can improve our efforts and work toward creating and developing a workforce that is culturally and linguistically responsive and promotes educational equity. We thereby hope that when the question "And how are the children?" is asked, our responses within early childhood education can be "All is well!"

> ⟩ **What steps are we taking to decolonize early childhood education (practices, policies, teacher education)?**

We must recruit, retain, train, and provide ongoing professional development for culturally relevant and competent teachers as well as bilingual/ESL teachers—no exceptions (Haberman 1996; García 2008; Goldhaber & Hansen 2010). If we have the will to educate all children, then we must be intentional in our work of recruiting and supporting the best and most promising teachers who express an interest and have skills in teaching RLM children. We want teachers who are effective, motivated, resilient, and transformative. We need teachers who engage in and seek educational experiences that help them to understand the central role of culture, language, and identity (García 2008; Durden, Escalante, & Blitch 2015) and those who create opportunities to critique the current educational system and strive toward developing as master teachers of RLM children. Not only must teachers (and teacher educators) adopt an ideology that is culturally and linguistically responsive, but they must also have a deep understanding that teaching is a sociopolitical act and how the classroom can support equity, justice, and opportunity (Curenton & Iruka 2013; García, Kleifgen, & Falchi 2008; Ladson-Billings 2014).

> ⟩ **What are culturally and linguistically responsive practices we can promote across the teacher development spectrum? How do we dismantle cultural and linguistic annihilation, classroom inequity, and mass miseducation from cradle to career?**

We must create measures of quality that capture anti-bias, culturally and linguistically responsive, and equitable teaching. There are tools being developed that help to measure culturally responsive education in preschool classrooms (i.e., ACSES; Curenton et al. 2020). Once validated, these tools can be used across the teacher developmental spectrum. Additionally, in most universities and colleges, there is a plethora of research that is being conducted that helps to advance our understanding of how to implement culturally and linguistically responsive education and innovative approaches that accelerate learning for children of color (Collier & Thomas 2017). We must be more intentional in translating this research to practice when preparing teachers and working with current teachers in the field. We must look to communities, schools and educators with *success* in educating children of color to assist in our systemic efforts to make success and educational equity a norm or expectation, not a distinction.

> ⟩ **How do we create professional standards that capture the complexity and dynamic nature of culture, language, and learning and the nuances of educational inequity?**

We must provide ongoing professional support to all individuals educating and caring for young children of color. Furthermore, professionals need ongoing professional development and support that also includes their prolonged immersion in the culture and close ties with community. They also need to be part of professional organizations such as NAEYC, the National Black Child Development Institute, the National Association for Bilingual Education, and the National Association for Multicultural Education to support advocacy efforts for the care and education of culturally and linguistically diverse children. Teacher education must also provide opportunities for observations and internships that effectively demonstrate culturally and linguistically relevant teaching and assessment with master teachers.

References

AAP (American Academy of Pediatrics). 2016. "SIDS and Other Sleep Related Infant Deaths: Updated 2016 Recommendations for a Safe Infant Sleeping Environment." *Pediatrics* 138 (5): e20162938.

Ball, H.L., & L.E. Volpe. 2013. "Sudden Infant Death Syndrome (SIDS) Risk Reduction and Infant Sleep Location—Moving the Discussion Forward." *Social Science & Medicine* 79: 84–91.

Benitez, M., Jr. 2010. "Resituating Culture Centers Within a Social Justice Framework." In *Culture Centers in Higher Education: Perspectives on Identity, Theory, and Practice*, ed. L. Patton, 119–134. Sterling, VA: Stylus.

Boutte, G.S. 2012. "Urban Schools: Challenges and Possibilities for Early Childhood and Elementary Education." *Urban Education* 47 (2): 515–550.

Burchinal, M.R., & D. Cryer. 2003. "Diversity, Child Care Quality, and Developmental Outcomes." *Early Childhood Research Quarterly* 18 (4): 401–426.

CAEP (Council for the Accreditation of Educator Preparation). 2013. *The CAEP Standards*. Washington, DC: CAEP. www .caepnet.org/standards.

Carter, D.J. 2008. "On Spotlighting and Ignoring Racial Group Members in the Classroom." In *Everyday Antiracism: Getting Real About Race in School*, ed. M. Pollack, 230–234. New York: The New Press.

CCSSO (Council of Chief State School Officers). 2011. *Interstate Teacher Assessment and Support Consortium (InTASC) Model Core Teaching Standards: A Resource for State Dialogue*. Washington, DC: CCSSO. https://ccsso.org/sites/default/files /2017-11/InTASC_Model_Core_Teaching_Standards _2011.pdf.

CDC (Centers for Disease Control and Prevention.) 2020. "Sudden Unexpected Infant Death and Sudden Infant Death Syndrome: Data and Statistics." Last modified September 18. www.cdc .gov/sids/data.htm.

Collier, V.P, & W.P. Thomas. 2017. "Validating the Power of Bilingual Schooling: Thirty-Two Years of Large-Scale, Longitudinal Research." *Annual Review of Applied Linguistics* 37: 203–217. doi:10.1017/S0267190517000034.

Curenton, S.M., & I.U. Iruka. 2013. *Cultural Competence in Early Childhood Education*. San Diego: Bridgepoint Education.

Curenton, S.M., I.U. Iruka, M. Humphries, B. Jensen, T. Durden, S.E. Rochester, J. Sims, J.V. Whittaker, & M.B. Kinzie. 2020. "Validity for the Assessing Classroom Sociocultural Equity Scale (ACSES) in Early Childhood Classrooms." *Early Education and Development* 31 (2): 269–288.

Derman-Sparks, L., & J.O. Edwards. With C.M. Goins. 2020. *Anti-Bias Education for Young Children and Ourselves*. 2nd ed. Washington, DC: NAEYC.

Durden, T.R., E. Escalante, & K. Blitch. 2015. "Start with Us! Culturally Relevant Pedagogy in the Preschool Classroom." *Early Childhood Education Journal* 43 (3): 223–232.

Escayg, K.A. 2018. "The Missing Links: Enhancing Anti-Bias Education with Anti-Racist Education." *Journal of Curriculum, Teaching, Learning, and Leadership in Education* 3 (1): 15–20.

García, O. 2008. "Multilingual Language Awareness and Teacher Education." In *Knowledge About Language*, ed. N.H. Hornberger, 385–400. Vol. 6 of *Encyclopedia of Language and Education*, 2nd ed. Boston: Springer.

García, O., J. Kleifgen, & L. Falchi. 2008. *Equity Perspectives: From English Language Learners to Emergent Bilinguals*. Equity Matters: Research Review No. 1. New York: Teachers College, Columbia University.

Gay, G. 2010. *Culturally Responsive Teaching: Theory, Research, and Practice*. New York: Teachers College Press.

Goldhaber, D., & M. Hansen. 2010. "Race, Gender, and Teacher Testing: How Informative a Tool is Teacher Licensure Testing?" *American Educational Research Journal* 47 (1): 218–251.

Gonzalez-Mena, J. 2008. *Diversity in Early Care and Education: Honoring Differences*. Burr Ridge, IL: McGraw-Hill Higher Education.

Haberman, M. 1996. "Selecting and Preparing Culturally Competent Teachers for Urban Schools." In *Handbook of Research on Teacher Education*, 2nd ed., eds. J. Sikula, T.J. Buttery, & E. Guyton, 747–760.

Hale, J.E. 2001. *Learning While Black: Creating Educational Excellence for African American Children*. Baltimore: The Johns Hopkins University Press.

Harms, T., R.M. Clifford, & D. Cryer. 2014. *Early Childhood Environment Rating Scale (ECERS-3)*. 3rd ed. New York: Teachers College Press.

Harms, T., D. Cryer, R.M. Clifford, & N. Yazejian. 2017. *Infant/ Toddler Environment Rating Scale (ITERS-3)*. 3rd ed. New York: Teachers College Press.

Hilliard, A.G., III. 1992. "Behavioral Style, Culture, and Teaching and Learning." *The Journal of Negro Education* 61 (3): 370–377.

Hilliard, A.G., III. 2000a. "Excellence in Education Versus High-Stakes Standardized Testing." *Journal of Teacher Education* 51 (4): 293–304.

Hilliard, A.G., III. 2000b. "The State of African Education." Paper presented at Annual Meeting of the American Educational Research Association in New Orleans, LA.

Hilliard, A.G., III [Baffour Amankwatia, N., II]. 2006. "Aliens in the Education Matrix: Recovering Freedom." *The New Educator* 2 (2): 87–102.

Humphries, M., & I.U. Iruka. 2017. "Ring the Alarm: Moving from Educational Gaps to Educational Opportunities for Black Students. In *African American Children in Early Childhood Education*, eds. I.U. Iruka, S.M. Curenton, & T.R. Durden, 15–34. Vol. 5 of *Advances in Race and Ethnicity in Education*. Bingley, UK: Emerald Publishing.

Kambon, K.K. 2004. "The Worldviews Paradigm as the Conceptual Framework for African/Black Psychology." In *Black Psychology*, 4th ed., ed. R.L. Jones, 73–92. Hampton, VA: Cobb & Henry.

King, J.E. 2015. "Dysconscious Racism: Ideology, Identity, and the Miseducation of Teachers." In *Dysconscious Racism, Afrocentric Praxis, and Education for Human Freedom: Through the Years I Keep on Toiling*, 125–139. New York: Routledge.

Ladson-Billings, G. 1995. "Toward a Theory of Culturally Relevant Pedagogy." *American Educational Research Journal* 32 (3): 465–491.

Ladson-Billings, G. 2014. "Culturally Relevant Pedagogy 2.0: a.k.a. the Remix." *Harvard Educational Review* 84 (1): 74–84.

Li, J. 2014. *Simple Interactions Tool*. Pittsburgh: Fred Rogers Center.

Minervino, J., & R.O.D. One. 2014. "Lessons from Research and the Classroom: Implementing High-Quality Pre-K that Makes a Difference for Young Children." Whitepaper. Seattle: Bill & Melinda Gates Foundation. https://docs.gatesfoundation.org /documents/lessons%20from%20research%20and%20the %20Classroom_September%202014.pdf.

NAEYC. 2016. *Code of Ethical Conduct and Statement of Commitment*. Brochure. Rev. ed. Washington, DC: NAEYC.

NAEYC. 2019. "Advancing Equity in Early Childhood Education." Position statement. Washington, DC: NAEYC. www.naeyc.org /resources/position-statements/equity.

NAEYC. 2020. "Professional Standards and Competencies for Early Childhood Educators." Position statement. Washington, DC: NAEYC. www.naeyc.org/resources/position-statements /professional-standards-competencies.

NBPTS (National Boards for Professional Teaching Standards) 2012. *Early Childhood Generalist Standards for Teachers of Students 3–8*. 3rd ed. Arlington, VA: NBPTS. www.nbpts.org /wp-content/uploads/EC-GEN.pdf.

Nxumalo, F., & S. Cedillo. 2017. "Decolonizing Place in Early Childhood Studies: Thinking with Indigenous Onto-Epistemologies and Black Feminist Geographies." *Global Studies of Childhood* 7 (2): 99–112.

Paris, D. 2012. "Culturally Sustaining Pedagogy: A Needed Change in Stance, Terminology and Practice." *Educational Researcher* 41 (3): 93–97.

Pianta, R.C., K.M. La Paro, & B.K. Hamre. 2008. *Classroom Assessment Scoring System (CLASS), K–3*. Baltimore: Brookes Publishing.

Safe to Sleep. n.d. "About SIDS and Safe Infant Sleep." Accessed October 20, 2020. https://safetosleep.nichd.nih.gov /safesleepbasics/about.

Sandilos, L.E., J.C. DiPerna, & The Family Life Project Key Investigators. 2014. "Measuring Quality in Kindergarten Classrooms: Structural Analysis of the Classroom Assessment Scoring System (CLASS K–3)." *Early Education and Development* 25 (6): 894–914. doi:10.1080/10409289.2014.883588.

Stewart, D.-L. 2013. "Racially Minoritized Students at US Four-Year Institutions." *The Journal of Negro Education* 82 (2): 184–197.

Trawick-Smith, J.W., & T. Smith. 2014. *Early Childhood Development: A Multicultural Perspective*. 6th ed. Upper Saddle River, NJ: Pearson.

Zepeda, M., J. Gonzalez-Mena, C. Rothstein-Fisch, & E. Trumbull. 2012. *Bridging Cultures in Early Care and Education: A Training Module*. New York: Routledge.

This chapter supports recommendations from the NAEYC position statement:

Recommendations for Everyone

Item 6: Recognize that the professional knowledge base is changing.

Recommendations for those Facilitating Educator Preparation and Professional Development

Item 1: Prepare current and prospective early childhood educators to provide equitable learning opportunities for all children.

Item 7: Provide regular time and space to foster a learning community among administrators, faculty, and staff.

Responsive Pedagogical Practices

There is extensive research that supports the need for early childhood teachers to have an expansive body of knowledge in order to produce quality outcomes for young children (IOM & NRC 2015). What early childhood educators do is a complex process. Aside from pedagogy and content knowledge, effective teachers of young children need to be

> Open-minded, flexible, culturally and linguistically responsive, and committed to the principles of social justice

> Dedicated to the ethics of inclusion and fairness in all of their interactions with children and their families

> Prepared to take an unpopular stand in order to advocate for the needs and rights of others

This part includes work from educators in the field who develop early learning through their relationships with children, families, and colleagues. Through an asset-based approach, authors interpret NAEYC's "Advancing Equity in Early Childhood Education" position statement and outline how to enact equitable contexts for children's learning. These chapters reveal the variety of ways we can advance the dialogue to transform the field of early childhood education. Each author considers how pedagogical practices leverage and capitalize on children's cultural and linguistic wealth as they design and facilitate instruction.

Through responsive and equitable interactions, early childhood educators promote trusting relationships with children while building on their knowledge and skills. The principles of developmentally appropriate practice establish the need for teachers to consider children's patterns of development, age, and sociocultural background when developing responsive education. Within this part of the text, you will find a variety of ways that teachers are actively engaged in activities that provide others with a sense of identity, community, and possibility. The authors remind us of the dynamic nature of learning and teaching as they situate the significant work teachers do within diverse early childhood contexts.

Reflection Questions

As you read the chapters in Part 2, we encourage you to reflect on the following questions:

1. How do these educators teach to children's differing strengths and needs?

2. How do these educators cultivate children's cultural and linguistic wealth?

3. What strategies do these educators use to foster children's cultural and linguistic identities?

4. How do you currently assess the cultural and linguistic capital of the families with whom you work?

5. What collaborative learning opportunities do you provide for children to be active learners and participants? In what way are you developing children's voice and agency?

6. What did you learn that you can put into practice in your learning environment?

Reference

IOM (Institute of Medicine) & NRC (National Research Council). 2015. *Transforming the Workforce for Children Birth Through Age 8: A Unifying Foundation*. Report of the National Academies of Sciences, Engineering, and Medicine. Washington, DC: National Academies Press. doi:10.17226/19401.

CHAPTER 6

Creating Caring Communities in Early Childhood Contexts

Garnett S. Booker III

Over the past decade, societal factors have shifted the structure of families in the United States. For example, in many cases both parents have pursued professional careers, or both parents are required to work for financial reasons. Subsequently, the concept of child care has adapted to fit the needs of working families. Due to the increased number of working parents, child care programs have witnessed a sharp increase in enrollment over the last decade. The number of hours children spend in such programs has increased as well. On average, children spend 33 hours per week in nonparental care programs (Snyder, de Brey, & Dillow 2019). During their time in such programs, children experience developmental milestones that are not only important to their families but also to their life trajectory. For example, children begin to develop social skills that pave the way for successful relationships when they are in child care programs. NAEYC's "Advancing Equity in Early Childhood Education" position statement (2019) acknowledges the need for early childhood educators to create a caring community of learners that embraces and celebrates such milestones.

A *caring community of learners* is defined as "a group or classroom in which children and adults engage in warm, positive relationships; treat each other with respect; and learn from and with each other" (Bredekamp 2014, 237). This definition should challenge teachers to re-examine the distribution of power within their classrooms. Traditionally teachers assume the greatest amount of power within the classroom hierarchy. Any power left over trickles down to the other individuals in the class. Consequently, adults tell children how to act, what they can play, and with whom they can play. In this chapter, I focus on four strategies educators can implement as they develop their own community of caring learners: (1) create warm, positive relationships; (2) create a community where children feel safe; (3) create a community that fosters respect; and (4) create a community in which everyone learns from and with each other.

Create Warm, Positive Relationships

When I think about the term *caring community of learners*, my thoughts instinctively take me to Maslow's hierarchy of needs (physiological, safety, love and belonging, esteem, and self-actualization) and how teachers must meet children's needs in order to ensure meaningful social interactions. In this sense, safeguarding children's safety and well-being paves the way for creating positive relationships. In most cases, my classroom provides some of the earliest social interactions for young children. As an early childhood teacher, I have noticed positive relationships begin with personal space. I utterly understand a child being wary when he or she first enters my room. When adults insist that children greet their teacher, the relationship is already unbalanced. Thus, my initial greeting is usually from a distance where I can observe the child's reaction as they enter the classroom and respond appropriately. There are times when space provides the opportunity for a child to safely observe the classroom environment. I also like to make a conscious effort to meet children at eye level after they have established a sense of security. I am six feet, four inches tall and the phrase "looking down on someone" resonates. Greeting children at their eye level helps them begin to understand my role as their teacher. For example, greeting a child at eye level has helped particularly with drop off. Young children begin to respond to familiar faces. I have observed children freely releasing their parents' hands and walking over to greet me. The teachers who take the time to build positive relationships with their students will spend less time responding to challenging behaviors (Bredekamp 2014).

Create a Community Where Children Feel Safe

In my community of learners, I intentionally set up an environment where children feel safe physically and emotionally. When children feel safe, they are more willing to take risks with their learning and their language. When children attend an early childhood classroom, they are experiencing a sense of the unknown. For example, they may wonder, "Where am I?," "Who are these people?," and "When is my family going to pick me up?" The unknown can create a stressful situation. Creating predictable routines and schedules alleviates some of that stress.

Setting developmentally appropriate expectations also helps children learn how to interact within the classroom. My students understand that our classroom is an organized and safe environment designed to support individual learning needs. In our classroom, we support this idea using photos as a visual learning tool. The photos display children engaged in various routine activities using socially acceptable behavior. When children are aware of what to expect and when schedules are predictable, they feel a sense of security as they develop self-regulation skills. Ultimately, they experience a strong sense of belonging.

Create a Community that Fosters Respect

A classroom community is grounded in mutual respect that extends beyond adult–child interactions to include child–child and child–materials interactions. Our classroom guidelines (that we respect our bodies, we respect others, and we respect the materials) are centered on mutual respect. During the creation of the guidelines, I help children understand the meaning of respect by explaining, "It's something that you can feel, see, and hear." I then get children's feedback on how they want to be treated and explain how to treat classroom materials during this discussion. To help with this process, I may ask, "How do you feel when people hit you?" or "Do you like when someone is yelling at you?" I follow up with a discussion about how such behaviors make us feel, and what we might do or say instead.

I also engage children in a discussion about the purpose and use of our classroom materials. I focus on how we respect the classroom materials. For example, by explaining "We build with blocks instead of throwing them" and asking "What should I do when I am done playing with the blocks?," I am always amazed with children's imagination and creativity. Some children want to use blocks in the dramatic play area or Unifix cubes in the kitchen area. What is important to me is the child's reasoning for this decision. When I take the time to ask children what they are thinking, I discover that they are using blocks as a cell phone or, as one child said about the LEGO bricks, "pretending to eat Chex cereal." As a sign of respect, I acknowledge the children's creativity and just remind them to place the materials back where they belong when they are done.

We also discuss the concept of friendships. Most people assume friendships develop automatically in early learning classrooms. However, I teach children that friendship is a voluntary social behavior based on a mutual relationship that takes time to develop. There are times when I have observed students become upset when another child states, "I am not your friend." During this social exchange I immediately try to highlight the concept of mutual respect. For example, my response to the child is typically, "It's okay that he is not your friend, I am pretty sure he respects you." As friendships are established, children learn that respect is at the root of all relationships. I am aware that it is developmentally appropriate for children to struggle with this situation (Taaffe 2019). Before I know it, the two children begin to establish a friendship.

Create a Community in Which Everyone Learns from and with Each Other

Within a community of learners, teachers create increased opportunities for children to interact with their peers. Such interactions help young children learn a wide range of social skills needed to develop their self-regulation and language capabilities. Traditionally, educators place a significant amount of emphasis on the interactions that take place between adults and children within early learning classrooms. Subsequently, the goal of my classroom community is to provide a space where children learn about themselves and others through social interactions. It is through these social interactions that children will learn about similarities, differences, and the need to respect each other. To facilitate these interactions, I create a shared space that works for everyone. That means acknowledging children's feelings. I *encourage* my students to share with others versus *requiring* them to share. I also provide children with the strategies that help them navigate these social interactions. This includes helping them use phrases such as "May I borrow that when you are finished with it?" or "Is it my turn now?" I also develop activities where children learn to work together to accomplish a task. Together we create a warm, safe, and respectful environment designed to support individual learning needs and the needs of the collective group.

Conclusion

NAEYC's "Advancing Equity in Early Childhood Education" position statement reminds us to "develop trusting relationships with children and nurture relationships among them while building on their knowledge and skills" (2019, 7). When children feel safe and secure, they are more likely to take the educational risks necessary to learn and grow. In most cases, respectfully providing space for children to become accustomed to their new learning environment is the beginning stage of creating classroom community. In due time, children feel free to explore and interact with their environment and peers. Creating a caring classroom community is a worthwhile investment not only to the participants within the class, but to their families and their communities. Effective teachers design a caring, safe, and respectful community of learners to increase positive social interactions amongst all members. The responses children get from their peers creates a different learning experience and power dynamic from the adult–child interaction. The caring community of learners framework encourages teachers to re-examine the distribution of power in classrooms. The knowledge children gain from such an environment will provide them with the necessary skills to be productive members of our society.

Key Points

> Creating predictable routines and schedules alleviates some of the stress of the unknown for young children. Setting developmentally appropriate expectations also helps children learn how to interact within the classroom.

> Providing a space where children learn about themselves and others through social interactions helps children learn about similarities, differences, and the need to respect each other.

> Effective teachers design a caring, safe, and respectful community of learners to increase positive social interactions among all members.

References

Bredekamp, S. 2014. *Effective Practices in Early Childhood Education: Building a Foundation.* 2nd ed. Upper Saddle River, NJ: Pearson.

NAEYC. 2019. "Advancing Equity in Early Childhood Education." Position statement. Washington, DC: NAEYC. www.naeyc.org/resources/position-statements/equity.

Snyder, T.D., C. de Brey, & S.A. Dillow. 2019. *Digest of Education Statistics 2018* (NCES 2020-009). Report. Washington, DC: National Center for Education Statistics, Institute of Education Sciences, US Department of Education. https://nces.ed.gov/pubs2020/2020009.pdf.

Taaffe, C.R. 2019. "Two's Company, Three's a Crowd: Peer Interactions in a Preschool Social Triangle." *Young Children* 74 (4): 74–83.

Recommendations for Early Childhood Educators

Create a Caring, Equitable Community of Engaged Learners

This chapter supports recommendations from the NAEYC position statement:

Item 3: Develop trusting relationships with children and nurture relationships among them while building on their knowledge and skills.

Item 6: Actively promote children's agency.

CHAPTER 7

Focusing on What Really Counts

How Noticing and Appreciating Simple, Ordinary Moments in Early Childhood Care and Education Can Enrich Human Relationships and Promote Professional Equity

Junlei Li and Dana Winters

From 2017 to 2019, we had the opportunity to drive across the state of Georgia, from Atlanta to the small rural towns, to observe teachers and children in child care centers that served communities experiencing persistent economic insecurity. These centers were involved in a statewide initiative to improve the quality of language and literacy experiences for their students. Though we are researchers by profession, our role was not to evaluate their results but simply to discover and appreciate the ordinary moments of their work with children. Below is a written description of one of the many small, ordinary, and beautiful moments we were fortunate to have captured on video.

> In an infant and toddler classroom serving a working-class neighborhood just outside Atlanta, we found Ms. Nikki, a young Black caregiver, sitting on the floor with three children around her—a baby boy and two toddler girls. She helped baby Jonah stand up so that he could see her eye to eye. Holding on to her hands, he leaned back, pursed his lips, locked eyes with her, and blew a raspberry. She feigned surprise, leaned back, and blew right back. Jonah leaned in, made the same sound again; she leaned in and reciprocated, again. The two of them went back and forth for a little while until he got tired of standing and plopped down. Ms. Nikki moved a small toy car toward him while making a *vroom, vroom* engine sound. The older toddler girl, Kimber, clutching her stuffed animal, looked at them curiously and moved closer.

> "You wanna play with us?!" Ms. Nikki looked up with an extra dose of welcoming enthusiasm. Kimber did not answer but dashed away as if on a mission. The third child, Marielle, a quieter toddler girl, moved in to be closer to the action. "Vroom, vroom," Ms. Nikki continued, as Jonah tried to grasp what this new game was about. Kimber returned, now with an oversized bus. "You brought us a bus!" Ms. Nikki welcomed her back with equal enthusiasm, "Now you are going to play with us?" Kimber put the bus down between Ms. Nikki and Jonah and, without making the *vroom* sound, moved it back and forth as Ms. Nikki did.

> "All right, high five!" Ms. Nikki reached out one open palm high enough that the girl had to stretch to reach it. The girl made it with a nice smack. Pleased, Ms. Nikki put up both hands, upping the bar. "High ten?" This time, both Kimber and Marielle squeezed their way in to reach her raised hands. While they played that for a few rounds, Jonah, not to be outdone, shifted from sitting to crawling to get on Ms. Nikki's lap. A new round of blowing raspberries soon proceeded.

Ordinary moments like this take place all across Georgia as well as in child care centers and homes all over the country. While human interactions across age groups, social settings, and cultural contexts may look outwardly different, the underlying dynamics of the foundation-building caregiving and early learning experiences are universal (Li & Julian 2012; National

Scientific Council on the Developing Child 2015; Osher et al. 2018). Such interactions are so intuitive and routine that they could easily have gone unnoticed, not only by an outside observer but by caregivers and educators like Ms. Nikki herself.

There are hundreds of research articles in the vast academic journal collections in university libraries that lend support to the intuitive ways Ms. Nikki tuned in to the developmental variations in the children's temperaments, abilities, and needs. In the domain of language development, her interactions exemplified the sensitive and adaptive adult responsiveness to each child's age-related learning, or *developmental sequence* (Rowe & Zuckerman 2016). To some observers, her use of relatively few words in her interactions might signal the shallow, deficit-based, and culturally biased regurgitation of the "30 million word gap" (Kamenetz 2018; McKenna 2018)—that families of color with low income (and, by association, providers of color with low income) say far fewer words to young children when compared with White professional families. The evolving scientific knowledge, however, affirms that Ms. Nikki appropriately focused on the *quality* of interactions—exemplified by her responsiveness, enthusiasm, and inclusiveness, with or without spoken words—over mere quantity of words spoken (Rowe 2012; Rowe & Zuckerman 2016).

Each day, through countless ordinary but powerful moments, children of diverse social and cultural backgrounds count on professionals like Ms. Nikki, many of whom are women of color. In Georgia, for example, 60 percent of frontline infant and toddler teachers are people of color, though they only make up less than a quarter of the school directors (Georgia DECAL 2016). Persistent gender and racial inequity in compensation and recognition undervalues the early childhood educator and caregiver, particularly those of color and those who serve the youngest children (Austin et al. 2019).

In this chapter, we use the case of Ms. Nikki to highlight the importance of recognizing high-quality practices in simple, everyday adult–child interactions and the need to support early childhood teachers and caregivers in equitable ways that benefit educators, children, and families.

Developing Responsive and Equitable Interactions

Even the simplest moments of human interactions can be *developmental* if they embody one or more of these four dynamic characteristics (Li, Akiva, & Winters 2018; Li & Winters 2019):

> **Connection.** Children and adults seek to be present and in tune with each other. The ways Ms. Nikki makes each child feel seen, heard, and felt creates space for such connections.

> **Reciprocity.** The flow of control in any joint activity incorporates a balance of "serve and return" exchanges. Ms. Nikki listens, watches, follows the children's leads, and takes turns to offer a few leads of her own.

> **Opportunities to Grow.** Children are incrementally supported to stretch beyond comfort zones of their current competence and confidence. Both the simple shift from Ms. Nikki's "high five" to "high ten" and mixing up mirroring the baby's sounds to leading the baby into more sophisticated play are examples of such individually differentiated and scaffolded opportunities.

> **Inclusion.** All children, especially those who are the least likely to engage due to ability, temperament, or other factors, are being invited and welcomed into a community of peers. Ms. Nikki notices each child's bid for her attention and invites each one into the common space and joint play whenever feasible.

Recognizing the value of the daily interactions between adults and children through these lenses can focus and align our collective efforts—teachers, administrators, coaches, and policymakers—toward what matters most in the lives of educators and children. When we oversimplify quality standards to accounting books or toy blocks or measuring the size of playgrounds or overlook the skills and experiences of educators who could neither afford nor access higher education, we confuse what can be easily counted (e.g., physical materials or spaces, degrees or certificates) with what really counts in the day-to-day interactions among educators, children, and families.

How do we focus on what really counts? One, we need to recognize that quality practices exist and can grow in places with both high and low economic resources

(Li 2019). While it is important to support early childhood professionals with material resources (e.g., books, blocks, furniture), we cannot lose sight of the resourcefulness of caregivers and educators who work in places with fewer material resources. The single most important resource that we need to recognize and nourish are the people who care for and teach our children. Two, we need to develop the kind of quality standards and quality improvement efforts that prioritize what happens in the interactions between teachers and children. Our existing system puts enormous pressure on "moving up the ratings" for coaches and providers alike (Smith et al. 2012). A reimagined system can put more emphasis on "recognition" over "rating," affirming what providers are already doing well and directing resources that can further strengthen the relationships among educators, children, and families. Third, we need to expand access to academic preparation and enrich professional development opportunities as one important strategy in addressing the persistently inequitable system of recognition and compensation between early childhood educators and other comparable professions, as well as within the early childhood profession itself. We can support providers with time and money to match their high-quality practices with educational opportunities that can advance their credentials and compensation. We can make professional development relevant, respectful, and reciprocal by both affirming the practices of frontline practitioners and expanding their strategies to meet the evolving and emerging needs of children and their families.

Within such a system—one that is more equitable not just for the children but for the professionals—educators like Ms. Nikki can have access to equitable compensation and practice-relevant professional development. They could afford to stay and grow *in* their classrooms year after year rather than leaving or switching jobs frequently just to earn a living that is marginally above poverty (Grant, Jeon, & Buettner 2019; Whitebook, Phillips, & Howes 2014). They could expand the toolbox of their experiences by engaging deeply with families and contributing to a community of practice with peers. All of these are the requisite features of the adult learning environment that supported pioneering teachers in one of the most successful and enduring demonstrations for early childhood education—the Perry Preschool Project (Derman-Sparks & Moore 2016).

Conclusion

Like Ms. Nikki, millions of caregivers all across this country do not yet have access to some, or *any*, of these financial resources or academic and professional opportunities. Through Power to the Profession, NAEYC (n.d.) continues to focus on "equitably advancing an effective, diverse, and well-compensated early childhood education profession across states and settings." There is much work to be done to advocate and provide equitable opportunities in professional learning, fair compensation, and respect. For our profession to advance equity along with quality, we need to identify the strengths and meet the developmental needs of professionals like Ms. Nikki, just as she and millions like her are striving to do for the children and families they serve.

We can start by noticing and appreciating what educators and caregivers *already* do in simple, everyday moments and supporting them to grow such practices in intentional ways. We can work to translate such appreciation into how we define *early childhood professional*, how we define and measure quality, and how and for whom we advocate for just compensation.

Key Points

> While it is important to support early childhood professionals with material resources (e.g., books, blocks, furniture), we cannot lose sight of the resourcefulness of caregivers and educators who work in places with fewer material resources.

> We need to develop the kind of quality standards and quality improvement efforts that prioritize what happens in the interactions between teachers and children.

> We need to expand access to academic preparation and enrich professional development opportunities as one important strategy in addressing the persistently inequitable system of recognition and compensation between early childhood educators and other comparable professions, as well as within the early childhood profession itself.

References

Austin, L.J.E, B. Edwards, R. Chávez, & M. Whitebook. 2019. *Racial Wage Gaps in Early Education Employment*. Report. Berkeley, CA: Center for the Study of Child Care Employment, University of California, Berkeley. https://cscce.berkeley.edu /racial-wage-gaps-in-early-education-employment.

Derman-Sparks, L., & E.K. Moore. 2016. "Two Teachers Look Back: The Ypsilanti Perry Preschool." *Young Children* 71 (4): 82–87.

Georgia DECAL (Georgia Department of Early Care and Learning). 2016. *Economic Impact of the Early Care and Education Industry in Georgia*. Report. Atlanta: Georgia DECAL. www .decal.ga.gov/documents/attachments/EconImpactReport.pdf.

Grant, A.A., L. Jeon, & C.K. Buettner. 2019. "Relating Early Childhood Teachers' Working Conditions and Well-Being to Their Turnover Intentions." *Educational Psychology* 39 (3): 294–312.

Kamenetz, A. 2018. "Let's Stop Talking About the '30 Million Word Gap.'" *All Things Considered*. National Public Radio, June 1. www.npr.org/sections/ed/2018/06/01/615188051/lets-stop -talking-about-the-30-million-word-gap.

Li, J. 2019. "Achieving Quality with Equity: Recognizing and Supporting High Quality Practices and Professionals in Low-Resource Communities." *ZERO TO THREE Journal* 40 (2): 5–9.

Li, J., T. Akiva, & D. Winters. 2018. *Simple Interactions Tool*. www.simpleinteractions.org/the-si-tool.html.

Li, J., & M.M. Julian. 2012. "Developmental Relationships as the Active Ingredient: A Unifying Working Hypothesis of 'What Works' Across Intervention Settings." *American Journal of Orthopsychiatry* 82 (2): 157–166.

Li, J., & D. Winters. 2019. "Simple, Everyday Interactions as the Active Ingredient of Early Childhood Education." *Exchange* 41 (1): 60–65.

McKenna, L. 2018. "The Long, Contentious History of the 'Word Gap' Study." *The Atlantic*, June 15. www.theatlantic.com /education/archive/2018/06/the-long-contentious-history -of-the-word-gap-study/562850.

NAEYC. n.d. "Power to the Profession Overview." Accessed November 13, 2020. www.naeyc.org/our-work/initiatives /profession/overview.

National Scientific Council on the Developing Child. 2015. "Supportive Relationships and Active Skill-Building Strengthen the Foundations of Resilience." Working paper no. 13. www.developingchild.harvard.edu/resources /supportive-relationships-and-active-skill-building -strengthen-the-foundations-of-resilience.

Osher, D., P. Cantor, J. Berg, L. Steyer, & T. Rose. 2018. "Drivers of Human Development: How Relationships and Context Shape Learning and Development." *Applied Developmental Science* 24 (1): 6–36. doi:10.1080/10888691.2017.1398650.

Rowe, M.L. 2012. "A Longitudinal Investigation of the Role of Quantity and Quality of Child-Directed Speech in Vocabulary Development." *Child Development* 83 (5): 1762–1774.

Rowe, M.L., & B. Zuckerman. 2016. "Word Gap Redux: Developmental Sequence and Quality." *JAMA Pediatrics* 170 (9): 827–828.

Smith, S., T. Robbins, W. Schneider, J.L. Kreader, & C. Ong. 2012. *Coaching and Quality Assistance in Quality Rating Improvement Systems: Approaches Used by TA Providers to Improve Quality in Early Care and Education Programs and Home-Based Settings*. Report. New York: National Center for Children in Poverty. www.nccp.org/publication /coaching-and-quality-assistance-in-quality-rating -improvement-systems.

Whitebook, M., D. Phillips, & C. Howes. 2014. *Worthy Work, STILL Unlivable Wages: The Early Childhood Workforce 25 Years After the National Child Care Staffing Study*. Report. Berkeley, CA: Center for the Study of Child Care Employment, University of California, Berkeley. https://cscce.berkeley.edu /files/2014/ReportFINAL.pdf.

This chapter supports recommendations from the NAEYC position statement:

Recommendations for Early Childhood Educators

Create a Caring, Equitable Community of Engaged Learners

Item 3: Develop trusting relationships with children and nurture relationships among them while building on their knowledge and skills.

Item 9: Recognize and be prepared to provide different levels of support to different children depending on what they need.

Recommendations for Public Policymakers

Item 8: Establish comparable compensation (including benefits) across settings for early childhood educators with comparable qualifications, experience, and responsibilities.

CHAPTER 8

Developing the Three Cs of Reciprocity

Zeynep Isik-Ercan

Early childhood educators have historically viewed families as the primary caregivers and experts in their children's education (NAEYC 2016). NAEYC's recent position statement on advancing equity encourages us to "embrace the primary role of families in children's development and learning" (NAEYC 2019, 8). To understand families' viewpoints, educators can draw from a practical framework for reciprocal relationships, as illustrated below, called *the three Cs of reciprocity*: communication, collaboration, and coordination (see Figure 8.1). In this chapter, I will expand on each area.

The main goal in a reciprocal relationship is targeting growth for all participants, not just for child outcomes but for the professional growth of the educator and positive change in interactions with families. A key to establishing relationships with families is to rethink power structures (MacNaughton & Williams 2004). Families often view teachers as experts related to child development.

Parents, however, might worry teachers will critique their family's core identities and cultural perspectives. When families position teachers this way, they may expect them to provide suggestions for child growth and learning but may not trust them with the intricacies of their family dynamics.

If, instead, early childhood educators view the parent–teacher dialogue as a way to support their professional learning, this relationship can be truly reciprocal. As this relationship develops, consider your own goals for professional development. Perhaps you want to overcome your own prejudices (Souto-Manning 2018), learn about a different cultural viewpoint (Isik-Ercan 2010), or inquire into the family dynamics of multiple siblings. When you approach the family with an inquiry mindset that situates both parties as learners and partners in the process, you facilitate trust and communication.

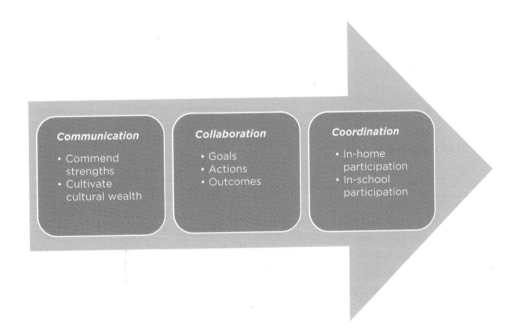

Figure 8.1. The Three Cs of Reciprocity

Communication

The first step in this reciprocal process is communication. Initial conferences allow teachers to reach out to each family. During this first conversation, there are specific questions teachers can use in verbal or written format to help identify family strengths and avoid prejudicial assumptions based on identity indicators such as low socioeconomic status, immigrant status, or single-parent households (Adair 2012). These questions might include the following:

1. What are the family's language skills and resources? If parents speak another language at home, how is the native language used beyond daily language?

2. How have the family members arrived in the United States (e.g., because of a difficulty, for education, for professional purposes)?

3. Do you know about this family's funds of knowledge? What types of talents, skills, wisdom, and experiences can be cultivated to support your center and children's learning?

4. Are parents interested in sharing some of their knowledge by volunteering at the center (in person or virtually)? What are the days and times they might be available?

5. Does the child have older siblings that are in the school system? Do parents have prior experiences with the curricula and practices of local schools or child care centers?

The more you understand about the family, the easier it will be for you to meet their needs. One strategy for understanding families' daily lives is drawing together a weekly schedule that depicts what children typically do on a weekly basis. This may provide some ideas about informal child care arrangements or significant individuals that might be important in the child's life. A weekly schedule example may have timeslots for what is happening before and after school and over the weekends. For example, perhaps you notice that a little girl in your class named Ava seems very restless and sleepy. You may begin to assume that Ava goes to bed late. However, as you communicate with the family, you learn that according to the family schedule, Ava and her infant brother are taken to another family to be cared for at 5:30 a.m. so their mother can catch her shift at work.

Acknowledging the family for their strengths and cultivating their cultural wealth will establish reciprocity in power dynamics and help family members realize the collective accountability in supporting children's growth. For instance, in my work with Burmese refugee families, I often observed how children as young as 5 years old have such high levels of self-regulation to sit together with adults for longer than expected and eagerly listen to adult conversations. This supports them to grow intuitive and sensitive, pick up social clues, develop connections to parents and adults, and share more daily activities that are of interest to both parents and children. This strength, however, may not be recognized as a special cultural wealth by the family itself since it seems natural to them. By getting to know the family in natural environments, the educators may be able to highlight these special strengths and cultivate them in their communication with families and in the learning environment.

Collaboration

Early childhood educators can collaborate with families on their child's care and education in three distinct ways: developing collaborative goals, developing an action plan, and sharing the outcomes.

Develop Collaborative Goals

Collaborative goals include a family's wishes, objectives, and desired outcomes for their child. Some families may not be willing to define goals for their children before being encouraged. However, each family has cultural practices and wishes for their child's developmental outcomes (Isik-Ercan 2017, 2018). Help families discover and fine-tune their goals and include them in your own goal setting for the year. For example, parents may want their child(ren) to be multilingual. Together, discuss how this can be achieved. Identify resources and strategies for native language maintenance and second or third language acquisition.

Develop an Action Plan

An action plan, designed in collaboration with families, should specify the goals developed for the child and clearly defined outcomes for physical, cognitive, or social-emotional growth. This plan should also include the resources and key people supporting the child with these goals. It will be helpful to develop a realistic timeline for progress and build in periodic check-ins where you and the family can share the progress achieved and reflect on growth.

Share the Outcomes

Teachers and families can share what they have observed at home and at school. Children's actions are influenced by their environment. As such, the way children act and respond at home may not always be the way they act or respond at school. Parents and teachers can share outcomes through conferences, emails, phone calls, or online platforms. Ask parents ahead of time about the best method of communication and what days or times of the week may work for a quick check-in.

Coordination

Early childhood practitioners would do well to coordinate family engagement and parent participation in broader ways than traditionally defined (Doucet 2011; Isik-Ercan 2018). For many families, the idea of involvement at home is as valuable as the participation in at-school activities. It is important for teachers to respect the different ways families define their purposes for involvement. Once you discover how parents are developing children's early literacy and numeracy skills through their daily activities, you can develop learning experiences in the classroom that individualize teaching to match children's strengths. This coordination helps both parties understand how children develop across multiple contexts (Caspe et al. 2018).

Although it is important for families to participate in at-school activities, it may not be feasible for some families. One way to support family involvement is to create free password-protected blogs (or share sites) online or use similar apps accessible through smart phones that are designed to share work and pictures and encourage a reaction from the family. These should include user-friendly and practical information for parents. It could also include examples about the program's curriculum or daily activities. Family members can view what the children are learning on a daily or weekly basis but also actively participate by adding comments and components of projects completed at home. While the physical presence of a family member may not be always possible, digital presence is practical for many families. An online platform also provides the possibility of free web-based translation tools, allowing multilingual families to participate actively in the learning process (Isik-Ercan 2012).

Early childhood educators need to rethink family involvement in their programs as a way to integrate families' expertise and leadership beyond just the limited role of helping with activities that teachers have already planned and structured (Isik-Ercan 2018; Souto-Manning 2016). A center director, for instance, may frame family volunteer hours as consultation hours based on families' funds of knowledge in areas like construction, technology, sewing, music, industrial repairs, health, nutrition, and cooking. This coordination is contingent on the communication at the beginning of the year.

Conclusion

Embed the three Cs—communication, collaboration, and coordination—as a practical framework in your plans to structure a strong relationship with families. With the advancement of technology and the digital communication tools available to us, it is vital that we reframe the concept of reciprocal communication with families. By commending strengths and cultivating talent; collaborating on developmental goals, action steps, and outcomes; and planning for both in-home and at-school participation, teachers can show their commitment to reciprocal relationships with families. The three Cs framework also supports equity-minded educators as it empowers families to collaborate, diversifies engagement practices at home and at school, and builds up strengths through communication by avoiding deficit perspectives toward families.

Key Points

> Approach the family with an inquiry mindset that situates both parties as learners and partners to build trust and open communication.

> Make an effort to understand families' cultural wealth and cultivate it in your communication with families and in teaching.

> Collaborate with families on their child's care and education in developing goals, developing an action plan, and sharing progress and outcomes.

> Instead of limiting family involvement to traditional events, such as visiting school for special days or fundraising, rethink family involvement as a way to integrate families' expertise and leadership at home and in school, virtually as well as in-person.

References

Adair, J.K. 2012. "Discrimination as a Contextualized Obstacle to Preschool Teaching of Young Latino Children of Immigrants." *Contemporary Issues in Early Childhood* 13 (3): 163–174.

Caspe, M., A. Seltzer, J. Lorenzo Kennedy, M. Cappio, & C. DeLorenzo. 2018. "Engaging Families in the Child Assessment Process." In *Spotlight on Young Children: Observation and Assessment*, eds. H. Bohart & R. Procopio, 31–39. Washington, DC: NAEYC.

Doucet, F. 2011. "Parent Involvement as a Ritual System." *Anthropology and Education Quarterly* 42 (4): 404–421.

Isik-Ercan, Z. 2010. "Looking at School from the House Window: Learning from Turkish-American Parents' Experiences with Early Elementary Education in the United States." *Early Childhood Education Journal* 38 (2): 133–142.

Isik-Ercan, Z. 2012. "In Pursuit of a New Perspective in the Education of Children of the Refugees: Advocacy for the 'Family.'" *Educational Sciences: Theory and Practice* 12 (4): 3025–3038.

Isik-Ercan, Z. 2017. "Culturally Appropriate Positive Guidance with Young Children." *Young Children* 72 (1): 15–21.

Isik-Ercan, Z. 2018. "Rethinking 'Parent Involvement': Perspectives of Immigrant and Refugee Parents." *Occasional Paper Series* 39 (7). https://educate.bankstreet.edu/occasional-paper-series/vol2018/iss39/7.

MacNaughton, G., & G. Williams. 2004. *Techniques for Teaching Young Children: Choices in Theory and Practice*. Buckingham, UK: Open University Press.

NAEYC. 2016. *Code of Ethical Conduct and Statement of Commitment*. Brochure. Rev. ed. Washington, DC: NAEYC.

Souto-Manning, M. 2016. "Honoring and Building on the Rich Literacy Practices of Young Bilingual and Multilingual Learners." *The Reading Teacher* 70 (3): 263–271.

Souto-Manning, M. 2018. "Disrupting Eurocentric Epistemologies: Re-Mediating Transitions to Centre Intersectionally-Minoritised Immigrant Children, Families, and Communities." *European Journal of Education* 53 (4): 456–468. doi:10.1111/ejed.12309.

Recommendations for Early Childhood Educators

Establish Reciprocal Relationships with Families

Item 1: Embrace the primary role of families in children's development and learning.

Item 2: Uphold every family's right to make decisions for and with their children.

Item 3: Be curious, making time to learn about the families with whom you work.

This chapter supports recommendations from the NAEYC position statement:

CHAPTER 9

What About the Children?
Teachers Cultivating and Nurturing the Voice and Agency of Young Children

Brian L. Wright

> What about the children?
>
> To ignore is so easy
>
> —Yolanda Adams, "What About the Children?"

This lyric from the chorus of gospel singer Yolanda Adams's "What About the Children?" captures the critical need for early childhood educators to listen to the insights of and pay close attention to the experiences, perspectives, and realities of *all* children. This need is conveyed further by the phrase "to ignore is so easy," especially given the reality that childhoods are unequal along lines of race, class, gender, language, ability, and disability. Therefore, children from marginalized groups often receive an education that does not recognize their worth, agency, potential, and brilliance (Wright with Counsell 2018).

Guided by this reality, the critical need for early childhood educators to be culturally competent in recognizing what children learn in their homes and communities as relevant to in-school learning is the focus of this chapter. Teachers' knowledge and understanding of the links between race, culture, and learning are vital to effectively cultivating and nurturing voice and agency in young children. Understanding how race and culture matter for learning manifests in bold and honest conversations and the delivery of creative lessons and activities in which teachers encourage children to explore their racial, ethnic, and cultural differences. Encouraging young children to share their perspectives, experiences, and realities based on their cultural worlds of home, school, and community provides opportunities to cultivate and nurture their voices and agency toward advancing equity in early childhood education. In the sections that follow, there is a discussion of the impact

of inequitable schooling on children of color in general and Black children, particularly Black boys. Then, the focus is on children's awareness of racial differences and why the silence about these matters allows children to draw their own often misguided conclusions. The chapter concludes with an explanation of why it is necessary to cultivate and nurture voice and agency in young children through meaningful activities and authentic multicultural children's books.

Schools as Sites of Inequality

Inequitable schooling contributes in substantive ways to missed essential opportunities to cultivate and nurture the ideas, interests, strengths, and abilities of children from culturally, linguistically, and economically diverse backgrounds. An example of inequitable schooling is the way in which Black boys—as early as preschool—are frequently viewed by White educators as older and less innocent than their White peers, a practice called *adultification*. Additionally, their play is perceived as more dangerous, violent, and not developmentally appropriate (Wright 2019; Wright with Counsell 2018).

According to a 2014 report from the US Department of Education's Office for Civil Rights, Black children make up 18 percent of preschool enrollment, but they represent 48 percent of preschool children receiving one or more out-of-school suspensions (OCR 2014). In comparison, White children represent 41 percent of preschool enrollment but only 28 percent of preschool children receiving one or more out-of-school suspensions. These data are telling and are a clarion call for positive changes in schools and classrooms related to race, diversity, equity, and inclusion. The lack of familiarity by educators to recognize the diverse ways that children organize their experiences and express meaning undermines children's sense of belonging, becoming, and being. This, in turn, places the self-identity, voice, and agency of Black boys and other marginalized children in jeopardy. Further, these deficit approaches create a clash between children of color and their languages, literacies, and cultural ways of being as deficiencies to be overcome in learning and, by extension, legitimize dominant language, literacy, and cultural ways of schooling as the sole gatekeepers to school success. Such a belief not only raises the question *What about the children?*, but, more specifically, *What about the languages and other cultural practices that children of color bring to the early childhood education classroom?* Moreover, these questions are a reminder of why early childhood educators must be culturally competent about matters of race, diversity, equity, and inclusion.

They're Not Too Young to Talk About Race

It is a mistake to assume that young children are unaware of racial differences and that they do not discriminate based on race, class, and gender. It is well documented (Kuh et al. 2016; Ramsey 2015; Souto-Manning 2013) that children quickly learn from their environment to attach beliefs, attitudes, and values to differences and to mimic dominant society's discriminatory practices unless such biases and behaviors are challenged using anti-bias and anti-racist teachings (Derman-Sparks & Edwards with Goins 2020; Kendi 2019). Comments and interactions that children notice as well as their curiosity about racial and cultural differences cannot be ignored. Children want to know more about the world in which they live. Teachers, therefore, must be culturally competent and astute in their observations of young children to understand and accurately interpret their sense-making practices to cultivate, nurture, and recognize each child's individuality and humanity in ways that develop their voice and

agency. This is especially true for teachers working with children marginalized by systems of inequality (Blackburn 2014).

In the remainder of this chapter, I describe two activities that teachers can use to facilitate the development of voice and agency in all children. These activities build on children's strengths and interests and go beyond the contributions level (i.e., surface-level topics) of food, fun, fashion, and folklore (Banks 1994, 2014; Ford et al. 2017). These activities are grounded in the following:

1. Children notice and think about racial differences, and they engage (perhaps unwittingly) in discriminatory practices based on race, class, gender, and other characteristics.

2. When adults allow children to draw their own conclusions based on what they see, hear, and read without critical and courageous conversations, racism and discrimination are reinforced.

3. Early childhood educators play an important role in helping children develop positive attitudes, individual voice, and personal agency to promote a more just future.

An Activity to Cultivate and Nurture Voice

One activity to cultivate and nurture voice in young children is centered around a poem by George Ella Lyon, "Where I'm From." To engage children in this activity, the teacher reads aloud the poem as the children read silently. The teacher draws attention to the poet's inclusion of specific details representing culture and ethnicity (e.g., food, family names, location). Children are given several options to represent their version of the poem to capture their cultural and personal identities. This poem invites children and their families' experiences and histories into the early childhood classroom. The poem follows a repeating pattern ("I am from . . .") that recalls details, evokes memories, and has the potential to encourage some excellent poetry writing by young children (Christensen 1997/1998). The power of this poem is its ability to bring together the individual and collective voices within the classroom.

As children work on their poems, teachers should encourage them to include aspects related to their cultural wealth, such as their home country or native language, the history of their name or names of family members (e.g., aunts, uncles, cousins), favorite dishes served during family gatherings, special places they go with their family, and more. As mentioned above, teachers should provide children with different options to choose from to represent their personal "Where I'm From" poems. For example, children can create a Me Poster that includes, but is not limited to, family photos, pictures from old magazines, and other cultural artifacts that represent and reflect the child's cultural and personal identity, family, and community. Or, children might create a diorama using a shoebox to represent different aspects of their cultural identity, family, and community. Children can also create a skit to dramatize an element of their culture or an illustrated poem that shows the beauty of their culture through color. Additionally, teachers should encourage bilingual children to choose the language(s) in which they wish to compose their poem. Teachers can invite children to share with their peers in either large or small group settings.

An Activity to Cultivate and Nurture Agency

Agency answers the questions *What actions can I take?* and *Will my actions make a difference?* Agency is children's ability to construct and co-construct their environment by negotiating different courses of action. For example, when children choose among different learning center activities or negotiate sharing props during dramatic play, they exercise agency by problem solving to satisfy both individual and group needs (Wright, Counsell, & Tate 2015; Wright with Counsell 2018).

Cultivating agency in young children requires the delivery of curriculum and instruction that encourages children to be actively involved in their own learning by asking questions, sharing insights, and providing opinions. Fostering agency in young children provides opportunities to build a child-centered and child-driven learning environment where multiple and opposing points of view, empowerment, equity, and social justice are at the center of recognizing each child's strengths and talents.

Authentic multicultural children's books serve as a developmentally appropriate way to cultivate and nurture agency in young children. They can introduce children to a variety of topics such as cultural pride, self-identity, gender expression, friendships, families, and much more.

All children, but especially children of color, need what Rudine Sims Bishop (1990) calls "mirror" books—that is, books that reflect themselves, their families, and their communities in positive ways. Currently there are far more "window" books—books that give a glimpse into the lives of other people (mainly in the White world)—than mirror books showing children of color their own communities. These mirror books highlight cultural histories, music, the arts, language varieties, fashion, cuisine, and other culturally rich experiences found in communities of color but not always found in school curricula.

Here is a list of picture books featuring topics that children from diverse cultural and linguistic backgrounds might see in their everyday lives and ways teachers can use them to cultivate and nurture children's agency and voice:

> *Hats of Faith*, by Medeia Cohan, exposes children to people around the world who share in the practice of covering their heads for similar and different reasons. Moreover, this book helps educate and prepare young children for a culturally diverse world in which they take a stand for inclusivity. Teachers can invite children to investigate the concrete, behavioral, and symbolic purposes of the head coverings that most interest them.

> *Hey Black Child*, by Useni Eugene Perkins, uses words and visuals to introduce readers to important people and events from Black American history. It encourages Black children to pursue their dreams and, by extension, all children to take pride in their cultural backgrounds.

> *Pancho Rabbit and the Coyote: A Migrant's Tale*, by Duncan Tonatiuh, uses an allegorical tale to discuss the hardships faced by thousands of families who illegally cross the border to make a better life for themselves and their children.

> *Pink Is for Boys*, by Robb Pearlman, challenges the gender stereotype that pink and purple are feminine colors. The author invites children to celebrate all the colors of the rainbow. Teachers can design their own celebration of the colors of the world and encourage each child to share how these colors enrich the world.

> *René Has Two Last Names/Rene tiene dos apellidos*, by René Colato-Laínez, is a bilingual book that describes a young boy's cultural pride when he uses the last names of both his mother's and father's families—an important Latino/a tradition.

When early childhood educators provide children with books that are mirrors and windows (Bishop 1990), children develop pride in their cultural and linguistic identity. They notice similarities and differences. These observations become conversation starters for rich dialogue based on children's insights, questions, and experiences.

Conclusion

It is a mistake to assume that young children are too young to utilize their voice and agency to develop deeper and richer learning experiences as well as take a stand for equity and social justice. Giving rise to children's voices in this way reaches far beyond their individual experiences and instead empowers them through agency to think about the experiences of others. When early childhood educators recognize that all children have a right to freedom of expression and the right to be heard, then questions about the children are not so easily ignored.

Key Points

› Inequitable schooling contributes in substantive ways to missed essential opportunities to cultivate and nurture the ideas, interests, strengths, and abilities of children from culturally, linguistically, and economically diverse backgrounds.

› It is well documented (Kuh et al. 2016; Ramsey 2015; Souto-Manning 2013) that children quickly learn from their environment to attach beliefs, attitudes, and values to differences and to mimic dominant society's discriminatory practices unless such biases and behaviors are challenged using anti-bias and anti-racist teaching (Derman-Sparks & Edwards with Goins 2020; Kendi 2019).

› Cultivating agency in young children requires the delivery of curriculum and instruction that encourages children to be actively involved in their own learning by asking questions, sharing insights, and providing opinions.

References

Banks, J.A. 1994. *Multiethnic Education: Theory and Practice.* 3rd ed. Boston: Allyn & Bacon.

Banks, J.A. 2014. *An Introduction to Multicultural Education.* 5th ed. New York: Pearson.

Bishop, R.S. 1990. "Mirrors, Windows, and Sliding Glass Doors." *Perspectives: Choosing and Using Books for the Classroom* 6 (3): ix–xi.

Blackburn, M.V. 2014. "Humanizing Research with LGBTQ Youth Through Dialogic Communication, Consciousness Raising, and Action." In *Humanizing Research: Decolonizing Qualitative Inquiry with Youth and Communities*, eds. D. Paris & M.T. Winn, 43–57. Thousand Oaks, CA: SAGE Publications.

Christensen, L. 1997/1998. "Where I'm From: Inviting Student Lives into the Classroom." *Rethinking Schools* 12 (2): 392–395.

Derman-Sparks, L., & J.O. Edwards. With C.M. Goins. 2020. *Anti-Bias Education for Young Children and Ourselves.* 2nd ed. Washington, DC: NAEYC.

Ford, D.Y., B.L. Wright, T.C. Grantham, & J.L. Moore III. 2017. "Infusing Culture and Equity in Gifted Education for Students of Color: Three Frameworks." In *From Giftedness to Gifted Education: Reflecting Theory in Practice*, eds. J. Plucker, A. Rinn-McCann, & M. Makel, 183–201. Waco, TX: Prufrock Press.

Kendi, I.X. 2019. *How to Be an Antiracist.* New York: One World.

Kuh, L.P., D. LeeKeenan, H. Given, & M.R. Beneke. 2016. "Moving Beyond Anti-Bias Activities: Supporting the Development of Anti-Bias Practices." *Young Children* 71 (1): 58–65.

OCR (US Department of Education Office of Civil Rights). 2014. *Data Snapshot: Early Childhood Education* (Issue Brief No. 2). Civil Rights Data Collection. www2.ed.gov/about/offices/list/ocr/docs/crdc-early-learning-snapshot.pdf.

Ramsey, P.G. 2015. *Teaching and Learning in a Diverse World: Multicultural Education for Young Children*, 4th ed. New York: Teachers College Press.

Souto-Manning, M. 2013. *Multicultural Teaching in the Early Childhood Classroom: Approaches, Strategies, and Tools Preschool–2nd Grade.* New York: Teachers College Press; Washington, DC: Association for Childhood Education International.

Wright, B.L. 2019. "Black Boys Matter: Cultivating Their Identity, Agency, and Voice." *Teaching Young Children* 12 (3): 4–7.

Wright, B.L., S.L. Counsell, & S.L. Tate. 2015. "We're Many Members, But One Body: Fostering a Healthy Self-Identity and Agency in African American Boys." *Young Children* 70 (3): 24–31.

Wright, B.L. With S.L. Counsell. 2018. *The Brilliance of Black Boys: Cultivating School Success in the Early Grades.* New York: Teachers College Press.

Recommendations for Early Childhood Educators

Create a Caring, Equitable Community of Engaged Learners

Item 1: Uphold the unique value and dignity of each child and family.

Item 4: Consider the developmental, cultural, and linguistic appropriateness of the learning environment and your teaching practices for each child.

Item 6: Actively promote children's agency.

This chapter supports recommendations from the NAEYC position statement:

CHAPTER 10
Equity, Diversity, and Child Development
Implications for Practice

Iliana Reyes, Mimi Gray, and Teresa Acevedo

Often, teachers hold preconceived ideas about the way children should learn and the types of language and literacy learning environments that should be in place at home. Unfortunately, these notions reflect a deficit perspective, sometimes because teachers' own privileged experiences have reinforced patterns and learning practices that are dominant in their communities. We argue for a paradigmatic shift from a deficit orientation toward an asset-based approach regarding the cultural experiences and language and literacy practices of immigrant and diverse families.

In this chapter, we focus on how educators and families can develop reciprocal, respectful relationships that foster linguistic and cultural knowledge and support diversity in all forms. We approach this theme from a *funds of knowledge* and *social justice* perspective. Studies provide evidence that the very basic concept of *respect for others' diverse backgrounds* supports teachers' learning about young children (González, Moll, & Amanti 2005).

Specifically, the concept of *diversity education* invites us to recognize "the pluralism that students embody (racial/ethnic, social class, gender, and other [identities]) as resources to be used in the service of their education" (Nieto 2009, 19). Educators like Sonia Nieto note that diversity in education is not a concept that we can simply acknowledge but one that necessitates action. Doing so requires early childhood educators in the United States to push an agenda of multiculturalism and diversity through public policies that support multilingualism in the classroom, as Canada and Australia have done. From our own perspective, we emphasize change for teacher action and practice. Teachers should be in continuous self-reflection—deepening their understanding of their own cultural and linguistic roots, as well as class, gender, and race. This is especially critical for dominant culture educators, who in general cannot expect to relate with deeper understanding to the ethnic and racial diversity of families and communities, including Indigenous peoples and their families, in their work environment without their own deep inquiry and reflection into race and class issues.

Innovative early childhood programs have emphasized the importance for an ecological lens and approach through critical awareness, or what Freire (1970) called *conscientização* (critical awareness). To awaken conscientização, educators are invited to question "monologic institutional views and to create new possibilities for addressing the *rights* of linguistically and culturally diverse children and their families" (Da Silva Iddings & Reyes 2017, 36). This questioning is key, in particular, in developing an awareness of the unconscious biases and prejudices that affect our interactions with young children and families.

As teachers engage with families and learn more about their unique funds of knowledge, it is essential that they remain aware of how preconceived ideas influence their pedagogy. There is a tendency, for example, to be so attached to the standardized approach to literacy development that individual funds of knowledge may not be acknowledged as sufficient resources to meet traditional goals and objectives. The *pedagogy of listening* is especially critical at this juncture (Rinaldi 2012). Listen, take it all in, and then in collaboration with colleagues reflect and consider the implications for how families' varied funds of knowledge, cultural traditions, and practices (for example, Day of the Dead and oral literacy events) will support and enhance a child's bilingual and biliteracy development (Reyes & Esteban-Guitart 2013). With this commitment, we can transform day-to-day practice by developing consistent, sustained, and respectful relationships with families and communities (Isik-Ercan, this volume; Rinaldi 2012).

With the intention of reaching some basic understanding of the impact of bilingualism on the literacy acquisition process of emergent bilingual children, we encourage educators to learn about children's home language and literacy experiences. Inviting families to share their stories and histories creates opportunities for teachers to learn about the cultural and linguistic resources children and families draw from in their day-to-day interactions. Teachers who participate in various family–school events can begin to acknowledge their students' home languages as linguistic resources (Hornberger 2016). And for many educators and administrators who are bilingual themselves, they become aware of how their own varied languages can also be utilized as assets to open dialogue with parents and primary caretakers.

Family–School Events

Educators within the school community can organize family engagement events in partnership with and for families. Such events are key in providing spaces and opportunities for teachers (including preservice teachers) to get to know the families they work with and their young children. Family–school events invite teachers and educators to place themselves as "learners in relation to their students and their families and provide the opportunity to socialize and to establish and sustain a caring relationship with the family" (Da Silva Iddings & Reyes 2017, 42). A family literacy and oral history night is an example of how families and teachers together can make connections with multicultural experiences and achieve schools' goals to support children's emergent literacy development. As a first step for families and educators to collaborate, do a walk-through of the school. Together, look carefully at displays such as postings, bulletin boards, and signage for inclusive welcoming—language, images, announcements, celebrations, and more. Although this is an "informal" but purposefully planned event, it suggests that the school is serious about their commitment to creating a respectful and thoughtful school environment that embraces all families.

An additional example of specific efforts in developing a partnership between teachers and families is the Tucson Hopes and Dreams project (Reyes et al. 2015). This initiative began as a local project but has now traveled and inspired many programs across the United States and beyond. A main objective is to learn about the hopes for the young child as part of a larger community (e.g., neighborhood, classroom). Educators, in collaboration with families, engage in ongoing discussions about the hopes and dreams we all have for children. In this dialogue, teachers listen and learn about the families' histories, vision, and hopes for their children through documentation (e.g., family pictures, artifacts) of important events for them. Through this documentation, the diversity of families and their resources are visible to teachers and others in the school context across communities. This exchange deepens also families' relationships with their young children's teachers and invites the construction of other spaces for dialogue. Moreover, bringing diversity at the forefront of dialogue encourages *action* toward advocacy for all children.

Conclusion

Early childhood educators have engaged in significant efforts as they grow and learn together with families and children. They continue to strengthen advocacy efforts that target the improvement of educational possibilities for all young children and their families who represent the broad scope of diversity in classrooms across the United States. NAEYC's position statement on advancing equity challenges each of us to join efforts in celebrating the diversity that exists in every classroom and community. The learning that takes place through projects and everyday interactions builds trust among teachers, children, families, and the community. The teacher–family partnerships that emerge will be stronger as teachers commit to listen, learn, and deepen their understanding of the hopes and dreams of all their families.

Key Points

> Teachers who are committed to continuous self-reflection will develop a deeper understanding of their own cultural and linguistic roots, as well as class, gender, and race.

> Educators have a professional responsibility to develop an awareness of the unconscious biases and prejudices that affect our interactions with young children and families.

> Educators learn about children's home languages and literacy experiences with the intention of reaching some basic understanding of the impact of bilingualism on the literacy acquisition process of emergent bilingual children.

References

Freire, P. 1970. *Pedagogy of the Oppressed*. New York: Herder and Herder.

Hornberger, N.H., ed. 2016. *Honoring Richard Ruiz and His Work on Language Planning and Bilingual Education*. Blue Ridge Summit, PA: Multilingual Matters.

González, N., L.C. Moll, & C. Amanti. 2005. *Funds of Knowledge: Theorizing Practices in Households, Communities, and Classrooms*. Mahwah, NJ: Lawrence Erlbaum Associates.

Nieto, S. 2009. "Diversity Education: Lessons for a Just World." In *Thinking Diversity While Building Cohesion: A Transnational Dialogue on Education*, eds. M. Nkomo & S. Vandeyar, 17–40. Amsterdam: Rozenberg; Pretoria, South Africa: UNISA Press.

Da Silva Iddings, A.C., & I. Reyes. 2017. "Learning with Immigrant Children, Families, and Communities: The Imperative of Early Childhood Teacher Education." *Early Years* 37 (1): 34–46.

Reyes, I., P.M. Baker, T. Acevedo, P. McPheeters, A. Gomez, M. Gray, & M. Habib. 2015. "The Tucson Hopes and Dreams Project: Teachers and Families Share Their Visions for Young Children." *Young Children* 70 (2): 66–71.

Reyes, I., & M. Esteban-Guitart. 2013. "Exploring Multiple Literacies from Homes and Communities: A Cross-Cultural Comparative Analysis." In *International Handbook of Research on Children's Literacy, Learning, and Culture*, eds. K. Hall, T. Cremin, B. Comber, & L.C. Moll, 155–170. Hoboken, NJ: Wiley-Blackwell.

Rinaldi, C. 2012. "The Pedagogy of Listening: The Listening Perspective." In *The Hundred Languages of Children: The Reggio Emilia Experience in Transformation*, 3rd ed., eds. C. Edwards, L. Gandini, & G. Forman, 233–236. Santa Barbara, CA: Praeger.

This chapter supports recommendations from the NAEYC position statement:

Recommendations for Early Childhood Educators

Establish Reciprocal Relationships with Families

Item 1: Embrace the primary role of families in children's development and learning.

Item 4: Maintain consistently high expectations for family involvement, being open to multiple and varied forms of engagement and providing intentional and responsive supports.

Observe, Document, and Assess Children's Learning and Development

Item 1: Recognize the potential of your own culture and background affecting your judgment when observing, documenting, and assessing children's behavior, learning, or development.

Equitable Learning Opportunities for Young Bilingual Children

Strategies to Promote Oral Language Development

Dina C. Castro and Ximena Franco

> All children have the right to equitable learning opportunities that help them achieve their full potential as engaged learners and valued members of society.
>
> —NAEYC, "Advancing Equity in Early Childhood Education"

Recognizing the diversity in the characteristics and experiences of culturally and linguistically diverse children and responding to those specific characteristics and experiences are the first steps to providing equitable learning opportunities for all children. With this in mind, we ask, *What does it mean to provide equitable learning opportunities for young bilingual children?* Answering this question requires that early childhood educators gain an understanding of the extent to which bilingualism and bilingual children's sociocultural experiences affect their development and learning. Because of the inequities that affect them, we focus on the experiences of young bilingual children in minoritized and marginalized communities, such as children from non-White immigrant families, children in indigenous families, and children from families who speak African American English Vernacular or other dialects. These children are more likely to experience inequities that limit their access to an early education that supports their bilingual language development and learning.

A Note Regarding Terminology

We use the phrase *young bilingual children* in this chapter to refer to children from birth to age 5 "who use two or more languages (or dialects) in their everyday lives" (Grosjean 2008, 10). In other words, children who "are able to function . . . even to a very limited degree in more than one language" (Valdés 2015, 8). Other terms used in the United States for these children include *emergent bilingual, dual language learner, English language learner,* and *English learner.*

In this chapter, we emphasize the importance of language interactions and provide useful and practical information that can be implemented by early childhood educators. The context for the recommendations we present is early education classrooms that serve young bilingual children following an English-only program as a medium of instruction. These recommendations, however, can also be applied to classrooms where children receive home language support as they develop English language skills.

Promoting Oral Language Development of Young Bilingual Children

The amount of and diverse ways in which early childhood educators use language in the classroom play a crucial role in the acquisition of language and literacy skills for both monolingual and bilingual preschoolers (Dickinson & Porche 2011; Hoff et al. 2012). Furthermore, the extent to which adults talk and are engaged in complex conversations with children are among the strongest predictors of monolingual (Hoff 2006) and bilingual (Hoff et al. 2012) children's language and cognitive development as is expected in school.

An important aspect in the development of oral language is that adult language is more effective in promoting language growth when it is responsive to children's developmental level and presents language forms that are slightly more advanced than the child's ability level. Therefore, to promote language development of bilingual children, it is important for early childhood educators to be aware that children growing up with two languages, regardless of the level of competency in each language, will always use both languages to learn—not only in the early education setting but also in the various contexts they experience at home and in their communities. Furthermore, bilingual children have unique characteristics (including family structures, multiple languages, and racial, ethnic, and cultural differences) that provide rich environments for language development.

Teaching Strategies: Listening and Speaking

The important role that oral language plays in both monolingual (Dickinson et al. 2003; Vellutino et al. 2007) and bilingual children's literacy skills (Davison, Hammer, & Lawrence 2011; Rinaldi & Páez 2008) has been well documented. Research has shown that reading books, singing, playing word games, and simply talking to and with children builds their vocabulary while providing increased opportunities to develop listening skills. These strategies are particularly beneficial for young bilingual children (Gillanders, Castro, & Franco 2014). Teachers are encouraged to be intentional in planning and implementation of the strategies to support bilingual children's language development.

To promote oral language development, teachers should consider the following (Castro et al. 2010):

> Listening to stories and read-alouds helps children develop an understanding of the grammatical structure of the language and an understanding of spoken language.

> Listening to the early childhood educator helps young bilingual children understand the world around them and construct meaning. Conversations in English and in their home language facilitate bilingual children's acquisition of oral language proficiency in both languages.

> Exposure to early childhood educator talk—in directives, conversations, and deliberately tailored language to foster understanding—is essential for young bilingual children. Providing an environment rich in oral languages will help young bilingual children learn new words and lead to an increase in their vocabulary.

> Oral language development includes an array of skills, and many of them are closely related to literacy development. Talking provides the foundation that leads to vocabulary acquisition, understanding of syntax and use, comprehension of decontextualized language, and phonological awareness.

> Children who acquire a variety of words (vocabulary) through conversations will have less difficulty reading those words when they find them in a text.

> Children need a lot of exposure to conversations about things that are not present in the here and now. Understanding of this kind of talk (decontextualized language) will facilitate children's comprehension of text and story narratives.

> Because of the exposure to two languages, bilingual children tend to find it easy to analyze the structure of the sounds of language (phonological awareness).

> Bilingual children can communicate seamlessly by making use of the languages they have to convey their message. Some authors called this characteristic *code-switching* (Genesee 2010); more recently, the term *translanguaging* has been proposed to encompass the broader aspect of linguistic repertoire (García & Wei 2014). Young bilingual children will use their entire language repertoire when they are communicating with others.

Language Interactions in the Early Childhood Classroom

Early childhood educators' use of sustained conversations (taking two or more turns), with elaborated language (e.g., using contextualized and decontextualized language) can improve children's language and academic skills (Cabell et al. 2015). The more interesting and interactive conversations are, the more language children learn (Magruder et al. 2013).

What Is Contextualized or Decontextualized Language?

Contextualized language has a context to help the child understand the teacher's words. It refers to talking about the "here and now." *Decontextualized language* requires children to remember an association between the words he or she is using and a thing or concept that is not visually or physically present. There are no cues. Young children need a lot of exposure to decontextualized language, which is the language of school, to develop their understanding of texts. In Table 11.1, we provide some examples of these two types of language interactions and describe the situations in which they occur.

Other practices to promote oral language development include the following:

1. Ask open-ended questions. When asking open-ended questions, take into consideration the child's level of oral language comprehension (e.g., children with beginning abilities in English may not be able to fully understand or respond to this type of question in English but may be able to do it if you can ask the question in their home language).

2. Ensure that there are many opportunities for child-initiated interactions with teachers and peers within different contexts in the classrooms, such as at mealtimes, during center time, and during whole group activities.

3. Connect new words to what the child already knows or has experienced.

4. Designate a time and place for sustained conversations.

5. Create opportunities for peer interactions, encouraging sustained conversations among peers in their home language or English. Sustained conversations involve taking at least two turns by each speaker within the same topic of conversation.

6. Encourage bilingual children to use their home language in the classroom.

7. Use bilingual children's home language in a positive manner, and avoid using the home language only to discipline.

Table 11.1. Examples of Contextualized and Decontextualized Language	
Contextualized	**Decontextualized**
"We are going back inside." *(Children are waiting in line.)*	"We are going back inside in a few minutes." *(Child is riding a tricycle.)*
"O is for orange. In Spanish, an orange is called *naranja*." *(Looking at a picture of an orange.)*	"Oranges grow on trees." *(No orange or picture of an orange present.)*
"Maria is happy. Look at her smile." *(Points to Maria, who is smiling.)*	"Sometimes children are sad, and sometimes they are happy." *(In a small group discussion about feelings.)*
"We have milk." *(Children are drinking milk.)*	"Yesterday, we had chocolate milk for breakfast!" *(Children are not drinking milk.)*
"You are reading a book." *(Child is reading a book.)*	"Did you read a book at home?" *(Book reading took place in the past, question is occurring away from home.)*

Conclusion

Bilingualism goes beyond being able to use two languages. **It defines children's identity and the way they see and interpret the world around them**. Thus, providing equitable early childhood education to young bilingual children means providing them with opportunities and support to develop and maintain both of their languages, taking into account their unique strengths and characteristics, and fostering inclusive environments.

Key Points

> Bilingual children will use both of their languages, within the same phrases and sentences, in linguistic interactions with adults and peers.

> Teachers should use children's home languages in the classroom with intentionality. Random and scattered use of the home language without a purpose and planning will not generate the positive expected impact in bilingual children that planned activities will.

> Bilingual children have diverse language backgrounds, including children who speak different dialects and those who have diverse language systems.

References

Cabell, S.Q., L.M. Justice, A.S. McGinty, J. Decoster, & L.D. Forston. 2015. "Teacher-Child Conversations in Preschool Classrooms: Contributions to Children's Vocabulary Development." *Early Childhood Research Quarterly* 30 (1): 80–92. doi:10.1016/j.ecresq.2014.09.004.

Castro, D.C., C. Gillanders, X. Franco, & M. Zepeda. 2010. *Nuestros Niños School Readiness Program: Teachers' Handbook*. Chapel Hill, NC: Frank Porter Graham Child Development Institute, The University of North Carolina at Chapel Hill.

Davison, M.D., C. Hammer, & F.R. Lawrence. 2011. "Associations Between Preschool Language and First Grade Reading Outcomes in Bilingual Children." *Journal of Communication Disorders* 44 (4): 444–458. doi:10.1016/j.jcomdis.2011 .02.003.

Dickinson, D.K., A. McCabe, L. Anastasopoulos, E.S. Peisner-Feinberg, & M.D. Poe. 2003. "The Comprehensive Language Approach to Early Literacy: The Interrelationships Among Vocabulary, Phonological Sensitivity, and Print Knowledge Among Preschool-Aged Children." *Journal of Educational Psychology* 95 (3): 465–481. doi:10.1037/0022-0663.95.3.465.

Dickinson, D.K., & M.V. Porche. 2011. "Relation Between Language Experiences in Preschool Classrooms and Children's Kindergarten and Fourth-Grade Language and Reading Abilities." *Child Development* 82 (3): 870–886.

García, O., & L. Wei. 2014. *Translanguaging: Language, Bilingualism, and Education*. London: Palgrave Macmillan.

Gillanders, C., D.C. Castro, & X. Franco. 2014. "Learning Words for Life: Promoting Vocabulary in Dual Language Learners." *The Reading Teacher* 68 (3): 213–221.

Genesee, F. 2010. "Dual Language Development in Preschool Children." In *Young English Language Learners*, eds. E.E. Garcia & E.C. Frede, 59–79. New York: Teachers College Press.

Grosjean, F. 2008. *Studying Bilinguals*. New York: Oxford University Press.

Hoff, E. 2006. "How Social Contexts Support and Shape Language Development." *Developmental Review* 26 (1): 55–88. doi:10.1016/j.dr.2005.11.002.

Hoff, E., C. Core, S. Place, R. Rumiche, M. Señor, & M. Parra. 2012. "Dual Language Exposure and Early Bilingual Development." *Journal of Child Language* 39 (1): 1–27.

Magruder, E.S., W.W. Hayslip, L.M. Espinosa, & C. Matera. 2013. "Many Languages, One Teacher: Supporting Language and Literacy Development for Preschool Dual Language Learners." *Young Children* 68 (1): 8–12, 15.

Rinaldi, C., & M. Páez. 2008. "Preschool Matters: Predicting Reading Difficulties for Spanish-Speaking Bilingual Students in First Grade." *Learning Disabilities: A Contemporary Journal* 6 (1): 71–86.

Valdés, G. 2015. "Latin@s and the Intergenerational Continuity of Spanish: The Challenges of Curricularizing Language." *International Multilingual Research Journal* 9 (4): 253–273. doi:10.1080/19313152.2015.1086625.

Vellutino, F.R., W.E. Tunmer, J.J. Jaccard, & R. Chen. 2007. "Components of Reading Ability: Multivariate Evidence for a Convergent Skills Model of Reading Development." *Scientific Studies of Reading* 11 (1): 3–32. doi:10.1207 /s1532799xssr1101_2.

Recommendations for Early Childhood Educators

This chapter supports recommendations from the NAEYC position statement:

Create a Caring, Equitable Community of Engaged Learners

Item 2: Recognize each child's unique strengths and support the full inclusion of all children—given differences in culture, family structure, language, racial identity, gender, abilities and disabilities, religious beliefs, or economic class.

Item 9: Recognize and be prepared to provide different levels of support to different children depending on what they need.

Establish Reciprocal Relationships with Families

Item 4: Maintain consistently high expectations for family involvement, being open to multiple and varied forms of engagement and providing intentional and responsive supports.

CHAPTER 12

Creating High-Quality STEM Experiences for All Young Learners
What Do Teachers of Young Children Need to Know?

Jie-Qi Chen

In a high-quality preschool setting, children often enthusiastically enjoy a range of playful activities—stacking blocks to see which tower is the highest, playing games outdoors with shadows and light, building a "house" for a classroom pet, or trying to figure out how many creatures are chasing the Gingerbread Man as they joyfully reenact the story. These young learners are engaged in science, technology, engineering, and mathematics (STEM) learning that was once believed to be "too hard" for preschoolers but is now known to be the necessary fabric for their growing understanding of the world.

High-quality STEM experiences provide young children with opportunities to develop critical thinking, executive functioning, and problem-solving skills that set the stage across content areas for future learning and development (Early Childhood STEM Working Group 2017; McClure et al. 2017). Of critical importance to the provision of high-quality STEM experiences for all young learners, however, is their teachers' understanding of guiding tenets in early STEM education and ways to carry them out in practice. NAEYC's "Advancing Equity in Early Childhood Education" position statement outlines the need for educators to "scaffold children's learning to achieve meaningful goals" (NAEYC 2019, 7). To do so, NAEYC urges early childhood educators to set challenging but achievable goals for each child; build on children's strengths and interests to affirm their identities and help them gain new skills, understanding, and vocabulary; and provide supports as needed while communicating authentic confidence in each child's ability to achieve these goals. Aligned closely with NAEYC's position statement on advancing equity, this chapter

briefly outlines several ways to effectively bring early STEM learning into the classroom to meet the needs of all young learners.

Understand a Working Definition of STEM

The STEM disciplines—science, technology, engineering, and mathematics—share a set of foundational processes and practices but also possess distinct, discipline-specific characteristics and knowledge (Early Childhood STEM Working Group 2017). This working definition acknowledges both the *connections* and *distinctions* of the STEM disciplines. The commonalities across the disciplines align well with developmentally appropriate practice, such as inquiry-based learning and learning through meaningful play. The "big ideas" of different STEM fields include concepts and skills that are central to disciplinary learning, appropriate to children's thinking, and generative to future learning. These big ideas are a useful way to help teachers of young children understand the distinctive knowledge base of each STEM discipline (Early Math Collaborative 2014). Armed with such working knowledge, teachers are more likely to set challenging but achievable STEM goals for young learners.

Make Meaningful STEM Connections

Good STEM activities engage children in learning about STEM disciplines in meaningful contexts. Ways to support meaningful STEM learning include making connections to young children's personal and cultural experiences, their play activities, and other curriculum areas.

Personal experiences for children include observations about themselves and how they relate to others. For example, young children love to know that they grow bigger or taller. To approach the subject of growing for each child, a teacher can use a variety of resources and activities such as storybooks and read-alouds. For example, *The Growing Story*, by Ruth Krauss, is a classic celebration of how a little boy sees the growth in farm animals and plants over the course of several seasons but keeps wondering if he himself is growing. This is a great story to engage children in the discussion of what growing means, and using additional diverse books or stories in the lesson can make for a richer learning experience.

Another story that discusses the topic of growth is "The Knee-High Man," a traditional Black folktale (which can be found in *The Knee-High Man and Other Tales*, by Julius Lester) that tells the story of a man who wants to be taller, but then sees that size is relative and learns to accept who he is. Adding this story to the lesson creates a unique opportunity to celebrate diversity while also advancing the lesson of how things grow and what that can mean for each child individually. Using the stories as an entry point, the teacher can invite children to a playful learning experience of measuring nonliving things, such as desks and blocks, and living things, such as plants and themselves. Such activities link children's experience of growing to playful learning of math and science concepts, such as measurement tools and living and nonliving things.

Foreground One Area for Integrated STEM Learning

A meaningful STEM connection emphasizes integration rather than isolation in children's learning. Successful integration across STEM disciplines is challenging, however, as it requires deliberate planning. One approach to meaningful integration involves one discipline in the *foreground*, or as the focus of the activity, and one or more other disciplines serving as the background (Early Childhood STEM Working Group 2017). For example, when children work to build a "house" for their classroom's pet turtle, teachers can foreground the engineering design process by involving children in identifying and solving problems using different materials while still integrating mathematics in the

background as children discuss the size and shape of the house. This same activity can foreground mathematics if the teacher draws the children's attention to concepts and procedures in measurement, while using house building as a meaningful context for children to learn about the usefulness of mathematics in real-life situations. The decision of what content knowledge should be foregrounded depends on teachers' understanding of developmentally appropriate learning goals and children's readiness as a group and individually. An authentic STEM activity always involves more than one area of learning. Background knowledge helps contextualize the foreground knowledge, making the focus of the activity more authentic, connected, and meaningful.

Make STEM Learning and Thinking Visible

Documentation, representation, and communication are three integrally related components that are essential to STEM learning. Working in tandem, they make children's STEM learning and thinking visible, individually and in groups. *Documentation* helps foreground the primary goal of the activity, record changes or patterns, and serve as a memory of learning, allowing children and adults to reflect on, evaluate, and build on their previous work and ideas. Necessary to documentation is the representation of children's thinking, such as when teachers invite children to talk about, write about, draw, or graph their ideas. *Representation*, or using multiple symbol systems and different tools, allows children to express their thinking and feelings in ways that are comfortable to them, which is particularly salient to young dual language learners. Of particular importance to diversity, equity, and inclusion is the encouragement and celebration of the use of the hundred languages in children's expression of learning (Edwards, Gandini, & Forman 2011). The primary purpose of documentation and representation is *communication*, through which children learn from and with each other. Learning in groups or with a partner helps children develop critical human capacities for participating in a democratic society, including the ability to share our views and listen to others, entertain multiple perspectives, seek connections, change our ideas, and negotiate conflict (Krechevsky et al. 2014).

Use Language to Activate STEM Thinking

Teachers of young children know well the importance of hands-on experiences in STEM learning. While it is important to engage young learners with math manipulatives, science tools, and technology gadgets, it is also important to know that "although kinesthetic experience can enhance perception and thinking, understanding does not travel through the fingertips and up the arm" (Ball 1992, 47). Of critical importance when activating young children's thinking and developing their conceptual understanding is their use of language (NRC 2009). For example, asking questions such as "How can we know for sure which of the two buckets is taller and heavier without moving them together?" or "I see you've made an interesting pattern here. Can you explain it to me?" introduces children to vocabulary and invites them to share their thinking process. Young children do not learn by simply doing, they learn by *thinking and talking about what they are doing*. When children engage in conversations about what they are learning, they articulate their ideas, clarify misunderstandings, and facilitate their thinking. Keenly aware of the developmental needs of dual language learners, NAEYC's position statement on advancing equity asks early educators to "design and implement learning activities using language(s) that the children understand. Support the development of children's first languages while simultaneously promoting proficiency in English. Similarly, recognize and support dialectal differences as children gain proficiency in the Standard Academic English they are expected to use in school" (NAEYC 2019, 7).

Instigate a Positive Mindset About STEM

Many early childhood teachers do not believe themselves competent in STEM-related fields and, consequently, often demonstrate STEM anxiety (Ginet & Itzkowich 2019). Teachers' negative attitudes and beliefs not only affect their own knowledge acquisition and classroom practices but also contribute to the inadvertent, often subtle or subconscious, transmission of low STEM expectations to the children they educate, especially to young girls, dual language learners, or children from households with low income or families with less education (Maloney et al. 2015). While research clearly indicates the long-term benefits of early STEM experiences, including high school graduation rate and adult employment and earnings (Duncan et al. 2007; Geary et al. 2013), engaging the traditionally underrepresented population in playful, quality STEM learning has to be a high priority in promoting equity in early education. A positive mindset invites teachers to take the risk to explore and learn things that they do not know but which are important to know. STEM competence is not an inborn trait; rather, it develops through productive struggles and engagement in a community of learners using all available resources.

Learn About Family Uses of STEM at Home

The critical importance of family involvement in children's STEM learning is well documented (Donohue 2016; Legnard & Austin 2014). To ensure all children have a high-quality STEM experience, it is vital that teachers learn how families are already integrating STEM understanding at home. School and family partnerships start when teachers ask families about their funds of knowledge. Teachers can learn how families are engaging children in STEM learning opportunities in their everyday activities. Perhaps Ricky's dad loves to bake or Alexis's grandmother enjoys cultivating herbs. Learning about families' cultural wealth allows teachers to extend what is taking place at home into the classroom. By embracing children's home activities, daily routines, or cultural customs in the classroom learning experience, the teacher develops *respectful and trusting relationships* with family. Such partnership capitalizes the knowledge "that children and families bring as members of their cultures and communities while also sparking children's interest and engagement" (NAEYC 2019, 7).

Conclusion

The growth of our national economy has led to a call for richer and more meaningful STEM education in the United States. To ensure our nation retains its competitive edge, we must offer our young children high-quality, meaningful STEM education that inspires, informs, and prompts their development in STEM disciplines. Of significance to the equity practice in STEM is to set developmentally appropriate learning goals and implement effective pedagogies that support the full inclusion of all children regardless of their differences in culture, family structure, language, racial identity, gender, learning differences, or socioeconomic status. High-quality early STEM education will build the foundation children need to succeed and thrive throughout their school years, feeding the nation's efforts to excel. Teachers of young children assume this important role to provide high-quality STEM experiences for all young learners. What teachers know about children and how they integrate this knowledge into their practice is the ultimate measure of high-quality STEM education in early childhood settings.

Key Points

> Educators should set challenging and achievable goals for each child to build on children's strengths and interests to affirm their identities and help them gain new skills, understanding, and vocabulary while expressing confidence in child's ability to achieve these goals.

> To ensure all children have a high-quality STEM experience, it is vital that teachers understand the guiding tenets in early STEM education and learn how families are already integrating STEM understanding at home. School and family partnerships start when teachers ask families about their funds of knowledge.

> A positive mindset invites teachers to take the risk to explore and learn things that they do not know but which are important to know. STEM competence is not an inborn trait; rather, it develops through productive struggles and engagement in a community of learners using all available resources.

References

Ball, D.L. 1992. "Magical Hopes: Manipulatives and the Reform of Mathematics Education." *American Educator* 16 (2): 14–18, 46–47.

Donohue, C. 2016. *Family Engagement in the Digital Age: Early Childhood Educators as Media Mentors.* New York: Routledge.

Duncan, G.J., C.J. Dowsett, A. Claessens, K. Magnuson, A.C. Huston, P. Klebanov, L.S. Pagani, L. Feinstein, M. Engel, J. Brooks-Gunn, H. Sexton, K. Duckworth, & C. Japel. 2007. "School Readiness and Later Achievement." *Developmental Psychology* 43 (6): 1428–1446.

Early Childhood STEM Working Group. 2017. *Early STEM Matters: Providing High-Quality STEM Experiences for All Young Learners.* Policy report. Chicago: Early Childhood STEM Working Group.

Early Math Collaborative (Early Math Collaborative at Erikson Institute). 2014. *Big Ideas of Early Mathematics: What Teachers of Young Children Need to Know.* Upper Saddle River, NJ: Pearson.

Edwards, C., L. Gandini, & G. Forman, eds. 2011. *The Hundred Languages of Children: The Reggio Emilia Experience in Transformation.* 3rd ed. Santa Barbara, CA: ABC-CLIO.

Geary, D.C., M.K. Hoard, L. Nugent, & D.H. Bailey. 2013. "Adolescents' Functional Numeracy Is Predicted by Their School Entry Number System Knowledge." *PLoS ONE* 8 (1): e54651.

Ginet, L., & R. Itzkowich. 2019. "Math Anxiety and Math Performance: How Do They Relate?" In *Growing Mathematical Minds: Conversations Between Developmental Psychologists and Classroom Teachers*, eds. J. McCray, J.Q. Chen, & J. Sorkin, 173–200. New York: Routledge.

Krechevsky, M., B. Mardell, M. Rivard, & D. Wilson. 2014. *Visible Learners: Promoting Reggio-Inspired Approaches in All Schools.* San Francisco: John Wiley & Sons.

Legnard, D., & S. Austin. 2014. "The Math Promise: Celebrating at Home and School." *Teaching Children Mathematics* 21 (3): 178–184.

McClure, E.R., L. Guernsey, D.H. Clements, S.N. Bales, J. Nichols, N. Kendall-Taylor, & M.H. Levine. 2017. *STEM Starts Early: Grounding Science, Technology, Engineering, and Math Education in Early Childhood.* New York: The Joan Ganz Cooney Center at Sesame Workshop.

Maloney, E.A., G. Ramirez, E.A. Gunderson, S.C. Levine, & S.L. Beilock. 2015. "Intergenerational Effects of Parents' Math Anxiety on Children's Math Achievement and Anxiety." *Psychological Science* 26 (9): 1400–1488.

NAEYC. 2019. "Advancing Equity in Early Childhood Education." Position statement. Washington, DC: NAEYC. www.naeyc.org/resources/position-statements/equity.

NRC (National Research Council). 2009. *Mathematics Learning in Early Childhood: Paths Toward Excellence and Equity.* Report. Washington, DC: National Academies Press. doi:10.17226/12519.

This chapter supports recommendations from the NAEYC position statement:

Recommendations for Early Childhood Educators

Create a Caring, Equitable Community of Engaged Learners

Item 5: Involve children, families, and the community in the design and implementation of learning activities.

Item 7: Scaffold children's learning to achieve meaningful goals.

Item 9: Recognize and be prepared to provide different levels of support to different children depending on what they need.

Establish Reciprocal Relationships with Families

Item 4: Maintain consistently high expectations for family involvement, being open to multiple and varied forms of engagement and providing intentional and responsive supports.

CHAPTER 13

Developing Meaningful and Relevant Writing with K–3 Dual Language Learner Students

Daniel R. Meier

Although K–3 dual language learners (DLLs) benefit from the very same rigorous and high-quality writing program and approach to literacy that all students receive, they specifically benefit from specialized instructional goals and strategies that support their integrated oral and written language growth.

This chapter emphasizes developmentally appropriate and linguistically accessible opportunities specifically for K–3 dual language learners to improve their school-based oral and written language development in multiple languages. In doing so, the chapter pays special attention to relevant theory and practice for K–3 teachers to support the writing talents, abilities, and needs of dual language learners, empowering young children to attain the requisite skills and knowledge to access their personal, cultural, familial, and linguistic talents and abilitites.

Relevant Research: Social Interaction, Oral Language, and Writing

Effective teaching approaches and strategies for supporting the writing of dual language learners are based upon selected aspects of seminal research on writing development over the last 40 years. This research has deepened our knowledge of important connections between students' sociocultural resources for language and literacy learning, and the most effective approaches and strategies for effective classroom writing instruction.

Cognition, Language, and Social Interaction

There are powerful connections for DLLs when we help them link cognition, language, and social interaction with their internal mental operations and their capabilities for writing (Vygotsky [1930–35] 1978, 1986). For Vygotsky, *internal mental operations* refer to the intellectual and cognitive

abilities of the mind to organize and express information, ideas, and thoughts. This social and cognitive view of writing development shows us that writing is a process whereby children learn to control writing as a symbol system within the particular ways that oral and written language are socially and culturally constructed in classrooms.

When DLLs have access to their familiar forms and functions of oral language through social interaction, they can use these social and linguistic strengths to support their writing development. For example, when teachers provide DLLs with enriching, daily opportunities to access their oral language skills through oral storytelling, high-quality read-alouds, reader's theater, drama, and conversation about texts, we can fashion a holistic approach to writing instruction based upon the totality of students' strengths and talents. For young writers, what happens off the page in terms of social interaction and talk with peers in socially and culturally responsive ways influences the forms and functions of their writing (Dyson & Genishi 2009). Entirely quiet or silent writing sessions prevent students from bringing their social and linguistic knowledge to bear on their writing. For this reason, DLLs need writing experiences that encourage talking and interaction with peers and adults on a daily basis (Arreguín-Anderson & Alanís 2019). Further, students and their families benefit from active, project-based learning that promotes home-community-school connections around child and family experiences, knowledge, and interests (Alvarez 2018).

Integrating Reading and Writing

DLLs also benefit from a literacy curriculum that integrates reading and writing both within the specific language arts period and across the entire curriculum (Gregory 2008; Mermelstein 2006; Samway 2006). In this way, students actively look for patterns and connections within the complementary symbolic processes of decoding (reading) and encoding (writing). The integration of reading and writing also supports DLLs' identities as

Table 13.1. Examples of Language-Reading-Writing Integration

Strategy	Linguistic Focus	Reading Activity	Writing Activity
Read aloud *Henny Penny*, by Paul Galdone	Highlight the text's repeated dialogue pattern of "May I go with you?" and "Yes, indeed."	*Reader's Theater* Ask students to act out the story. This enables them to practice the syntactic structures of story book language.	*Write, Pair, Share* Have students build in patterned phrases for dialogue in their own writing and share them with their peers.
Read aloud *Where the Mountain Meets the Moon*, by Grace Lin	Point out the literary language and imagery, "Far away from here, following the Jade River, there was once a black mountain that cut into the sky like a jagged piece of rough metal."	*Conversations About Text* Engage students in a partner-based activity where they discuss similar literary language and imagery throughout the text and/or other examples.	*Partner Writing* Ask students to co-create their own versions of Grace Lin's literary language through a partner-based writing activity.

agentic learners, readers, and writers who are capable of making text-to-text, text-to-self, and text-to-world connections to support their comprehension of written language texts (Keene & Zimmerman 2007).

When DLLs are immersed on a daily basis in integrated reading-writing activities, they gain knowledge about academic vocabulary, literary conventions, and syntactical structures that they can apply in their written language composition and revision. To promote these skills, consider the examples in Table 13.1.

Written Language Content and Mechanics Integration

Effective teachers also emphasize writing as a process in which students choose their own topics based upon their personal interests and knowledge of the world, and then create opportunities for students to engage in daily writing with peers as they edit and revise multiple drafts of a piece of writing (Calkins 2017). It is important in this process that students receive scaffolded instruction and feedback from teachers and peers that connect and integrate written language mechanics and content (Meier 2011, 2013). For example, attention to students' written language mechanics such as spelling, punctuation, code-switching, and syntax are integrated with attention to the story lines and characters of students' fiction writing, and to the ideas and information in their nonfiction writing. Further, when we explicitly teach and guide students to recognize and engage with a range

of socially and academically valued texts, students gain important access to the "codes of power" (Delpit 1987) in writing instruction and classroom discourse that are critical for students' academic achievement and school success.

Clues for Meaning

Effective content and mechanics integration is also founded upon targeted attention to specific semantic (the meaning behind words), syntactic (the structure of a particular language), bibliographic (text patterns), lexical (words and their immediate linguistic context), and grapho-phonic (orthographic and phonological knowledge) literacy clues (Gregory 2008). Taken together, these clues greatly assist students in recognizing and integrating essential elements of written texts that perform a range of functions—telling a well-told story, evoking powerful images and feelings, conveying important information, and convincing an audience of a particular stance or argument.

Conclusion

Developmentally appropriate and culturally sustaining approaches and strategies, some of which are presented in this chapter, must speak to DLLs as members of particular cultural and linguistic communities, traditions, and worldviews. Students learn to write well when their familiar ways of using languages and of interacting with others are recognized and incorporated into the daily writing curriculum. DLLs specifically benefit from regular, scaffolded opportunities to bring their oral language and interactional talents to bear on writing activities, connect the processes of reading and writing, integrate written language content and mechanics, and gain access to important clues for meaning. K–3 DLLs are highly capable of learning to write well, and engaging in writing is a critical pathway for social inclusion, academic achievement, and school success.

Teachers play the most critical role in this process, as the depth and breadth of our conceptual knowledge about theory-to-practice connections provides the foundation for a thoughtful, sensitive, and transformative writing program for connecting students with their families. For example, activities and projects that invite participation from children's families, such as dictated and written stories co-constructed with families at home, afford increased home–school connections for children. Other examples include the sharing of treasured family stories, legends, and recipes that families can directly share with students in classrooms or send in as additional activities and projects to celebrate and extend children's multiliteracy writing development.

Key Points

> When dual language learners have access to their familiar forms and functions of oral language through social interaction, they can use these social and linguistic strengths to support their writing development.

> As DLLs are immersed on a daily basis in integrated reading-writing activities, they gain knowledge about academic vocabulary, literary conventions, and syntactical structures that they can apply in their written language composition and revision.

References

Alvarez, A. 2018. "Experiential Knowledge and Project-Based Learning in Bilingual Classrooms." *Occasional Paper Series* 39: 84–101.

Arreguín-Anderson, M.G., & I. Alanís. 2019. *Translingual Partners in Early Childhood Elementary-Education: Pedagogies on Linguistic and Cognitive Engagement.* New York: Peter Lang.

Calkins, L.M. 2017. *A Guide to the Writing Workshop.* Portsmouth, NH: Heinemann.

Dyson, A.H., & C. Genishi. 2009. *Children, Language, and Literacy: Diverse Learners in Diverse Times.* New York: Teachers College Press.

Gregory, E. 2008. *Learning to Read in a New Language.* London: SAGE Publications.

Keene, E.O., & S. Zimmerman. 2007. *Mosaic of Thought: The Power of Comprehension Strategy Instruction.* 2nd ed. Portsmouth, NH: Heinemann.

Meier, D.R. 2011. *Teaching Children to Write: Constructing Meaning and Mastering Mechanics.* New York: Teachers College Press; Berkeley: National Writing Project.

Meier, D.R. 2013. "Promoting Content and Mechanics Integration for Young Dual Language Learners." *Young Children* 68 (1): 20–26.

Mermelstein, L. 2006. *Reading/Writing Connections in the K–2 Classroom: Find the Clarity and Then Blur the Lines.* New York: Pearson.

Samway, K.D. 2006. *When English Learners Write: Connecting Research to Practice, K–8.* Portsmouth, NH: Heinemann.

Vygotsky, L.S. [1930–35] 1978. *Mind in Society: The Development of Higher Psychological Processes.* Ed. and trans. M. Cole, V. John-Steiner, S. Scribner, & E. Souberman. Cambridge, MA: Harvard University Press.

Vygotsky, L.S. 1986. *Thought and Language.* Ed. and trans. A. Kozulin, E. Hanfmann, & G. Vakar. Cambridge, MA: MIT Press.

Recommendations for Early Childhood Educators

Create a Caring, Equitable Community of Engaged Learners

Item 6: Actively promote children's agency.

Item 7: Scaffold children's learning to achieve meaningful goals.

Item 9: Recognize and be prepared to provide different levels of support to different children depending on what they need.

This chapter supports recommendations from the NAEYC position statement:

CHAPTER 14

Providing Responsive Supports to Dual Language Learners with Disabilities

Lillian Durán

Young children who speak a language other than English are one of the fastest growing populations in the United States (NASEM 2017). These children are often referred to as dual language learners (DLLs) because they will need to maintain their home language(s) to communicate with their families and also learn English as they begin participating in early education programs or attend kindergarten. DLLs are a diverse group and include children born in and outside of the United States to parents who are native-born and immigrants.

Not only do DLLs come from many different countries and cultures, but they also speak a wide variety of languages. There are over 350 different languages spoken in the United States (US Census Bureau 2015). The timing and amount of exposure to children's home languages and English also varies considerably (Phillips, Lonigan, & McDowell 2014). Some children are *simultaneously bilingual*, meaning that they are learning both English and another language in their homes. Other young children are *sequential bilinguals*; they may only speak their home language with family and are formally introduced to English through early education programs (Paradis, Genesee, & Crago 2011). Ultimately, this variation in language background leads to a broad range of language proficiencies in both home languages and English. It also implies that DLLs bring many strengths and funds of knowledge in their home languages and cultures to the task of learning in school.

It is important to recognize that young children who are bilingual may also be diagnosed with a disability. These children require special considerations as their disability may affect their language development. A one-size-fits-all approach to educating DLLs is not appropriate. One challenge lies in the disproportionate number of DLLs represented in special education programs with both over- and underrepresentation being documented

(Guiberson 2009; Harry & Klingner 2014; Morgan et al. 2012). Often educators confuse the process of second language acquisition with the presence of a disability; other times, because of a lack of training, they might be reluctant to assess bilingual children, unsure about how to tell the difference between bilingual acquisition and a language delay. Other challenges include the lack of bilingual special education teachers and of bilingual assessments with adequate evidence of reliability and validity to determine children's strengths and needs. In this chapter, I briefly discuss these issues and provide recommendations for practice.

Holistic Support and Services
Working Collaboratively

Several studies document that culturally and linguistically diverse families often feel isolated from and uninvolved in the special education process (Durán, Cycyk, & Batz, under review; Wolfe & Durán 2013). Given the significant challenges often faced by DLLs and their families, early childhood special and general education teachers should work collaboratively to holistically support families through the difficult process of special education eligibility determination. If a child qualifies, families will also need support to actively participate in the development of individualized education programs (IEPs) or service plans. Ortiz and colleagues (2011) indicate that bilingual educators can be instrumental in building bridges between special education professionals and families and may prevent inappropriate referrals of DLLs to special education. Skilled interpreters are also needed to ensure a child's family understands the process and can be actively involved.

Using the Home Language as a Resource

Research indicates that DLLs with disabilities who receive bilingual intervention demonstrate greater growth in both languages (Guiberson & Ferris 2019; Simon-Cereijido & Gutiérrez-Clellen 2013; Kay-Raining Bird et al. 2005). As IEPs are developed, teams need to consider how to incorporate all languages a child speaks into intervention, including working closely with the family to support their child's home language development. If bilingual staff are not available, programs may need to consider hiring bilingual teaching assistants to support equity and maximize the benefits the child will receive from intervention. Using a child's home language during targeted instruction builds a strong foundation for improved academic performance (NASEM 2017).

Instructional Competencies

To work effectively with young DLLs who also have special needs, Zepeda, Castro, and Cronin (2011) describe several competencies early childhood educators should possess. These include

> A knowledge of language development generally and, more specifically, bilingual development

> The ability to implement effective practices for DLLs

> An understanding of the link between language, culture, and learning

> Accurate information about dual language assessment practices

> Strategies for engaging in the culturally and linguistically appropriate delivery of services

All of these competencies are necessary to provide opportunities for meaningful involvement of families in their children's early education and to meet the social, linguistic, and cognitive needs of DLLs with disabilities. For example, if early childhood professionals are knowledgeable about bilingual development and the link between language, culture, and learning, they will be better equipped to provide information to the family about the importance of home language maintenance and the connection of home language to the child's cultural identity, learning, and future academic success. For many families, the messages they receive in the community lead them to believe that they should rapidly transition to English with the false belief that children with disabilities will face greater challenges with language learning if they are bilingual. This position is not supported by research; therefore, it is critical that teachers of DLLs with disabilities are able to provide them with accurate information (Cheatham, Santos, & Kerkutluoglu 2012).

Bilingual Screening

Screening is a critical practice to increase the likelihood that children will have access to the services they need, should they present with a disability. Often, early educators are the first involved in screening young DLLs to identify those who may need to be referred for a special education evaluation. Importantly, early educators need to carefully consider their screening practices with young DLLs. To distinguish between a disability and issues of learning in a second language, educators must ensure that DLLs are tested for a disability in their dominant language or, in the case of simultaneous bilinguals, in both languages (DEC 2014; Peña & Halle 2011). When a bilingual assessor is not available, educators should use a trained interpreter. Additionally, teachers must meaningfully involve families in an information gathering process to learn more about the child's functioning in their home and community settings.

Many programs use screening tools such as the *Ages & Stages Questionnaires*, Third Edition ([ASQ-3]; Squires & Bricker 2009), which involves families reporting on important developmental milestones. Even though the ASQ-3 is available in multiple languages, it is critical to consider how the family might view the questions on the ASQ-3 through their own cultural lens. Therefore, even when screening using a parent report tool, it is important to facilitate the family's completion of the questionnaire to support their understanding of the items and to gather additional information about the child's development that may be culturally relevant but not included on the questionnaire.

Conclusion

Early childhood education programs have the responsibility of serving some of America's most vulnerable children. With this responsibility comes a significant opportunity to improve developmental trajectories and equity in long-term academic outcomes. This requires educators to develop the skills necessary to effectively serve young bilingual children with disabilities and delays. Thus, to best prepare educators to serve DLLs with disabilities, more attention is needed to develop teachers' knowledge about this population and their educational needs and rights (Kangas 2017). Ultimately, the quality of the investment we make today in our youngest and most diverse population will provide a return on investment for generations to come.

Key Points

> Teachers must have access to high quality professional development opportunities to build their knowledge base and increase their confidence in effectively educating DLLs with disabilities.

> Early childhood systems need to invest in more bilingual staff and educators who speak the languages of the local community and can deliver high-quality assessment and instruction in children's home languages.

> Administrators need to invest in the future of these children by allocating the necessary resources now and developing program policies, practices, and priorities that promote equity in the services delivered to families and children who speak languages other than English.

References

Cheatham, G.A., R.M. Santos, & A. Kerkutluoglu. 2012. "Review of Comparison Studies Investigating Bilingualism and Bilingual Instruction for Students with Disabilities." *Focus on Exceptional Children* 45 (3): 1–12.

DEC (Division for Early Childhood of the Council for Exceptional Children). 2014. *DEC Recommended Practices in Early Intervention/Early Childhood Special Education*. Arlington, VA: DEC. www.dec-sped.org/dec-recommended-practices.

Durán, L.K., L. Cycyk, & R. Batz. Under review. "Voces de la Gente: Perspectives of Spanish-Speaking Latinx Families on Early Intervention and Early Childhood Special Education." *Journal of Early Intervention*.

Guiberson, M. 2009. "Hispanic Representation in Special Education: Patterns and Implications." *Preventing School Failure: Alternative Education for Children and Youth* 53 (3): 167–176.

Guiberson, M., & K.P. Ferris. 2019. "Early Language Interventions for Young Dual Language Learners: A Scoping Review." *American Journal of Speech-Language Pathology* 28 (3): 945–963.

Harry, B., & J. Klingner. 2014. *Why Are So Many Minority Students in Special Education? Understanding Race and Disability in Schools*. New York: Teachers College Press.

Kangas, S.E.N. 2017. "'That's Where the Rubber Meets the Road': The Intersection of Special Education and Dual Language Education." *Teachers College Record* 119 (7): 1–36.

Kay-Raining Bird, E., P. Cleave, N. Trudeau, E. Thordardottir, A. Sutton, & A. Thorpe. 2005. "The Language Abilities of Bilinguals with Down Syndrome." *American Journal of Speech-Language Pathology* 14 (3): 187–199.

Morgan, P.L., G. Farkas, M.M. Hillemeier, & S. Maczuga. 2012. "Are Minority Children Disproportionately Represented in Early Intervention and Early Childhood Special Education?" *Educational Researcher* 41 (9): 339–351.

NASEM (National Academies of Sciences, Engineering, and Medicine). 2017. *Promoting the Educational Success of Children and Youth Learning English*. Report. Washington, DC: National Academies Press. doi:10.17226/24677.

Ortiz, A.A., P.M. Robertson, C.Y. Wilkinson, Y. Liu, B.D. McGhee, & M.I. Kushner. 2011. "The Role of Bilingual Education Teachers in Preventing Inappropriate Referrals of ELLs to Special Education: Implications for Response to Intervention." *Bilingual Research Journal* 34 (3): 316–333.

Paradis, J., F. Genesee, & M. Crago. 2011. *Dual Language Development and Disorders: A Handbook on Bilingualism and Second Language Learning*. 2nd ed. Baltimore: Brookes Publishing.

Peña, E.D., & T.G. Halle. 2011. "Assessing Preschool Dual Language Learners: Traveling a Multiforked Road." *Child Development Perspectives* 5 (1): 28–32.

Phillips, B.M., C.J. Lonigan, & K.D. McDowell. 2014. "Home Environment Predictors of Language Minority Preschool Children's English and Spanish Skills." Paper presented at the 21st Annual Meeting of the Society for the Scientific Study of Reading, in Santa Fe, NM.

Simon-Cereijido, G., & V.F. Gutiérrez-Clellen. 2013. "Bilingual Education for All: Latino Dual Language Learners with Language Disabilities." *International Journal of Bilingual Education and Bilingualism* 17 (2): 235–254.

Squires, J., & D. Bricker. 2009. *Ages & Stages Questionnaires, Third Edition (ASQ-3)*. Baltimore: Brookes Publishing.

US Census Bureau. 2015. "Census Bureau Reports at Least 350 Languages Spoken in US Homes." Press release CB15-185. www.census.gov/newsroom/press-releases /2015/cb15-185.html.

Wolfe, K., & L.K. Durán. 2013. "Culturally and Linguistically Diverse Parents' Perceptions of the IEP Process: A Review of Current Research." *Multiple Voices for Ethnically Diverse Exceptional Learners* 13 (2): 4–18.

Zepeda, M., D.C. Castro, & S. Cronin. 2011. "Preparing Early Childhood Teachers to Work with Young Dual Language Learners." *Child Development Perspectives* 5 (1): 10–14.

Recommendations for Early Childhood Educators

Create a Caring, Equitable Community of Engaged Learners

This chapter supports recommendations from the NAEYC position statement:

Item 2: Recognize each child's unique strengths and support the full inclusion of all children—given differences in culture, family structure, language, racial identity, gender, abilities and disabilities, religious beliefs, or economic class.

Item 5: Involve children, families, and the community in the design and implementation of learning activities.

Establish Reciprocal Relationships with Families

Item 1: Embrace the primary role of families in children's development and learning.

CHAPTER 15

Making Thinking, Learning, and Development Visible and Inclusive Through Authentic Assessment

Hilary Seitz

Close your eyes and imagine a child walking on a playground. There are flowers in large pots in the center; around the flowerpots are gravel pathways with trees lining the edges. Beyond the trees are other children playing, talking, running, and laughing. Open your eyes and think about what you saw in your mind. Did you notice the child's facial expressions? Were they tentative to join in with other children or were they excited and ready to explore on their own? Did you notice the walking gait or other motor movements? Did you notice the different physical elements in the playground environment and how the individual child interacted with it? Did the playground inspire creativity and inquiry for this child? Could they be successful? Did you notice how the children engaged with each other in their play? Did you see the outdoor environment as a whole that supports various areas of development and curriculum?

Learning to really see each individual child, to see their abilities, their strengths, and their possibilities, is an art. Documenting this and making the thinking, learning, and development visible helps us understand the child better and helps others value their capabilities. Documentation takes practice, collaboration, and support from those around you. It also takes an internal motivation to truly understand the children with whom you work. In this chapter, I discuss how learning to use authentic assessment strategies (such as documentation of a child's skills and interests) starts with learning to see and observe children in their environments and then unpacking and reflecting on your learning. Learning about children's communities, traditions, families, and backgrounds will strengthen the assessment and help tell the whole story in an inclusive way.

What Is Authentic Assessment?

Authentic assessment is a process of learning about all the capabilities that a child has, including where they are and where they are going. Such assessment is thoughtful and intentional, with adequate time and resources for support. These capabilities are skills, attributes, characteristics, and dispositions that help teachers understand all children in their classrooms. This process also helps tell the "whole story" of the child, including their developmental and cultural story, their thinking story, and how a child interacts within a group, including the group story.

Authentic Assessment Strategies Are Strengths-Based

The process of authentic assessment helps to shift the concept of assessment from a narrow view of comparing children with numbers that reflect what they *don't* know to a system that demonstrates what children *do* know and can do (Escamilla, this volume). One way to document visual and auditory evidence of a child's growth and learning abilities is to create a portfolio, hard copy or digital, that includes photos, transcripts, and videos (Derman-Sparks, LeeKeenan, & Nimmo 2015; Seitz 2018). To do this, teachers need to have an ongoing system to collect documentation (e.g., observations, photos, work samples) on each child. For example, to document a child's ability to write, begin by collecting a writing sample with a photo of how the child holds the writing implement as well as notes about the experience. This provides assessment data for a particular date. If this process is repeated every month or two and then put together, the pieces tell a story and the documentation (authentic assessment) will show how the child is growing and developing.

Authentic Assessment Strategies Are Culturally Responsive

Hammond (2014) defines *culturally responsive teaching* as "an educator's ability to recognize students' cultural displays of learning and meaning making and respond positively and constructively with teaching moves that use cultural knowledge as a scaffold to connect what the student knows to new concepts and content" (15). Culturally responsive means that we, as early educators, learn about, build upon, and provide opportunities to understand all the children and families we work with in our programs. This includes learning about family values and cultural traditions so the classroom is a safe and inviting place that reflects the classroom community. The classroom community consists of many parts that make a whole. Each group of children (the class) looks and acts differently depending on the prior knowledge of the children and the experiences and expectations of their families. When the teacher looks at these elements holistically and builds opportunities based on these assets, the whole classroom community comes together and is culturally relevant to the children and families.

Authentic Assessment Strategies Promote Equity in a Digital World

Some educators are challenged when it comes to determining how to assess children's learning authentically when children are using digital tools. Relevant and important skills for young children to learn in digitally driven learning experiences are similar to skills educators should be looking for in nondigital learning experiences. These include collaboration, critical thinking, creative problem solving, and communication. Within the context of a more digitally driven learning experience, these skills can prepare young students for the future. But are all learning experiences equitable for all children? How can technology in the form of apps, social media platforms, and websites support authentic assessment when the digital landscape is not equitable for everyone? Teachers need to teach *how* to find, process, and use the information learned through these sources in a responsible and equitable way. Teachers can document this learning through multiple avenues as part of authentic assessment.

How Do We Make Thinking, Learning, and Development Visible?

There are four steps in the authentic assessment cycle (see Figure 15.1). When a teacher applies these four steps, it helps various audiences—including the teacher, children, families, and the community—understand and value children's thinking, learning, and development. The complete cycle makes this visible in an appealing way that is culturally and linguistically appropriate and addresses the way children learn in a digital world.

The first step in the cycle is *observation*. Observation includes looking for thinking, learning, development, and engagement. To do this, one must practice watching children in and outside of the classroom. Take photographs of children engaged in activities, write down quotations of individual children, and notice the small things about each child. Some of the smallest things might be the most important, such as how often the child shares materials with a peer or where and how the child stands or sits in relation to other children or adults. It is important to note that these observations should be factual and not based on interpretations. All of us come with a variety of preconceived ideas and a different cultural lens, so we need to observe carefully.

After careful observation, the early childhood educator begins the second step in the cycle—*documentation*. Documentation involves looking at all of the observational notes and records, photographs, and other materials collected. We put these things together to tell the child's story. Documentation can take a number of different forms, from a notebook to an ePortfolio to a website or other platform (such as a private share site accessible only to the children's families), and provides photos, short videos, or comments about a classroom community. Think about the audience for the documentation. If the audience is the family, then you want an accessible format for the family to see their child's story. Different devices manage documentation in various ways. Administrators and community members may want a different story told. That is to say, administrators and community members want to know how a classroom community as a whole (all the children) is successful, engaged, learning, growing, and meeting developmental milestones rather than a specific child. Often a website can show how learning is visible in a classroom without identifying individual children. In all cases, the educator must communicate their ideas

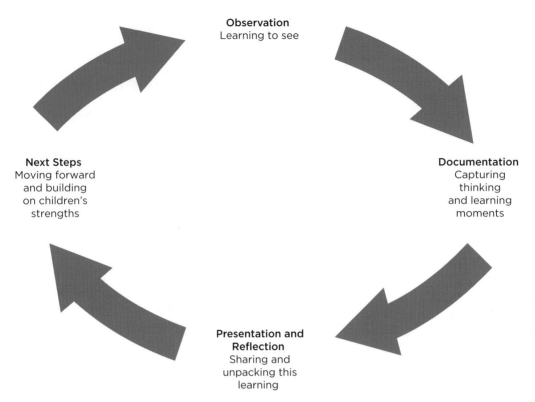

Observation
Learning to see

Documentation
Capturing
thinking
and learning
moments

Presentation and
Reflection
Sharing and
unpacking this
learning

Next Steps
Moving forward
and building
on children's
strengths

Figure 15.1. Authentic Assessment Cycle

to families beforehand and seek permission, particularly for posting photos or videos and other personalized information sharing.

The third step in the cycle is *presentation and reflection*. This is important for children, teachers, families, and the community. The actual sharing and unpacking of the learning help to underscore the value and purpose of the experience. The presentation and reflection can be done in several formats; each has value in a different way. A presentation may be as simple as inviting a family into the classroom at the end of the day and having the child share their work from a documentation piece such as their ePortfolio or work that is displayed as on a bulletin board. Having a child become the center of the experience tells the child that their work, abilities, and ideas are important and special. The teacher may facilitate a more formal gathering or family celebration to share the collective work and documentation of the group. This more formal sharing may be done in the evening, at a class lunch, or even on a weekend, depending on the communities' access and schedules. The actual event, whether it is sitting at a group

lunch or in the evening, can be a presentation by the teachers with children, or through a video or a series of documentation panels that are unveiled at a certain time. These sharings are celebrations of the children's strengths, imaginations, and abilities. These formal gatherings of presentation are also outlets for families to build a sense of community based on their children's learning and cultural connections. After the presentation, it is important to have time to reflect on the experience. This leads to the last step of the process.

The *next steps* portion, which is the fourth and final step in the authentic assessment cycle, helps the educator think about where the children are developmentally and emotionally and consider what to do next. Do some of the children need more time with building blocks? Are others ready to take the next step toward writing sight words? Educators and families can answer these questions together as they look at the authentic assessments and build curriculum around them. In this way, the curriculum will be more meaningful and more connected to the children and families as well as their community and cultural values.

Advancing Equity and Embracing Diversity in Early Childhood Education

Conclusion

The authentic assessment process is a valuable tool in today's diverse early childhood classroom. Learning how to observe, document, and present and reflect guides teachers to the next steps needed to help children grow and thrive. Authentic assessment will help to build community in the classroom and become a way to really know and understand each child's cultural and linguistic story.

Key Points

> Authentic assessment is an important process to learn about a child's unique capabilities.

> Authentic assessment is strengths-based and culturally responsive.

> Authentic assessment promotes an equitable system to learn about children.

References

Derman-Sparks, L., D. LeeKeenan, & J. Nimmo. 2015. *Leading Anti-Bias Early Childhood Programs: A Guide for Change.* New York: Teachers College Press; Washington, DC: NAEYC.

Hammond, Z. 2014. *Culturally Responsive Teaching and the Brain: Promoting Authentic Engagement and Rigor Among Culturally and Linguistically Diverse Students.* Thousand Oaks, CA: Corwin Press.

Seitz, H. 2018. "The Power of Documentation in the Early Childhood Classroom." In *Spotlight on Young Children*: *Observation and Assessment*, eds. H. Bohart & R. Procopio, 50–57. Washington, DC: NAEYC.

naeyc®

This chapter supports recommendations from the NAEYC position statement:

Recommendations for Early Childhood Educators

Observe, Document, and Assess Children's Learning and Development

Item 1: Recognize the potential of your own culture and background affecting your judgment when observing, documenting, and assessing children's behavior, learning, or development.

Item 2: Use authentic assessments that seek to identify children's strengths and provide a well-rounded picture of development.

Item 3: Focus on strengths.

CHAPTER 16

Learning Stories

Observation, Reflection, and Narrative in Early Childhood Education

Isauro M. Escamilla

As a preschool teacher in a dual language public preschool, I am required to conduct classroom observations to assess children's learning. This has led me to the following questions: *How can early childhood educators support and make visible children's emergent cultural and linguistic identities? Moreover, within this process, how can teachers embed story and narrative to document children's growth and strengthen families' participation in their children's education?* This chapter examines the use of an authentic assessment approach in the form of Learning Stories, a narrative-based formative assessment created by New Zealand early childhood education leaders to highlight children's strengths and improve instruction based on the interests, talents, and expertise of children and their families (Carr & Lee 2012).

Narrative in Marginalized Communities

A *learning story* is a record of a child's life in the classroom and school community based on teachers' observations of the child at play and work. It tells a story written *to* the child that is meant to be shared with the family. Learning stories are based on individual or family narratives. For native, Indigenous, and marginalized communities, the telling of stories or historical memoirs may be conceived as something deeply personal and even part of a sacred whole (Benham 2007). Narratives recognize the value of Indigenous knowledge. As an example, the learning story journey starts by honoring and respecting the process of observing, listening, reflecting, and sharing. When we engage in writing and reading classroom stories—knowing how they are told, to whom, and why—we uncover who we are as communities and, perhaps, develop a deeper appreciation and understanding of other people's stories.

Learning Stories Capture Children's Learning

NAEYC's "Advancing Equity in Early Childhood Education" position statement (2019) states that educators should "use authentic assessments that seek to identify children's strengths and provide a well-rounded picture of development" (8). Learning stories encompass this philosophical approach and serve as a meaningful pedagogical tool to assess children's strengths and help educators reflect on their roles in the complex processes of teaching and learning (Carr & Lee 2012; Carr & Lee 2019). As formative assessments, learning stories offer the possibility of reimagining all children as competent, inquisitive learners and educators as critical thinkers and creative writers, genuinely invested in their work.

The school where I teach is located in San Francisco's Mission District. My students reflect the ethnic, economic, cultural, and linguistic mosaic of the school's immediate neighborhood, which consists of mostly first- and second-generation immigrant families from Mexico, Central America, and Asia. Most students receive subsidized services, and their families primarily work as housekeepers, babysitters, cooks, painters and construction workers, while some hold office jobs. The school has three preschool-age classrooms: one Spanish-English dual language classroom with 24 children, one Cantonese-English dual language classroom with 24 children, and one classroom of children with special needs with 12 children.

The preschool's academic framework is based on the project approach, which embraces children's interests and the immediate environment for engaging in an in-depth study of a specific topic from multiple perspectives (Helm & Katz 2010). The investigation is usually undertaken by a small group of children within a class, sometimes by a whole class, and occasionally by an individual child. Each project is a research effort focused on finding answers to questions about a topic posed by the children, teachers, or teachers and children together. Classroom investigations, which may last from a few days to several months, are carefully documented by teachers and children through photographs, recorded conversations, short videos, children's artwork and dictations, and classroom-made booklets, as well as teachers' reflections and interpretations. We are also required to administer several district- and state-mandated assessments multiple times during the year and require the teachers to collect work and play samples from all the children on a regular basis. The Learning Stories approach provides additional opportunities for teachers to observe and document developmental paths within the context of each child's individuality.

Working on these projects made the teachers realize that we play a pivotal role in preserving a child's language in relation to family, culture, and traditions. If, for example, children lose their ability to speak Spanish in an effort to learn English, they risk losing a link to their own heritage. In our classroom, we have seen that second-generation children have more difficulty acquiring the basics of Spanish and feel much more comfortable speaking English in their social interactions with peers and siblings. Some children respond in English to bilingual parents, even though these parents address them in Spanish. The situation worsens in the case of grandparents who speak Spanish only and children don't make the effort to communicate in Spanish or do so in a very limited manner. Children and families are encouraged to communicate in the language with which they feel most comfortable. As equity-mindful teachers, we must engage in projects that are relevant to children's and families' lived experiences. Reading books in children's diverse languages is a way to do this while developing children's bilingual identity.

As an example, in my class, we read a book to connect with children's cultural and linguistic heritage. It is titled *A Movie in My Pillow/Una película en mi almohada*, by Salvadorean writer Jorge Argueta, and it's written in Spanish and English. The children I teach enjoyed this collection of poems where the main character, young Jorgito, lives in the San Francisco's Mission District, a predominantly Latino/a community; but he hasn't forgotten his native El Salvador. Just like the young boy in the book of poems, we discovered that many of the children in our classroom had "memories"

of the places from which their families had emigrated. One of Jorge Argueta's poems, entitled "When We Left El Salvador," opened the door to children's creativity and imagination.

In a real-life example, a different young boy, Zahid, would uncover his hidden talents in our classroom. Zahid was a cheerful, talkative boy who didn't much enjoy tracing random letters but had a talent for expressing his feelings and telling a good story. He was also skillful in using different tools, such as an easel, canvas, paints, maps, and markers, to express his thoughts and convey his ideas. Zahid revealed his storytelling skills and talent by sharing a story of his father trying to cross the border between Mexico and the United States. The following is a story I wrote addressed to Zahid, talking about what he shared with the teachers, its meaning, and possible future activities based on his genuine interest.

"Waiting for Dad on This Side of the Border": Zahid's Learning Story

What's the Story?

Zahid, I admire your initiative to tell us the tale of the travels your dad has undertaken to reunite with you and your family in California. On a map, you showed us Mexico City, where you said your dad started his journey to the North. You spoke about the *frontera* (the border), and you asked us to help you find Nebraska and Texas on our map because that's where you said your dad was detained. We asked you, *"¿Qué es la frontera?"* (What is the border?), and you answered in Spanish, "It is a place where they arrest you because you are an immigrant. My dad was detained because he wanted to go to California to be with me."

Why Is this Story Significant?

Zahid, through this story where you narrate the failed attempt of your dad to get reunited with you and your family, you reveal an understanding that goes well beyond your 5.4 years. In the beginning you referred to the map as a *planet*, but perhaps that's how you understand your world: a planet with lines that divide cities, states, and countries. A particular area that called your attention was the line between Mexico and the United States, which you retraced in blue ink to highlight the place where you said your dad crossed the border. It is indeed admirable to see you standing so self-assured in front of the class ready to explain to your classmates your feelings and ideas and to guide us through your map so eloquently.

What Activities Could We Plan to Support You in Exploring this Topic?

Zahid, we could invite you to share with your classmates the tale of your dad's travels and invite your friends to share the stories of their families too. We could take dictations of what it means for you to be waiting for dad on this side of the border. We could support you to put into practice your interest in writing so that you could write a letter or message to your dad. Perhaps you would be interested in making a painting on a canvas representing your ideas and feelings.

What Does Zahid's Family Think?

"A Zahid casi no le gusta escribir, pero habla mucho y entiende mucho también. Casi no le gusta dibujar, pero a ver si con ustedes aquí en la escuela disfruta dibujar o pintar." –Mamá (Zahid is not very fond of writing, but he talks a lot and also understands quite a lot. He doesn't like drawing, but maybe with your support here at school he could find enjoyment in drawing or painting. –Mom)

Essentially the learning story provides a structure for documenting Zahid's developmental progression over time, collecting data on his language use, funds of knowledge, evolving talents, and curiosity for the natural world.

Developing a Learning Story

Although all learning stories will be a little different, there are core principles that underlie any learning story. The foundational components include the following (Carr & Lee 2012; Carter 2010, 2017):

> An observation with accompanying photographs or short videos

> An analysis of the observation

> A plan to extend a child's learning

> The family's perspective on their child's learning experience

> Links to specific evaluation tools

Educators can use learning stories to identify developmental milestones with links to specific assessment measures; however, the purpose is not to test a hypothesis or to evaluate. At the root of any learning story is a genuine interest in understanding children's lived experiences and the meaning teachers, families, and children themselves make of those experiences to augment their learning.

Suggested Format of a Learning Story

1. **Title:** Any great story begins with a good title that captures the essence of the tale being told.

2. **Observation:** The teacher begins the story with his or her own interest in what the child has taken the initiative to do, describing what the child does and says.

3. **What It Means:** The teacher's reflection to interpret and write about the significance of what was observed.

4. **Opportunities and Possibilities:** The teacher's description of what he or she could do next to extend the child's learning.

5. **Questions to the Family:** The child's family responds with their point of view and reaction to what the teacher wrote.

6. **Milestones or Skills:** Links to specific evaluative and assessment measures.

This suggested format has the potential to offer a helpful guide for alternative ways to observe and assess children's learning processes. It may also help teachers in organizing fleeting ideas into a coherent narrative to make sense of specific children's experiences or classroom observations. More importantly, the writing of learning stories encourages teachers to recognize children as competent explorers and learners in familiar settings at any given moment during the school day.

Conclusion

Learning stories are visual and written narratives about children's growth created by teachers from a strengths-based perspective. Through these child-centered stories, teachers engage minds, touch hearts, and enhance their pedagogical and intellectual work. They humanize the early childhood profession, paving the way toward innovative modes of observing, analyzing, and understanding the complexities of children's actions and behaviors. Children's active participation in classroom life and curriculum planning support a sense of inclusiveness and belonging when they see themselves as the protagonists of their own stories in a school environment that celebrates their voices, experiences, and talents.

Key Points

> The Learning Stories approach provides additional opportunities for teachers to observe and document developmental paths within the context of each child's individuality.

> When we engage in writing and reading classroom stories—knowing how they are told, to whom, and why—we uncover who we are as communities and, perhaps, develop a deeper appreciation and understanding of other people's stories.

> At the root of any learning story is a genuine interest in understanding children's lived experiences and the meaning teachers, families, and children themselves make of those experiences to augment their learning.

References

Benham, M.K. 2007. "Moʻōlelo: On Culturally Relevant Story Making from an Indigenous Perspective." In *Handbook of Narrative Inquiry: Mapping a Methodology*, ed. D.J. Clandinin, 512–533. Thousand Oaks, CA: SAGE Publications.

Carr, M., & W. Lee. 2012. *Learning Stories: Constructing Learner Identities in Early Education*. London: SAGE Publications.

Carr, M., & W. Lee. 2019. *Learning Stories in Practice*. London: SAGE Publications.

Carter, M. 2010. "Using Learning Stories to Strengthen Teachers' Relationships with Children." *Exchange* 32 (6): 40–44.

Carter, M. 2017. "Growing Ourselves as Leaders: A Conversation with Annie White." *Exchange* 39 (6): 46–51.

Helm, J.H., & L.G. Katz. 2010. Young Investigators: The Project Approach in the Early Years. 2nd ed. New York: Teachers College Press.

NAEYC. 2019. "Advancing Equity in Early Childhood Education." Position statement. Washington, DC: NAEYC. www.naeyc.org /resources/position-statements/equity.

---

naeyc®

This chapter supports recommendations from the NAEYC position statement:

Recommendations for Early Childhood Educators

Create a Caring, Equitable Community of Engaged Learners

Item 1: Uphold the unique value and dignity of each child and family.

Observe, Document, and Assess Children's Learning and Development

Item 2: Use authentic assessments that seek to identify children's strengths and provide a well-rounded picture of development.

Moving Forward as a Profession

Throughout this text, we have presented individual reflections and discussed teacher responsibilities in an effort to provide more context for NAEYC's "Advancing Equity in Early Childhood Education" position statement. To achieve social justice and equity within the early childhood education system, we need also to engage with the administrators and higher education faculty who reinforce and support the work of teachers and teacher candidates. Furthermore, we need to discuss next steps for what equity and social justice means for our profession as a whole.

Administrators of center-based programs, schools, and home-based family child care play a key role in supporting the early childhood educator. To advance equity, early childhood educators need work settings that also embrace equitable goals for all children as well as the early childhood professional. The administrator's role is more than supervising curriculum, managing budgets, and evaluating teachers; it is also the role of an advocate who rejects deficit perspectives and promotes the acceptance and integration of all cultural and linguistic groups. To provide teachers with continuous support and opportunities for sustained transformative

change, administrators must provide teachers with effective professional development, time, and space for critical reflection.

Likewise, faculty members in teacher preparation programs also play a significant role in promoting social justice and equity for their teacher candidates and the communities they serve. This requires courageous conversations about the structural inequities that affect their efforts, the education of teacher candidates, and young children of color. Excellence in teaching requires a continuous interplay of theory, research, and practice. Early childhood teacher candidates develop cultural competence through coursework and supervised field experiences that provide multiple opportunities to use developmental knowledge to create healthy, respectful, supportive, and challenging learning environments for all young children. These experiences, however, must be purposeful and selected to expose students to a variety of cultural, linguistic, and ethnic settings within early childhood education. Finally, teacher candidates should have opportunities to build a strong identification and involvement with the early childhood profession to equitably serve young children and their families.

In this part, we have collected essays in the form of chapters which pull together all of these perspectives with an eye to the future. These chapters ask us to really challenge our assumptions about what is excellence and what the field must do to ensure that all children reach their potential. By doing nothing, we are complicit in inequitable access and learning opportunities. In order to reach the North Star or our vision of the goal of early childhood education, these authors ask us to recognize the historical harm and trauma that have been visited upon various groups and to use our political will to address the root causes while also recognizing the humanity and capacity in all children, families, and communities.

The authors in this section call to action the ways that early childhood professionals and system leaders can better equip themselves to be thoughtful and active in ensuring children have equitable learning experiences regardless of their race, ethnicity, language, nativity status, and ability level. Spending time to gap-gaze on all the disparities and inequities inherent in US systems, including early childhood, will not help children to meet their potential without active behaviors from adults. The authors seek to identify ways that early childhood professionals, including system leaders, can engage in creating and implementing a social justice agenda for early childhood education.

Reflection Questions

As you read the chapters in Part 3, we encourage you to reflect on the following questions:

1. What steps can you take to shift the culture of your school to one that reflects the values and principles of NAEYC's position statement on advancing equity?

2. What are other examples of how educators should make culture and language the center of educational experiences instead of a generic "developmentally appropriate" practice?

3. In what ways do your curriculum, course readings, and assignments need to be adjusted to reflect your teacher candidates' cultural and linguistic resources?

4. What is second-generation work and how much have you engaged in it?

5. What do you see as the barrier to engaging in second-generation work?

6. What do you see as the systems that perpetuate inequities?

7. What role do you play as gatekeeper, if any, in potentially perpetuating or dismantling inequities?

8. What is the one thing you can do today to address marginalized communities' historical trauma?

CHAPTER 17

The Work

Promoting Equity and Justice in Early Childhood

Jen Neitzel

In recent years, there has been increased attention on equity within the educational system, particularly related to addressing the long-standing disparities in achievement. Educators have made distinct efforts at addressing cultural and linguistic diversity and providing more inclusive learning experiences for all children; however, the keen focus on these issues actually prevents us from true equity work and allows us to avoid talking about and acknowledging the truths of our country's past that have led to hundreds of years of oppression and subjugation within the educational system. The work of equity will take a concerted effort from system leaders, educators, policymakers, and the larger community to achieve specific goals that will ultimately lead to positive outcomes for all children and families.

Merriam-Webster (n.d. b) defines *work* as something that is produced or accomplished through effort or exertion. True equity work—work that is grounded in dismantling inequitable policies, practices, and structural barriers—will require more than becoming culturally proficient or making environments more inclusive for diverse children and families. Rather, educators, policymakers, administrators, and community members must be challenged to examine the roots of the current disparities, particularly related to discipline, the quality of instruction, and how teachers form relationships with children (Bowman, Comer, & Johns 2018). This work will require a great deal of effort and a move beyond superficial solutions. This chapter will define the concept of second-generation equity work and discuss specific strategies and recommendations for policymakers and system leaders to move the work of systems change forward in the field of early childhood education.

Second-Generation Equity Work

The field of education, including early childhood, is still entrenched within "first-generation" equity work, in which we superficially approach the opportunity and achievement gaps by implementing variations of the same practices rather than focusing on the underlying causes of the inequities that need to be addressed. A "second-generation" approach to equity focuses on identifying and addressing structural barriers and root causes that prevent equitable access and outcomes for children and families of color (Neitzel 2020). The term *second-generation work* is borrowed from a chapter written by Michael J. Guralnick in the early 1990s. In his writing, Guralnick (1993) argued that early intervention was in the midst of a period of rapid change that was marked by a movement away from superficial analyses regarding the effectiveness of services and supports for young children with disabilities into a new era in which researchers and policymakers were being pushed to ask more specific questions and develop a more nuanced understanding about how to meet the needs of young children and their families.

With respect to equity, the field of early childhood education is in a similar period of rapid change; however, we have not yet moved into work that is focused on developing a nuanced understanding of the issues and how to address them. As we move forward in this work, it is imperative that educators and policymakers shift their focus away from what has always been done to a more thoughtful and systematic approach to equity. Moving too quickly or resting our hopes solely on high-quality early childhood education will keep us firmly planted within first-generation equity work.

For generations, we have focused on solving disparities in achievement by implementing highly specific educational practices that are centered on promoting literacy, social-emotional, or math skills, which are grounded in a "blame the victim" ideology. The conscious and unconscious beliefs that drive first-generation equity work assume that children of color are in need of "fixing" because of their culture and language, their families, or their economic status rather than turning the attention back to the system itself—one that expects children of color and their families to fit into early childhood programs that are grounded in White European ideology about how children develop, what social skills are appropriate, and what school readiness looks like (Vaught 2011). This type of mentality allows us to overlook the root causes of the inequities that lay deep within the history of our nation and perpetuate the ongoing disparities.

As a field, we have yet to emerge from a first-generation approach to equity in which we are in a constant cycle of implementing the latest intervention or relying on what we have always done without thinking critically and examining the underlying issues surrounding equity in education. Ladson-Billings and Tate (1995) argue that a fixation on the achievement gap actually prevents educators from examining and addressing the underlying problems and perpetuates a reliance on short-term solutions. Second-generation equity work requires that we shift the way we think about children and families of color and how we approach equitable education. It is the system, not the children, that needs to change.

Another characteristic of first-generation equity work is our tendency as a field to focus on buzzwords (e.g., equity, trauma-informed care) without developing an understanding of the issues and how to address them effectively. To understand equity, we also have to understand privilege. According to Merriam-Webster (n.d. a), *privilege* is a special right, advantage, or immunity granted or available only to a particular person or group of people. Conversely, *equity* is the elimination of privilege, oppression, disparities, and disadvantage. Racial equity, in particular, is achieved when one's racial identity no longer predicts access to education or success in life (National Equity Project, n.d.). To get to this place, a significant paradigm shift will need to take place in which we move away from a paternalistic approach to early childhood education (e.g., implementing

trauma-informed interventions that are based on White European norms and values) by viewing all educational policies and practices through an equity lens. That is, we need to work to identify and eliminate policies and practices that privilege one group but oppress another (Neitzel 2020). By doing so, we will be able to engage in a more careful examination of the underlying problems, barriers, and causes of the inequities that currently exist so that we can finally address equity and promote justice in a meaningful way. Only then will the field begin to shift into a second-generation mindset.

Beginning the Work

Working toward equity in early childhood education ensures high outcomes for all children by removing the predictability of success or failure based on race, ethnicity, or language; interrupts inequitable practices; examines biases; and creates inclusive early learning environments (National Equity Project, n.d.). In addition, those working toward educational equity take into account key issues within our current society that prevent culturally and linguistically diverse children from attaining long-term academic success.

Understanding the complexity of the issues and how each of the institutions within our country intertwine to create one big system of oppression is critical to this work (Neitzel 2020). As the field of early childhood begins to focus on second-generation work, several key activities must be put into place to provide a strong foundation:

1. Working across early childhood sectors to align equity-based policies and practices

2. Examining early childhood data to identify where disparities exist and the barriers that sustain them

3. Developing more equitable policies and practices that are focused on children's cultural and linguistic wealth

A Cross-Sector Approach to Equity

Within the field of early childhood education, there is a tendency to work in silos with specific policies and practices that are unique to each. Because of the complex nature of equity and children's development, there is a growing need to work together to minimize the complex web of services that can be difficult for families to navigate. Effective cross-sector collaboration includes meaningful dialogue and relationship building between Head Start, public pre-K, child care, and early childhood mental health. All sectors that touch the lives of young children and their families should be a part of the collaborative equity work going forward.

In addition, it is essential that families and community members who are directly impacted by the inequitable policies and practices be included in this collaborative work. Any type of cross-sector approach to early childhood equity must include an emphasis on listening to, learning from, and making space for those who are most affected to guide the work and be equal partners in bringing about real change within early childhood programs. The answers to our most pressing questions do not lie within the walls of offices and buildings but within the communities that have consistently faced structural barriers (Neitzel 2020).

Through this collective approach, the various early childhood sectors work together with community members to build a common agenda that allows for alignment and coordination across systems (Kania, Kramer, & Senge 2018). With a clear definition of equity and understanding of the current disparities, key stakeholders can then work toward creating a common vision, mission, goals, and theory of change, which is essentially a roadmap for the work ahead. These activities are fundamental to the success of any systems change efforts because they provide the infrastructure for success and support long-term sustainability.

Examining Data to Identify Disparities and Barriers

An additional task of cross-sector collaboration is to review data to determine current inequities within early childhood sectors (Alyn & Cabbil 2018). Most often, these inequities will be related to discipline and access to resources and services. Understanding where the disparities exist (e.g., in certain programs, for certain populations of children) is critical to disrupting current policies and practices.

A review of the current data also provides a context for drafting a vision, mission, and goals that should guide the work going forward. In particular, this cross-sector work can determine in what ways stakeholders (e.g., families,

children, teachers) are most affected by current policies and practices and how these stakeholders can be meaningfully engaged in shaping solutions and strategies that will address the continuing disparities within each sector (Annie E. Casey Foundation 2018).

Analysis of data trends within sectors and individual programs provides a context for implementing high-quality professional development activities that assist providers in implementing more equitable services for children and families of color. Having a mechanism for monitoring child outcomes, disciplinary exclusions (including being moved from one classroom to another), and access to services ensures that early childhood sectors better meet the needs of all children and provide the necessary resources to address disparities related to discipline, instruction, curricula, and the formation of adult–child relationships (Losen et al. 2015).

Developing More Equitable Policies and Practices

Key to all of this work is the development of more equitable policies and practices. Current policies and practices are one of the biggest barriers within the early childhood system because they generally reflect the views of the dominant White culture and often do not include standards related to inclusivity and equity (Johnson-Staub 2017). This can be seen in the policies related to suspension and expulsion, particularly within the child care sector.

Suspension, expulsion, and other exclusionary policies are particularly troublesome because they create a direct link between the educational system and the criminal justice system (Skiba, Arredondo, & Williams 2014). Current practices for managing behaviors are grounded in first-generation equity work. These types of exclusionary practices are wholly ineffective for all children and are counterproductive in helping children who are exposed to trauma heal and acquire key self-regulation and social-emotional skills. The use of suspensions and expulsions serves as a Band-Aid to a larger problem and does not address much larger issues within early childhood programs, such as ineffective behavior management practices, implicit bias, and unresolved trauma.

More emphasis should be placed on helping teachers acquire key knowledge related to child development (including what is truly a challenging behavior), how culture shapes behavior, and specific culturally and linguistically responsive anti-bias strategies that help teachers implement effective instructional practices, develop meaningful relationships with children, and manage behavior in a developmentally appropriate manner.

To truly address equitable policies and practices, early childhood educators will have to place a primary emphasis on mental health—not just the social and emotional well-being of children, but also teachers, families, and other staff. This mindset shift is significant because it is counter to the current educational culture of academic achievement. Focusing on the mental health of the entire early childhood community is a key piece of the puzzle that has yet to be addressed in a real and meaningful way. When we place a priority on helping children acquire key social-emotional skills, they will be better equipped to interact with others, develop relationships, and learn. When teachers are emotionally supported and have key competencies, they will be more effective in their work with children in early learning programs (Neitzel 2020). All of these efforts will require significant and critical changes to both policy and practice.

Putting It All Together

At the surface, the work of equity can seem like a daunting task. As we gain a deeper understanding of the history of our country and the hold that racism and oppression has on all aspects of society, including early childhood education, we come to realize that addressing the deep disparities will not be a quick and easy fix. The work of equity will take time, perseverance, and a commitment to peeling back the layers of inequity to effectively eliminate barriers and structures within the early childhood system.

If we are to make the choice to work toward equity, this also will require a significant amount of self-reflection, active listening, and acquiescence of power on the part of those in leadership positions. As individuals, we will need to acknowledge our role in the continuing disparities. Many people remain complicit simply because they accept their experiences as the norm. That is the product of living

and operating within a racist society. If we are to achieve equity, teachers, policymakers, and administrators also will need to pause their tendency to provide immediate solutions without reflection. It is also time for those in leadership positions to relinquish a great deal of control. If we are to have equity, we must allow those who have experienced the reality of inequitable early childhood policies and practices lead the way in devising meaningful solutions.

Policymakers, administrators, and educators do not, and should not, have all the answers. We must clear the path so that those who are most affected can lead us forward. Their lived experiences and knowledge are needed when developing more equitable policies and practices. A community-wide cross-sector team that includes leadership from each sector as well as members of traditionally marginalized neighborhoods will guide this larger work going forward. A cohesive framework that includes key strategies for pursuing equity creates a context in which long-term change can occur so that all young children and their families have the same access to resources, supports, and services. This is the second-generation work of equity and justice in early childhood education.

> **Key Points**
>
> › There is a great need to move beyond the current Band-Aid approach to equity that is focused on implementing isolated interventions and curricula that do not address the root cause of the disparities between Black and White children.
>
> › A cross-sector approach is needed within the field of early childhood so that policymakers, system leaders, and educators have a shared language and common understanding of the issues, which will lead to a collective effort to create more equitable policies and practices.
>
> › Listening to the voices of families and other community members who are most affected by the inequitable policies and practices will guide our work.

References

Alyn, J., & L. Cabbil. 2018. "Silence Is Violence and Inaction Gives Traction to White Supremacy." *Understanding and Dismantling Privilege* 7 (1): 112–120.

Annie E. Casey Foundation. 2018. "Race Equity Crosswalk Tool: Targeted and Universal Strategies to Achieve Better and More Equitable Results." Baltimore: Annie E. Casey Foundation. www.aecf.org/m/blogdoc/aecf-raceequitycrosswalk -2018.pdf.

Bowman, B.T., J.P. Comer, & D.J. Johns. 2018. "Addressing the African American Achievement Gap: Three Leading Educators Issue a Call to Action." *Young Children* 73 (2): 14–23.

Guralnick, M.J. 1993. "Second Generation Research on the Effectiveness of Early Intervention." *Early Education and Development* 4 (4): 366–378.

Johnson-Staub, C. 2017. *Equity Starts Early: Addressing Racial Inequities in Child Care and Early Education Policy.* Report. Washington, DC: CLASP. www.clasp.org/sites /default/files/publications/2017/12/2017_EquityStartsEarly _0.pdf.

Kania, J., M. Kramer, & P. Senge. 2018. *The Water of Systems Change.* Report. Washington, DC: FSG. www.fsg.org /publications/water_of_systems_change.

Ladson-Billings, G., & W. Tate. 1995. "Towards a Critical Race Theory of Education." *Teachers College Record* 97 (1): 47–68.

Losen, D., C. Hodson, M.A. Keith II, K. Morrison, & S. Belway. 2015. *Are We Closing the School Discipline Gap?* Report. Los Angeles: UCLA, The Center for Civil Rights Remedies. https://civilrightsproject.ucla.edu/resources/projects /center-for-civil-rights-remedies/school-to-prison-folder /federal-reports/are-we-closing-the-school-discipline-gap /AreWeClosingTheSchoolDisciplineGap_FINAL221.pdf.

Merriam-Webster, s.v. "privilege." n.d. a. Accessed October 31, 2020. www.merriam-webster.com/dictionary/privilege.

Merriam-Webster, s.v. "work." n.d. b. Accessed October 31, 2020. www.merriam-webster.com/dictionary/work.

National Equity Project. n.d. "Educational Equity: A Definition." Accessed October 29, 2020. www.nationalequityproject.org /education-equity-definition.

Neitzel, J. 2020. *Achieving Equity and Justice in Education Through the Work of Systems Change.* Lanham, MD: Lexington Books.

Skiba, R.J., M.I. Arrenondo, & N.T. Williams. 2014. "More than a Metaphor: The Contribution of Exclusionary Discipline to the School-to-Prison Pipeline." *Equity and Excellence in Education* 47 (4): 546–564.

Vaught, S.E. 2011. *Racism, Public Schooling, and the Entrenchment of White Supremacy: A Critical Race Ethnography.* Albany, NY: State University of New York Press.

This chapter supports recommendations from the NAEYC position statement:

Recommendations for Everyone

Item 4: Acknowledge and seek to understand structural inequities and their impact over time.

Item 6: Recognize that the professional knowledge base is changing.

Recommendations for Early Childhood Educators

Create a Caring, Equitable Community of Engaged Learners

Item 4: Consider the developmental, cultural, and linguistic appropriateness of the learning environment and your teaching practices for each child.

Recommendations for Administrators of Schools, Centers, Family Child Care Homes, and Other Early Childhood Education Settings

Item 9: Create meaningful, ongoing opportunities for multiple voices with diverse perspectives to engage in leadership and decision making.

Agency and Power in Young Children's Lives

Five Ways to Advocate for Social Justice as an Early Childhood Educator

Jennifer Keys Adair and Shubhi Sachdeva

Early childhood education is increasingly positioned as an important part of making societies more equitable and prosperous. Strong early childhood systems can be both a safety net and an accelerator for families experiencing poverty and other oppressive forces. However, there are also ways in which early childhood education can perpetuate social injustices through White-centric curriculum, deficit-oriented programs, and intense pressure (even if unintentional) on families of color and/or families experiencing poverty to behave as White, middle-class families to be seen as successful.

In this chapter, we describe how and why social justice education is important for early childhood education. We offer a district and classroom example of how social justice approaches to early childhood education can increase the positive impact of early childhood education in children's lives. Then we suggest five ways to shift thinking and practice to be more oriented toward social justice in our work with young children.

Our main goal in this chapter is to demonstrate that social justice in early childhood education requires an "interrogation of power" (De Lissovoy 2019, 42) by all of us who work with and make policies for young children. Social justice requires deference to marginalized communities' ways of knowing and learning as well as a willingness to confront institutions and systems that oppress and/or privilege us. We hope that this chapter will add to the growing body of voices calling for the intersecting fields of early childhood education and child development to appreciate the wealth and real lives of families and children as well as to insist that systems and institutions need fixing, rather than children and families.

We begin with two stories of social justice. The first took place in a preschool classroom and the second at a district superintendent meeting. Both are meant to illustrate the effort and thinking necessary for social justice work and how our collective effort can begin in small and simple ways.

Welcoming a Child Surviving Homelessness

In a Head Start classroom in San Antonio, 4-year-old Luis often arrived at school tired and grumpy. He would quickly end up getting irritated and hitting his classmates. The teachers had a strong and meaningful relationship with his mother, and they knew that his family had lost their home. Because they were sharing a motel room with other relatives, they did not have a regular schedule for eating and sleeping. Instead of blaming the family or calling his behavior problematic, they understood that he needed care and understanding. The teachers gave him a bed to sleep in for a few minutes in the morning, and that was enough to transform his day. He would wake up happy and ready to learn. When the principal learned about Luis's need for sleep and the teachers' response to it, she made an official school policy that each teacher should look out for children who could be in a similar situation and need extra care.

The children engaged in welcoming Luis by considering his need as something that required accommodation rather than judgment. Instead of changing Luis, the children in the class began to build train tracks or construct buildings with blocks or pathways for their cars around where Luis was sleeping. They played next to Luis while being conscious of where he was laying and sleeping. Providing a bed for a quick nap or including Luis in play even while he was sleeping were both small but important ways to change the context rather than to blame or speak negatively about the child.

The children did not hear teachers and other school staff speak negatively about Luis or his family. They only knew that Luis did not have a home sometimes. The children worked to validate his situation through their inclusion efforts, all without specific teacher direction.

Superintendent Decision-Making to Address Racial Justice in Early Childhood Education Social Justice

The San Antonio Independent School District (SAISD) has been improving standardized test scores and state ratings quickly over the past five years. Between 2016 and 2019, SAISD went from an F rating to a B rating as a district, surpassing both national and state performance standards on national- and state-level assessments. Still, the superintendent, Pedro Martinez, was not satisfied with early childhood education achievement scores on national assessments. Instead of deciding to create intervention programs aimed at family education or mandated pull-out or tutoring services, Superintendent Martinez decided to redesign the district approach and professional development for pre-K–3 classrooms to be more focused on agency and racial justice. This effort led to the Dynamic Innovation for Young Children (DIFYC) professional development program. In a planning meeting for DIFYC, racial justice was offered as a primary framework for opening up classrooms to support children's agency. Instead of narrowing classroom practices, as is what often happens in schools serving children of color experiencing economic hardships, the goal was to offer equitable learning experiences that valued children's stories, cognitive sophistication, inquiry learning, and high-level academics led by children's interests. Superintendent Martinez explained in the meeting that the primary motivation for redesigning early childhood education in the district was because all children deserve these kinds of learning experiences, saying, "Our motivation is justice, as much as it is achievement."

Social Justice Requires Belief and Effort

In both stories, educators valued equity and worked toward it in their own spaces, even when it was not convenient or comfortable. Social justice in early childhood education requires both belief and effort: a belief that everyone deserves equal economic, political, and social rights and opportunities *and* significant effort to transform the institutions and systems that sustain unequal relationships and realities. All of those involved with social justice education—including young children—are learning about how institutional racism and other social injustices impact their lives. Young children are not too young for social justice because "young children can think about fairness and are deeply moved and highly motivated by the recognition of injustice" (Cowhey 2006, 18).

Social justice acknowledges the political nature of teaching and learning and supports children (along with their teachers, administrators, and policymakers) in understanding their own realities as well as the realities of others in the context of justice so they can recognize discrimination and other injustices and have the tools to act against them. Learning for Justice (formerly Teaching Tolerance [2018]) offers five outcomes of social justice teaching, all of which can be applied to work with young children:

1. Recognizing stereotypes

2. Recognizing unfairness on individual and institutional levels

3. Understanding how bias and injustice harms us in the past and present

4. Recognizing their relationships to power and privilege

5. Identifying diverse examples and ways to work hard for social justice

NAEYC's "Advancing Equity in Early Childhood Education" position statement (2019) builds upon this work by specifically outlining ways that young children and their educator-leaders can work hard for social justice.

The underlying importance of recognizing injustice and supporting children in working against those injustices is paramount for all children—those who are at risk of being oppressed and those at risk of oppressing. It could mean teaching White children to recognize racism and providing the tools to take on responsibility for transforming spaces that feed or support racism in subtle or overt ways. This also means helping young children of immigrant families recognize linguistic discrimination so that they can value their parents' attempts to help them speak their native language and fight against policies, programs, or attitudes that try to make them think lesser of their languages and/or families. This also means empowering children to recognize ableism and how certain bodies and abilities are privileged so that they can all work toward changing policies and curriculum to be more inclusive. For all of these options, we, as educators, must challenge ourselves to think past our knowledge and backgrounds and seek knowledge from our families, communities, and a range of educational researchers that represent the diversity we serve in early childhood centers and classrooms.

We believe that working for social justice in early childhood education will require at least two major shifts in our field. The first is that instead of trying to fix children and families, we must look collectively at the systems and institutions that continue to create inequitable opportunities, resource allocation, and experiences. That is, we must acknowledge institutional and structural racism. The second is that instead of insisting on only biological, normalized versions of child development, we also need to depend on political and cultural understandings of development. We will explain both elements of social justice and then offer examples and practical next steps for educators.

Social Justice Fixes Systems, Not Families

Some educators believe that educational equity is best achieved through fixing individuals, families, or communities. This belief often leads to solutions such as home visiting interventions, parent education classes, English-only and/or biased assessments, family interventions, and individual behavior modification approaches. These types of programs tend to insist that children and/or families improve or change. One example comes from the case of the erroneous and persistent "word gap" argument, in which families, educators, and the larger public are told that if they speak more words to their children they will be able to overcome disparities often faced by children experiencing poverty (Hart & Risley 2003; Hindman, Wasik, & Snell 2016). Rather than blame poverty itself or the historical conditions that continue a racialized class system in the United States, families are asked to change their speaking and interaction patterns to more closely align with those of White, upper-middle-class families to be successful (Adair, Colegrove, & McManus 2017; Martínez 2018). This type of research is problematic because the methodology typically involves White researchers entering homes and schools of Black, Indigenous, and people of color (BIPOC) families and making judgements, observations and assumptions that become interventions,

assessments, and additional ways to mark and label BIPOC children. Researchers are not always grounded in respectful understanding and too often apply the White-centered expectations and studies of "foundational" White theorists that intersect most fields associated with child development and early childhood education (Pérez & Saavedra 2017).

Blaming people for their own oppression is destructive and ineffective. Flores (2018) challenges us to imagine fixing unjust systems rather than marginalized communities:

> What if instead of creating programs that seek to fix low-income students of color, we created programs that would support teachers in building on their linguistic resources in the classroom? What if instead of spending millions of dollars on modifying parenting practices in communities of color we invested that money in economic development in the segregated neighborhoods where most of them reside? Some people will think that the argument I am making here is biased. I certainly am. I reject the expectation that communities of color undo their own oppression by modifying their cultural and linguistic practices.

Most educators committed to social justice are looking for systemic solutions—ones that fix systems rather than blame or fix individuals, families, or communities. This orientation leads to solutions such as

> Student and parent agency

> Multilingual teacher recruitment

> Restorative justice discipline approaches

> Home visiting programs to learn from families

> Increased academic rigor and sophistication

> Curriculum that responds to children's real lives, interests, and social issues (such as ecological destruction, immigration raids, or police brutality)

> Inclusionary materials and curriculum

> Asset-based views of families and communities

> Programs that work to change institutions and the minds of those who are powerful within those institutions (e.g., administrators, police, policymakers, researchers, teacher educators, and teachers)

NAEYC's position statement on advancing equity engages educators and policymakers at all levels to see inequity as a systemic problem, rather than as one that fixes individuals.

Social Justice Makes Space for Cultural and Political Views of Development

Social justice requires a broad view of what is good and important for young children. Social justice runs the risk of becoming its own version of an extremist singular positionality in which one group has the right way of teaching and learning. To avoid this, we suggest that teaching and learning as social justice educators must make space for racial, gender, cultural, linguistic, ethnic, and contextual diversity in how and what children should be learning.

Narrow versions of how children learn and strict adherence to "ages and stages" views of young children can dismiss cultural variation in the actual development of children, as well as cultural and contextual variation in what makes sense to young children and needs to be learned for success in a variety of communities (Rogoff 2003). Singular ideas are often derived from the dominant group and/or borrowed from research conducted on White, middle-class children and then imposed onto other groups (Saavedra & Pérez 2018). Singular ideas about development are often hidden within the language and interpretations of developmentally appropriate practice (Nxumalo 2019; Gupta 2013). For example, the American Indian College Fund's (AICF) For the Wisdom of the Children initiative is an effort to increase the connection between developmentally appropriate practice (DAP) and indigenous ideas of how and what children should learn. Instead of forcing teachers, children, and communities to adopt White ways of being, learning, and teaching with young children, AICF is working to shift DAP and the larger early childhood teaching and assessment system to center on indigenous knowledge because "centering indigenous knowledge is paramount to the sustainability of the systems of care needed for the holistic development and well-being of children" (AICF, n.d.).

In similar work, Kaomea, Alvarez, and Pittman (2019) have worked with Hawaiian indigenous and Samoan teacher communities, respectively, to challenge ideas that DAP is natural or culturally relevant to everyone. Both studies use video-cued ethnography (VCE), which involves sharing filmed practices with cultural and community experts to understand the variance in what is considered developmentally appropriate and/or effective teaching for young children (Adair & Kurban

2019). In both cases, they found that teachers challenged White-normative ways of teaching and learning with young children and needed to center their culturally embedded practices to be culturally sustaining and effective educators.

At all levels, we can all work toward social justice in early childhood settings. Here are five ways to begin or continue this important work.

Reject Deficit Talk

Rejecting deficit talk in early childhood education means speaking positively about families and focusing on their assets, strengths, and everyday realities that go into their decision-making and way of seeing the world. It means speaking up when deficit talk is a part of the curriculum, teacher planning, or policies at the school, district, or state levels. Rejecting deficit talk means asking parents and communities what they think about curriculum and pedagogical practices and not speaking negatively about families. This doesn't mean that educators have to agree with everything parents and families do. Instead, social justice educators seek to understand and include parents and families in addressing the underlying inequities that are responsible for so much trauma and suffering in peoples' lives. And social justice educators work to find their role in perpetuating such inequities. Social justice educators operate under the assumption that everyone has a logic and rationale for the way they live, parent, and engage with the world. Just as there is danger in behaving as though there is only one best way of teaching children, there is also danger in believing that there is one way to parent or engage with one's family or larger community.

There is no space for negative assumptions or stereotypes in social justice teaching and learning. Deficit thinking justifies inequity. Deficit thinking normalizes oppression. Deficit approaches dismiss and devalue practices that are meaningful and important to communities other than White, upper-middle-class groups (Valencia 1997). Deficit thinking and approaches to teaching and learning view "the languages, literacies, and cultural ways of being of many students and communities of color as deficiencies to be overcome in learning the demanded and legitimized dominant language, literacy, and cultural ways of schooling" (Paris 2012, 93). Schools, classrooms, assessment companies, and community organizations can state upfront that deficit language will not be used to describe children or families. Educators who use deficit language should not *ever* be involved in assessing or teaching young children.

Deficit talk can include "at-risk" language ("We have a lot of at-risk children at our school, so we have behavior issues"); quick references to race and poverty without context ("Children don't get enough attention at home because their parents are urban poor"); assumptions about communities ("Immigrant parents don't care enough to learn English"); rationales for low expectations ("The children at our school cannot handle that curriculum"); or justifications for harsh discipline ("Children need to prove they are ready for more freedom"). See Brown (2016) for more examples.

Children cannot be described as *at risk* in the same way they can be described as *smart* or *young* or *capable*. *At risk* is not a label or an adjective, and it typically ignores the reality of children's lives. Young children are put at risk by larger, unjust societal systems that fail them and their families. Immigrant parents *do* care about their children, even if they show it in ways that White teachers or teachers from different backgrounds don't understand because they expect or want something different. Young children deserve to explore, talk, move around, and connect regardless of circumstance. It is the environment that must shift to accommodate and make such experiences possible when children are dealing with the ongoing impact of historic injustices. Strengths-based observations and assumptions position young children, families, and communities as knowledgeable and capable.

De-Privilege White-Centric, Western Philosophies and Approaches

Social justice necessitates that we think deeply about the role our background, experience, beliefs, and training play in interpreting children and families and approaching teaching and learning. Gutiérrez and Johnson (2017) call for us to check the lenses (e.g., curriculum, research, pedagogy models, materials, classroom management approaches) we look through and ask

> How can one *see* dignity in people's everyday lives when the operant analytical lens (e.g., urban, poor, English Learner, "gritless") has already defined the nature of possibility of people and their practices? (249)

If most of what guides our practice comes from White, upper-middle-class researchers and educators, our knowledge base will be too narrow. Knowledge and

learning need to be constantly redefined to be more representative of the voices that are silenced, erased, or unheard, rather than it being a prerogative of a few privileged ones. We can broaden the authors we read, the educators we consult for help, and the scientific ideas that come from various racial, linguistic, ethnic, LGBTQIA+, geographic, discipline, and cultural communities. In classrooms, teachers can provide materials, books, decorations, and conversation that privileges marginalized communities, including books focused on normalizing racial, cultural, linguistic, gender, economic, religious, and LGBTQIA+ diversity through everyday stories of empowered or nuanced characters told by decolonized authors and illustrators. Experiencing the normalization of diversity without colonizing deficit thinking serves young children from privileged and marginalized communities (Beneke, Park, & Taitingfong 2019).

There are often important skills and knowledge normalized within marginalized communities that go unrecognized or are devalued in larger institutions of schooling. Rogoff, Dahl, and Callanan (2018) have compared how young children from different cultural heritages approach learning. They have found that in indigenous Mexican and Central American communities, for example, young children develop "wide attention" that includes an ability to pay attention and notice what is going on around them. Wide attention is a skill that allows young children to observe a task and contribute as soon as they feel ready. Young children do not need specific invitations. Learning happens through observing, participating, and "pitching in" (Rogoff 2014). Coppens and Alcalá (2015) found that while European-heritage children most often learn to help through a list of chores or specifically assigned tasks, Mexican-heritage children most often learn to help by participating in collective work efforts. Young children can and do learn to help in different ways, and yet following strict instructions and learning independently is often valued more at school than observing and finding ways to help. Social justice means looking at the cultural variance in how young children learn and valuing a broad range of learning experiences and dispositions beyond following directions.

Prioritize Children's Agency Every Day

Creating socially just early childhood education classrooms and systems is as much (if not more) about how to teach than what is taught. Children need opportunities to use their agency every day to see themselves as leaders—those who can advocate, plan for, and make change for themselves and their communities.

Children being able to use their agency at school is critical to social justice in early childhood education and long-term social justice movements. Agency is the ability to influence or make decisions about what and how something is learned to expand capabilities (Adair, Colegrove, & McManus 2017). Agency is a core recommendation in NAEYC's "Advancing Equity in Early Childhood" position statement because agency is a mechanism to the development of the content as well as a means to expand the range of capabilities. Using their agency, children investigate ideas, relationships, or things around them that are meaningful to them. Being able to influence and make decisions about learning expands children's capabilities in broad and deep ways. Agency allows for leadership and meaningful development of ownership over one's life and learning along with education content. Multiple studies have shown that when young children can use their agency, they use it to help others and work together (Colegrove & Adair 2014). A collective sense of effort and understanding is key to fighting social injustice.

Children using their agency looks different across communities, so there are many ways to support agency. Children can choose the topics to study or be free to roam the room to help friends, observe others' learning activities, or get materials to build, experiment, or explain something to a classmate. Children can write books on their own topics or family stories with materials they determine from inside and outside of the classroom. Children can have agency to handle conflict or make an experiment or share stories from home without constant adult control or disruption. Children can create shared learning materials such as calendars, word walls, or letter and number posters that are often purchased at teacher-supply stores. Children can move and talk in all areas of the school and classroom, instead of walking in prison-like lines with bubbles in their mouths. Children can alter lessons, schedules, and plans when they have a rigorous idea to study. Children's families can share knowledge in class and suggest ideas for study or ways of teaching and learning. Children can move outside as well as engage with and care for the natural world in ways that expand their relationships and capabilities.

Because children learn in embodied ways, the kinds of learning experiences they have at school impact their view of themselves, their families, and what it means to be a learner in the short and long term (McManus 2019). During the ages of 3–8, young children are learning who they are in relation to the larger society outside the relationships of their family and/or immediate caretakers. They learn what society expects of them by what we offer them in terms of their learning experiences. If children's everyday learning experiences (seven to 10 hours of which are in school) are primarily following directions, task completion, individual assessments, checking in with behavior models, and being quiet and still, then children will see learning and being a learner as being a result of compliance, stillness, and quiet rather than multimodal knowledge construction, problem solving, agency, collective work, and leadership. Bang and colleagues (2012) argue that such low expectations or "settled expectations" is a continuing colonizing idea that some children (those in marginalized groups) cannot handle the sophisticated, agentic learning experiences that others (those in the dominant group) can, or are forced to learn ways that devalue their community knowledge. Distancing young children from their own agency at school is a continuation of the dominant/oppressor relationship that continues to privilege those (typically in the US context, White, wealthy children) who receive such learning experiences because they are thought to be deserving or ready for such experiences.

Instead of supporting a learning process that "becomes an act of depositing [. . .] deposits which the students patiently receive, memorize, and repeat" and in which "knowledge is a gift bestowed by those who consider themselves knowledgeable upon those whom they consider to know nothing," a socially just classroom is characterized by teachers and students co-constructing knowledge based on the problems and priorities of the students and their communities as well as children's interests (Freire 1970, 72). While children do not determine state or national standards for content, they and their families should have a significant role in how they learn such content. All children deserve to use their agency at school every day, even if that means sacrificing some adult comfort, efficiency, or control.

Make Space for Children's Realities and Community Knowledge

Detangling from singular or White-normative ways of viewing children also means making space for children's stories and real lives as they are being lived. Children need time every day to share, play, and communicate what is going on and what they are thinking about. Social justice education in early childhood education means bringing children's knowledge into curriculum and pedagogical approaches. We agree with Pelo (2008) that "social justice teaching grows from children's urgent concerns" (xi). Genishi and Dyson (2009) have written extensively about how high-quality literacy practices begin with ideas and stories from children's real lives. Vasquez (2016) explains that curriculum for young children should be built from children's interests and stories so that it will have a greater chance of having importance in their lives. She asks herself, "Are my students able to participate in the world differently as a result of the work we have done throughout the year?" (Vasquez 2016, 2).

Efforts to engage in social justice efforts require a commitment to listening and taking seriously the lives and realities of marginalized families and communities across the early childhood education system. Children are capable of having conversations about difficult subjects such as sexism, racism, and religious exclusion, especially if those conversations incorporate high-quality literature, children's questions, and an already spoken out-loud commitment to being a community that welcomes and values diversity.

Teachers can make space for children's stories through active and ongoing discussions that inform projects, even if some teaching and learning happens didactically as requested by the community, for example (Delpit 2012). While this may seem difficult, educators can begin by asking children and families to contribute their ideas about what should be studied and how. Classrooms that dismiss or ignore community realities and concerns, regardless of any progressive or high-quality teaching and learning practices, are not working toward social justice.

Creating Healing Spaces

Spaces where young children exist should be comforting and supportive of their well-being. Creating healing classrooms often means veering slightly from the script of lesson plans, schedules, and even protocols to attend to the immediate needs of children. Childhood is often idealized and seen as a worry-free, innocent time. For some, this may be true; however, a significant number of children witness and experience traumatizing events. Trauma can be racial slurs aimed at their parents from someone in line at the grocery store, abuse or neglect at home, experiencing homelessness, mass shootings media coverage, patterned violence and/or bullying, mistreatment, or intimidation. It is hard to define what could be traumatic for children because trauma is not an event but a response to an event (Anda et al. 2006). What is traumatizing for one child might not be traumatizing for another. Trauma and its effects look different across contexts, ages, and communities and continue across generations. Children's responses to trauma too often get mistaken for "bad behavior" or "learning difficulties" (Wright 2007, 2010, 2017). When teachers have bias or presume to understand children's lives without getting to know them or their families, attempts to discipline are unhelpful or, at worst, retraumatize.

In the current US political and media climate, children are experiencing, hearing about, or watching incidents of racial and gendered violence. They hear hurtful rhetoric that is aimed at people who look like and share identities with them, their families, and their communities. NAEYC's position statement on advancing equity also recommends trauma-informed care to address issues of inequity. It recognizes the role of historical and multigenerational trauma (Fast & Collin-Vézina 2010) "inflicted through slavery, genocide, sexual exploitation, segregation, incarceration, exclusion, and forced relocation" (NAEYC 2019, 14), which could often go unaddressed and therefore further inequities by denying access to sources of healing.

Conclusion

Early education spaces can and should be one of the primary spaces where children feel safe and can heal. This healing process is where social justice begins for some children and their families as a way to compensate for, or at least hold off, the personal and structural violence children experience. Teachers can create safe, healing spaces by bravely listening to children's stories and acknowledging and validating the difficult circumstances children are going through. Just as with Luis, teachers who care for their students and their families as human beings worthy of dignity create opportunities for them to feel welcome and safe. They help young children engage in social justice activities by caring for one another through engagement and compassion.

Key Points

Early childhood education programs committed to social justice

> Work on fixing environments and systems, not families

> Prioritize children's agency every day without them having to earn it

> Include children's realities, communities, and land relationships in all aspects of everyday teaching and learning at all levels of practice and policy

> Reject deficit thinking, "at-risk" labeling, and other ways researchers, policymakers, and educators dehumanize young children of color and their families

> Authentically center the scholarship, teaching approaches, methodologies, research questions, perspectives, theories, businesses, expertise, and programs that come from educators of color

---

References

Adair, J.K., K.S.S. Colegrove, & M.E. McManus. 2017. "How the Word Gap Argument Negatively Impacts Young Children of Latinx Immigrants' Conceptualizations of Learning." *Harvard Educational Review* 87 (3): 309–334.

Adair, J.K., & F. Kurban. 2019. "Video-Cued Ethnographic Data Collection as a Tool Toward Participant Voice." *Anthropology & Education Quarterly* 50 (3): 270–290.

AICF (American Indian College Fund). n.d. "For the Wisdom of the Children: Strengthening the Teacher of Color Pipeline." Accessed September 3, 2019. https://collegefund.org /programs/early-childhood-education/for-the-wisdom -of-the-children-strengthening-the-teacher-of -color-pipeline.

Anda, R.F., V.J. Felitti, J.D. Bremner, J.D. Walker, C.H. Whitfield, B.D. Perry, & W.H. Giles. 2006. "The Enduring Effects of Abuse and Related Adverse Experiences in Childhood." *European Archives of Psychiatry and Clinical Neuroscience* 256 (3): 174–186.

Bang, M., B. Warren, A.S. Rosebery, & D. Medin. 2012. "Desettling Expectations in Science Education." *Human Development* 55 (5–6): 302–318.

Beneke, M.R., C.C. Park, & J. Taitingfong. 2019. "An Inclusive, Anti-Bias Framework for Teaching and Learning About Race with Young Children." *Young Exceptional Children* 22 (2): 74–86.

Brown, K.D. 2016. *After the "At-Risk" Label: Reorienting Educational Policy and Practice*. New York: Teachers College Press.

Colegrove, K.S.S, & J.K. Adair. 2014. "Countering Deficit Thinking: Agency, Capabilities and the Early Learning Experiences of Children of Latina/o Immigrants." *Contemporary Issues in Early Childhood* 15 (2): 122–135.

Coppens, A.D., & L. Alcalá. 2015. "Supporting Children's Initiative: Appreciating Family Contributions or Paying Children for Chores." In *Children Learn by Observing and Contributing to Family and Community Endeavors*, eds. M. Correa-Chávez, R. Mejía-Arauz, & B. Rogoff, 91–112. Vol. 49 of *Advances in Child Development and Behavior*. Waltham, MA: Academic Press.

Cowhey, M. 2006. *Black Ants and Buddhists: Thinking Critically and Teaching Differently in the Primary Grades*. Portland, Maine: Stenhouse Publishers.

Delpit, L. 2012. *"Multiplication Is for White People:" Raising Expectations for Other People's Children*. New York: The New Press.

De Lissovoy, N. 2019. *Power, Crisis, and Education for Liberation*. New York: Palgrave Macmillan.

Fast, E., & D. Collin-Vézina. 2010. "Historical Trauma, Race-Based Trauma, and Resilience of Indigenous Peoples: A Literature Review." *First Peoples Child & Family Review* 14 (1): 166–181.

Flores, N. 2018. "Making Millions off of the 30-Million-Word Gap." *The Educational Linguist* (blog), May 31. https://educationallinguist.wordpress.com/2018/05/31/making-millions-off-of-the-30-million-word-gap.

Freire, P. 1970. *Pedagogy of the Oppressed.* New York: Continuum Publishing Group.

Genishi, C., & A.H. Dyson. 2009. *Children, Language, and Literacy.* New York: Teachers College Press.

Gupta, A. 2013. *Early Childhood Education, Postcolonial Theory, and Teaching Practices and Policies in India: Balancing Vygotsky and the Veda.* New York: Palgrave.

Gutiérrez, K.D., & Johnson, P. 2017. "Understanding Identity Sampling and Cultural Repertoires: Advancing a Historicizing and Syncretic System of Teaching and Learning in Justice Pedagogies." In *Culturally Sustaining Pedagogies: Teaching and Learning for Justice in a Changing World*, eds. D. Paris & H.S. Alim, 247–260. New York: Teachers College Press.

Hart, B., & T.R. Risley. 2003. "The Early Catastrophe: The 30 Million Word Gap by Age 3." *American Educator* 27 (1): 4–9.

Hindman, A.H., B.A. Wasik, & E.K. Snell. 2016. "Closing the 30 Million Word Gap: Next Steps in Designing Research to Inform Practice." *Child Development Perspectives* 10 (2): 134–139.

Kaomea, J., M.B. Alvarez, & M. Pittman. 2019. "Reclaiming, Sustaining, and Revitalizing Hawaiian Education Through Video-Cued Makawalu Ethnography." *Anthropology & Education Quarterly* 50 (3): 313–332.

Martínez, R.A. 2018. "Beyond the English Learner Label: Recognizing the Richness of Bi/Multilingual Students' Linguistic Repertoires." *Reading Teacher* 71 (5): 515–522.

McManus, M.E. 2019. "How Classroom Learning Experiences of Young Latinx Children from Immigrant Families Shape Their Beliefs About Learning." PhD diss., The University of Texas at Austin.

NAEYC. 2019. "Advancing Equity in Early Childhood Education." Position statement. Washington, DC: NAEYC. www.naeyc.org/resources/position-statements/equity.

Nxumalo, F. 2019. "Presencing: Decolonial Attunements to Children's Place Relations." In *Feminist Research for 21st-Century Childhoods: Common Worlds Methods*, ed. D. Hodgins, 159–169. London: Bloomsbury.

Paris, D. 2012. "Culturally Sustaining Pedagogy: A Needed Change in Stance, Terminology, and Practice." *Educational Researcher* 41 (3): 93–97.

Pelo, A., ed. 2008. *Rethinking Early Childhood Education.* Milwaukee, WI: Rethinking Schools.

Pérez, M.S., & C.M. Saavedra. 2017. "A Call for Onto-Epistemological Diversity in Early Childhood Education and Care: Centering Global South Conceptualizations of Childhoods." *Review of Research in Education* 41 (1): 1–29.

Rogoff, B. 2003. *The Cultural Nature of Human Development.* New York: Oxford University Press.

Rogoff, B. 2014. "Learning by Observing and Pitching in to Family and Community Endeavors: An Orientation." *Human Development* 57 (2–3): 69–81.

Rogoff, B., A. Dahl, & M. Callanan. 2018. "The Importance of Understanding Children's Lived Experience." *Developmental Review* 50 (Part A): 5–15.

Saavedra, C.M., & M.S. Pérez. 2018. "Global South Approaches to Bilingual and Early Childhood Teacher Education: Disrupting Global North Neoliberalism." *Policy Futures in Education* 16 (6): 749–763.

Teaching Tolerance. 2018. *Social Justice Standards: The Teaching Tolerance Anti-Bias Framework.* Montgomery, AL: Teaching Tolerance. www.learningforjustice.org/sites/default/files/2020-09/TT-Social-Justice-Standards-Anti-bias-framework-2020.pdf.

Valencia, R.R., ed. 1997. *The Evolution of Deficit Thinking: Educational Thought and Practice.* London: Routledge.

Vasquez, V.M. 2016. *Critical Literacy Across the K–6 Curriculum.* New York: Routledge.

Wright, T. 2007. "On Jorge Becoming a Boy: A Counselor's Perspective." *Harvard Educational Review* 77 (2): 164–186.

Wright, T. 2010. "Learning to Laugh: A Portrait of Risk and Resilience in Early Childhood." *Harvard Educational Review* 80 (4): 444–464.

Wright, T. 2017. "Supporting Students Who Have Experienced Trauma." *NAMTA Journal* 42 (2): 141–152.

Recommendations for Early Childhood Educators

Advocate on Behalf of Young Children, Families, and the Early Childhood Profession

Item 1: Speak out against unfair policies or practices and challenge biased perspectives.

Item 2: Look for ways to work collectively with others who are committed to equity.

This chapter supports recommendations from the NAEYC position statement:

CHAPTER 19

Creating Anti-Racist Early Childhood Spaces

Rosemarie Allen, Dorothy L. Shapland, Jen Neitzel, and Iheoma U. Iruka

The focus on racial equity following the murder of George Floyd has resulted in conversations about racism that were unheard of less than a year ago. A critical examination of race, bias, racial inequity, and racism is taking place at every level in our society, and researchers, educators, and advocates have proposed anti-racism strategies for a variety of settings, including in early childhood spaces. To enact and sustain an anti-racist approach, early childhood educators need to understand the racial history of early childhood programs and the racism in current early childhood programs. In this chapter, we outline the past and present along with strategies for creating anti-racist early childhood spaces.

Racial History of Early Childhood Programs

The history of early childhood education is vast and varied. The Perry Preschool Project stands out as a seminal program and longitudinal study in its history, and many early childhood advocates, supporters, and professionals tout the benefits of the Perry Preschool Program as an investment in the future of America, noting a 13 percent return on investment for every $1 invested in high-quality early childhood programs (Heckman 2006; Heckman & Karapakula 2019). The program also provides a key example of the racial history of early childhood programs, as it was designed to increase the IQ test scores of children from disadvantaged families (Derman-Sparks & Moore 2016).

In essence, the goal of the Perry Preschool Project was to address Black children's inherent deficits and to create better Americans. Initiated in the 1960s in a climate rife with civil unrest and overt racism, Black children were viewed as culturally, socially, and economically "deprived" and living in a culture of poverty. The term *disadvantaged*—and a viewpoint now identified as a *deficit perspective*—emerged around the time of the Perry Preschool Project, and it was code for being poor and Black. More specifically, Black preschoolers were identified as a population that could be fixed, whose deficits could be corrected, and whose future lives could be improved (Jackson 2014). Black families, especially Black single mothers, were viewed as pathological, inept, and incapable of providing an optimal environment for their children (Moynihan 1969; Jensen 1984). It was believed that Black families needed to be taught how to parent their children by the White teachers in the program (Derman-Sparks 2016). The fear of unruly, uneducated, and socially deviant children led to the implementation of preschool curricula focused on improving IQ scores, learning socially "appropriate behaviors," and responding positively to those in authority.

In addition, the focus on psychopathologic outcomes such as criminalization and teen pregnancy contributed to this deficit lens of Black children and communities. Weikart (1971) described the Perry Preschool Project as an experiment to enable culturally deprived children and children testing in the range of "educable mentally retarded" to enter into a regular classroom. From the onset, the Perry Preschool Project and other programs of this time—coupled with the War on Poverty—sought to fix children from families with low income rather than address the structural racism that led to the disproportionate numbers of Black children living in poverty and being labeled as "deprived."

While the Perry Preschool Project (and similar studies, such as the Carolina Abecedarian Study) did not significantly improve scores on measures of intelligence, children who participated in the program were more likely to graduate high school and have greater earning capacity as adults (Campbell et al. 2002; Schweinhart et al. 2005). They were also less likely to become teen parents and become involved in the justice system.

Although the Perry Preschool Project resulted in positive outcomes for children, such as increased parent engagement over time, employment stability, positive multigenerational effects, and positive adult health outcomes, its effects must be considered in light of its limitations too (Heckman & Karapakula 2019). A key limitation was that researchers failed to interview the teachers or gather a range of information from the families and children who were involved in the program and study. They did not investigate the attitudes of the teachers toward the children, nor the relationships between the home and school (Derman-Sparks 2016). As Derman-Sparks and Moore (2016) wrote,

> Most Perry Preschool teachers—including the two of us—held the empowerment perspective, while administrators mostly took the cultural deprivation perspective. The teachers' empowerment beliefs shaped actual practice with the children and families, although publications about the program reflected the administrators' cultural deprivation thinking. (85)

Such qualitative information could have informed and improved the practices not only of the Perry Preschool program, but of many early childhood education programs that came after.

Racism in Current Early Childhood Education Programs

More often than not, early childhood educators and programs think or teach about race, bias, and equity from one of two approaches: "the color-blind approach" or the "celebration of differences approach" (Doucet & Adair 2013). These stem from beliefs that if educators teach love, kindness, and fairness only, then they do not need to point out or discuss racial bias or inequities with our young learners.

These more common approaches fail to acknowledge that everyone has lived their lives in a system that is racist; that we all come with and act on biases, especially when unchecked or monitored; and that we are inundated with images and messages that influence how we think about and respond to one another. This has resulted in racist perceptions and beliefs that are embedded within the very fabric of our existence (Staats 2014). The system is designed for some to rise at the expense of others, and loving all children equally is not enough. Frankly, it is not the reality in our early childhood classrooms.

Statistics consistently show disparities in young Black children's experiences in early learning settings and in how teachers perceive and respond to children's behaviors based on race. For example, in one study,

educators were asked to be on the lookout for challenging behaviors in a video clip. The video clip showed two Black children (one male, one female) and two White children (one male, one female). Researchers found that participants watched the Black boy more than any other child. Forty-two percent of the participants reported that he required more of their attention, despite the fact that no challenging behaviors were demonstrated in the video and that all children were involved in the same level of play (Gilliam et al. 2016).

Research also shows that teachers tend to perceive Black children as older, less innocent, more culpable, and more criminal than other children (Goff et al. 2014). This *adultification* may contribute to the bias teachers hold, expecting negative behavior from Black children more than others (Gilliam et al. 2016).

National data find the following regarding disproportionate rates of preschool suspension and expulsion:

> Preschool children are expelled more than three times as often as children in all of K–12 combined (Gilliam 2005).

> Black children are three-and-a-half times more likely to be suspended than their White counterparts, despite the fact that they make up less than 20 percent of the population (OCR 2016).

> Black girls account for only 20 percent of the female preschool population, yet they comprise 54 percent of preschool girls who are suspended (OCR 2016).

These facts are significant indicators of the ways that early childhood classrooms contribute to societal racism and anti-Blackness, or the belief that "Black bodies become marginalized, disregarded, and disdained" (Dumas & Ross 2016, 417). Indeed, if teachers are not actively working toward an anti-racist early childhood space, then they may be teaching children to be racist by their own behaviors and words in the classroom.

Children in the preschool years are inquirers by nature. They are constantly observing, collecting information, analyzing, and trying to make sense of what they see and hear. For instance, they know who it is that teachers look at when something goes wrong, who is being held more accountable, who is granted second chances, and who is reprimanded most often in their classrooms. They notice the actions of teachers. They detect the implicit biases and unconscious prejudices, which come through in displays of favoritism and privileging of some children over others based on gender, race, and culture (Allen 2016). What children tend to observe, from early ages, is that boys get into trouble more than girls, that the darker-skinned children are more likely to be held accountable than the lighter-skinned children, and that White children are given the opportunity and time to share about themselves and their lives more often than darker-skinned children. In addition, the quality of interactions differs too: the more Black and Latino/a children there are in a classroom, the more teachers talk *at* them and not *with* them (Early et al. 2010). In current early childhood spaces, children seek and gain an internalized sense of how things are in school and in the world. In many early childhood spaces, racism exists as part of the early childhood experience.

Creating Anti-Racist Early Childhood Environments
Teaching Anti-Racism

In order to learn about race, children need the time, space, curriculum, and supports to talk about and make sense of what they are seeing and noticing. It requires teachers to embrace the conversation, even if they experience uncertainty or discomfort while doing so. Teachers must talk about race every day, because race exists every day. Children deserve mirrors that reflect themselves and windows to peer into other people's experiences (Wright with Counsell 2018). They deserve the opportunity to ask the questions that form in their minds about differences and similarities as they learn to categorize the world around them.

Unlike the more common approaches taken, being anti-racist is more than loving all children the same or teaching children more generally about kindness and fairness. It is more than celebrating diversity during special events and then moving on with the curriculum. Anti-racist teachers teach about racism throughout the day and the curriculum. They point it out and acknowledge it, and they invite children to discuss race, racism, and inequity when they see it. When teachers invite the conversation about how everyone is learning about race and that racism is all around us, we give children the space to name it and to become anti-racists themselves.

Noticing Racism in Your Classroom

As highlighted earlier, racial bias and inequity show up in various ways in the interactions between children, in the interactions between adults, and in the interactions between families and the school. Here are just some examples of how racism might show up in early childhood settings:

› Mispronouncing, making fun of, or shortening children's names that are not traditionally "White" names

› Assuming a Spanish-speaking Latino/a child is undocumented

› Assuming children eat only foods that are stereotypically assigned to a specific culture or ethnicity

› Favoring one group of children over other groups, such as calling on some children while ignoring others based on race, gender, language, class, etc.

› Treating a child differently because of their hair style, language, style of clothing, or other cultural ways of being

› Assigning roles based on gender or race, such as boys and White children being assigned leadership roles and girls and Black and Brown children being relegated to subservient roles

› Stereotyping Black girls as too loud, too angry, or too sassy and assuming big Black boys are aggressive

› Misinterpreting or inaccurately labeling children's actions and ways of being as defiant

› Assuming families of color don't care about their children (Iruka et al. 2020)

Racism Within Your Organization

Many organizations include diversity, inclusion, and equity in their mission statements. *Diversity* is the effort to increase the number of people of color, and *inclusion* (in this context) is the effort to incorporate the input of people of color. *Equity* is the relentless focus on eliminating racial inequities and increasing success for all groups (Nelson & Brooks 2015). To evaluate whether an organization's reality is aligned with its written statements, an equity audit should be conducted on a regular basis. It can reveal if equity is indeed valued in early childhood classrooms, administrations, and organizations.

Some of the ways in which racism is evident in early childhood organizations include when

> Most of those in leadership positions are White, and people of color are not invited to serve on committees, boards, or to take on higher level duties (Austin et al. 2019).

> Most of the teaching staff are Black or Brown and are rarely promoted within the organization (Austin et al. 2019).

> Employees of color experience closer, more intense examination of their work and behavior; are more frequently reprimanded, especially Black staff members; may have their hairstyles banned in dress codes; and may be discouraged from speaking their home language at work (Griffin 2019).

> Mispronouncing, making fun of, or shortening names that are not traditionally "White" names are accepted practices (Marrun 2018).

> Black men are expected to be the disciplinarians, and White teachers send Black children to Black teachers for discipline because "they know how to handle them" (Brockenbrough 2015).

> People of color are excluded from outside-of-work activities attended by White staff.

> There is no equity-focused discussion, strategy, or focus area.

Committing to Become Anti-Racist

The journey toward becoming anti-racist is not a check-the-box activity. Becoming anti-racist is an ongoing, continual commitment that is grounded in education, listening, self-reflection, and healing from the trauma of slavery and racism. Given our history and the present, how can people begin their journey toward becoming anti-racists? Here are specific actions that teachers, administrators, and others can take as daily practice. Only through practice will these become habits.

1. **Educate yourself through intentionally selected materials.** Read books on racism and the true history of our country. A few include the following:

   - *The 1619 Project*, by Nikole Hannah-Jones

   - *Between the World and Me*, by Ta-Nehisi Coates

   - *Caste*, by Isabel Wilkerson

   - *How to Be an Antiracist*, by Ibram X. Kendi

   - *Just Mercy*, by Bryan Stevenson

   - *Stamped from the Beginning*, by Ibram X. Kendi

   - *Waking Up White*, by Debby Irving

   - *White Fragility*, by Robin DiAngelo

   - *White Rage*, by Carol Anderson and Pamela Gibson

   Consider the perspective of the authors. If you are beginning this journey as a White person, reading White authors may be helpful, but don't stop there. Read authors who bring a different perspective and experience to the work. There are Black authors who write for White audiences, and there are also Black authors who write for Black audiences. These approaches present different entry points depending on where you are in your journey and include readers who want to continue being agitated in their complacency. Watch documentaries, such as *13th*, *When They See Us*, and *American Son* with Kerry Washington. Seek out presentations, webinars, and other multimedia materials. True equity work cannot begin until we are grounded in a common understanding about the unique realities and brutalities in our history and present, particularly the structures that have been put in place over time to benefit White people and to simultaneously oppress others.

2. **Follow Black men and women on social media, particularly Twitter.** Bree Newsome Bass, Bakari Sellers, Jamil Smith, Clint Smith, Yamiche Alcindor, Zerlina Maxwell, Karine Jean-Pierre, Goldie, Joy Reid, Nikole Hannah-Jones, ICE T, Soledad O'Brien, BrooklynDad_Defiant, BeAKing, Roxane Gay, Brittany Packnett-Cunningham, and Jonathan Capeheart are a few examples.

3. **Reflect.** Take time to journal your own experiences growing up within our racist society and how this has influenced how you operate in the world—where you live, where you send your children to school, and with whom you socialize. Do you self-isolate, and if so, is it out of fear or comfort? How have your experiences and your worldview contributed to how you understand what it means to be part of a high-quality early childhood program? Self-reflection and a thorough understanding of our history ensure that we begin to see how White dominance is the norm and racism is endemic within early childhood education.

4. **Commit to undoing your color-blindness.** We often say some version of "I choose to see the content of your character, not the color of your skin." This may be true; however, color-blind ideology is harmful and counterproductive to the cause. If you do not see your color, you also do not see the reality of others' experiences as different from the White experience. This leads to normalizing the White experience as a definition of "acceptable," "normal," or "typical." Gaining a better understanding of Black existence and the existence of other historically marginalized groups is critical to committing to being an ally in the cause of social justice.

5. **Stand beside, behind, but never in front of Black people.** An essential step toward equity is to actively listen, learn, and let Black people lead the way forward. Rather than look for solutions at this time, White educators, administrators, researchers, and policy makers should strive to be an ally to their Black peers. Be ready to give up privilege in the service of anti-racism so that others who have experienced more oppression than you can lead you.

Now is the time to make this commitment. We must all be involved in the cause; however, educators need to take these steps toward anti-racism before that can happen.

Conclusion

Fundamentally, to create anti-racist early childhood spaces, early childhood educators must embrace the concepts of anti-racism. They must take direct and intentional action against racist behaviors, practices, policies, and beliefs to dismantle and interrupt racism. Anti-racism posits there is no middle ground. There is no such thing as "not a racist." One is either anti-racist and fighting against racism, or they are racist by default. Racism is not defined by who you are but by your actions. It is what one does or fails to do that makes a person racist (Kendi 2019).

In early childhood classrooms are future doctors, police officers, government officials, and teachers who will live in a racial society. Creating an anti-racist early childhood program is essential for their survival and will ensure that today's young children are not tomorrow's protestors, demanding justice and chanting "Black Lives Matter."

Key Points

> To enact and sustain an anti-racist approach, early childhood educators need to understand the racial history of early childhood programs and the racism in current early childhood programs.

> Anti-racist educators teach about racism throughout the day and the curriculum. They point it out and acknowledge it, and they invite children to discuss race, racism, and inequity when they see it.

> If teachers are not actively working toward an anti-racist early childhood space, then they may be teaching children to be racist by their own behaviors and words in the classroom.

> Becoming anti-racist is an ongoing, continual commitment that is grounded in education, listening, self-reflection, and healing from the trauma of slavery and racism.

References

Allen, R. 2016. "School Suspensions Are an Adult Behavior." Talk presented and filmed at a TEDxMileHigh event in Denver, CO. www.youtube.com/watch?v=f8nkcRMZKV4.

Austin, L.J.E., B. Edwards, R. Chávez, & M. Whitebook. 2019. "Racial Wage Gaps in Early Education Employment." *Center for the Study of Child Care Employment*, December 19. https://cscce.berkeley.edu/racial-wage-gaps-in-early-education-employment.

Brockenbrough, E. 2015. "'The Discipline Stop:' Black Male Teachers and the Politics of Urban School Discipline." *Education and Urban Society* 47 (5): 499–522.

Campbell, F.A., C.T. Ramey, E. Pungello, J. Sparling, & S. Miller-Johnson. 2002. "Early Childhood Education: Young Adult Outcomes from the Abecedarian Project." *Applied Developmental Science* 6 (1): 42–57.

Derman-Sparks, L. 2016. "What I Learned from the Ypsilanti Perry Preschool Project: A Teacher's Reflections." *Journal of Pedagogy* 7 (1): 93–105.

Derman-Sparks, L., & E. Moore. 2016. "Two Teachers Look Back: The Ypsilanti Perry Preschool, Part I." Our Proud Heritage. *Young Children* 71 (4): 82–87.

Doucet, F., & J.K. Adair. 2013. "Addressing Race and Inequity in the Classroom." *Young Children* 68 (5): 88–97.

Early, D., I. Iruka, S. Ritchie, O. Barbarin, G. Crawford, P.M. Frome, R.M. Clifford, M. Burchinal, C. Howes, D.M. Bryant, & R. Pianta. 2010. "How Do Pre-Kindergarteners Spend Their Time? Gender, Ethnicity, and Income as Predictors of Experiences in Pre-Kindergarten Classrooms." *Early Childhood Research Quarterly* 25 (2): 177–193.

Dumas, M., & K. Ross. 2016. "'Be Real Black for Me:' Imagining BlackCrit in Education." *Urban Education* 5 (4): 415–442.

Gilliam, W. 2005. "Prekindergarteners Left Behind: Expulsion Rates in State Prekindergarten Systems." Policy brief. New York: Foundation for Child Development. www.fcd-us .org/prekindergartners-left-behind-expulsion-rates-in-state -prekindergarten-programs.

Gilliam, W., A. Maupin, C. Reyes, M. Accavitti, & F. Shic. 2016. "Do Early Educators' Implicit Biases Regarding Sex and Race Relate to Behavior Expectations and Recommendations of Preschool Expulsions and Suspensions?" Research brief. New Haven, CT: Yale University Child Study Center.

Goff, P.A., M.C. Jackson, B.A.L. Di Leone, C.M. Culotta, & N.A. DiTomasso. 2014. "The Essence of Innocence: Consequences of Dehumanizing Black Children." *Journal of Personality and Social Psychology* 106 (4): 526 –545.

Griffin, C. 2019. "How Natural Black Hair at Work Became a Civil Rights Issue." *JSTOR Daily*, July 3. https://daily.jstor .org/how-natural-black-hair-at-work-became-a-civil -rights-issue.

Heckman, J.J. 2006. "Skill Formation and the Economics of Investing in Disadvantaged Children. *Science* 312 (5782): 1900–1902.

Heckman, J.J., & G. Karapakula. 2019. "Intergenerational and Intragenerational Externalities of the Perry Preschool Project." NBER Working Paper No. w25889. Cambridge: National Bureau of Economic Research. www.nber.org /papers/w25889.

Iruka, I., S. Curenton, K.A. Escayg, & T. Durden. 2020. *Don't Look Away: Embracing Anti-Bias Classrooms*. Lewisville, NC: Gryphon House.

Jackson, P.S.B. 2014. "The Crisis of the 'Disadvantaged Child:' Poverty Research, IQ, and Muppet Diplomacy in the 1960s." *Antipode* 46 (1): 190–208.

Jensen, A. 1984. "Political Ideologies and Educational Research." *Phi Delta Kappan* 65 (7): 460–462.

Kendi, I.X. 2019. *How to Be an Antiracist*. New York: One World

Marrun, N.A. 2018. "Culturally Responsive Teaching Across PK–20: Honoring the Historical Naming Practices of Students of Color." *Taboo: The Journal of Culture and Education* 17 (3): 5–25.

Moynihan, D.P. 1969. "Professors and the Poor." In *On Understanding Poverty: Perspectives from the Social Sciences*, ed. D.P. Moynihan, 3–35. New York: Basic Books.

Nelson, J., & L. Brooks. 2015. *Racial Equity Toolkit: An Opportunity to Operationalize Equity*. Berkeley, CA: Government Alliance on Race and Equity. https:// racialequityalliance.org/wp-content/uploads/2015/10 /GARE-Racial_Equity_Toolkit.pdf.

OCR (US Department of Education Office for Civil Rights). 2016. *2013–2014 Civil Rights Data Collection: A First Look*. Washington, DC: OCR. www2.ed.gov/about/offices/list/ocr /docs/2013-14-first-look.pdf.

Schweinhart, L.J., J. Montie, Z. Xiang, W.S. Barnett, C.R. Belfield, & M. Nores. 2005. *Lifetime Effects: The High/Scope Perry Preschool Study Through Age 40*. Report. Ypsilanti, MI: High/Scope Press.

Staats, C. 2014. *State of the Science: Implicit Bias Review 2014*. Report. Columbus, OH: Kirwan Institute. www.kirwaninstitute .osu.edu/wp-content/uploads/2014/03/2014-implicit -bias.pdf.

Weikart, D. 1971. *Cognitively Oriented Curriculum, Ypsilanti, Michigan: A Program that Exposes Preschool Children to a Variety of Materials and Equipment to Teach Concepts Through Physical and Verbal Experiences*. Booklet. Washington, DC: United States Department of Health, Education, and Welfare. https://files.eric.ed.gov/fulltext/ED045217.pdf.

Wright, B.L. With S.L. Counsell. 2018. *The Brilliance of Black Boys: Cultivating School Success in the Early Grades*. New York: Teachers College Press.

This chapter supports recommendations from the NAEYC position statement:

Recommendations for Everyone

Item 6: Recognize that the professional knowledge base is changing.

Recommendations for Early Childhood Educators

Create a Caring, Equitable Community of Engaged Learners

Item 4: Consider the developmental, cultural, and linguistic appropriateness of the learning environment and your teaching practices for each child.

Observe, Document, and Assess Children's Learning and Development

Item 3: Focus on strengths.

CHAPTER 20

Early Childhood Teacher Educators' Critical Role

Preparing Culturally Efficacious Early Childhood Teachers

Belinda Bustos Flores, Socorro Herrera, and Janelle Beth Flores

NAEYC's "Advancing Equity in Early Childhood Education" position statement is a bold call for early childhood teacher educators (ECTEs) to assume ethical and professional responsibility in advancing equity and social justice. Although early childhood professional organizations recognize the value of diversity and social justice, and early childhood teacher educators integrate aspects of social justice into the curricula and educator programs, Boutte (2008) contends that the actualization of equitable practices and curricula has yet to be realized. DeVore, Fox, Heimer, and Winchell (2015) conclude that the teaching practices of ECTEs must be continuously examined to determine the impact on teacher candidates' notions and dispositions toward social justice issues. Essentially, the exploration of diversity issues requires a multifaceted analysis of the sociocultural, historical, linguistic, and political contexts and structural inequities that perpetuate the marginalization of diverse populations. The purpose of this chapter is to examine NAEYC's position statement on advancing equity and bring a critical consciousness to the roles of language and culture assets evident in diverse communities. Grounded in the Culturally Efficacious Evolution Model to enact the NAEYC position statement, this chapter provides exemplars for preparing early childhood educators to meet the needs of young diverse children and their families.

Achieving equity is complicated given the lack of representation in the early childhood educator force within the United States as compared to the ethno-racial and linguistic demographic shift evident in our young children. According to the National Center for Educational Statistics (Snyder, de Brey, & Dillow 2016), the majority of faculty are White. In contrast, according to KIDS COUNT Data Center (2020), only 49 percent of children ages 0–4 are White, while the remainder are Hispanic or Latino/a (26 percent), Black (14 percent),

Asian (5 percent), mixed-race (5 percent), American Indian/Alaskan Native (1 percent), and Hawaiian/Pacific Islander (less than .05 percent).

Many White ECTEs have not had significant personal or teaching experiences with diverse learners (Lee 2011; Nganga 2015). Therefore, we suggest that to ensure equitable learning opportunities for young diverse learners, critical reflection on self (as educators), the curriculum, and the preparation program is indispensable. Ethical professionalism demands that ECTEs approach decision-making about diverse young learners from a social justice stance (Giovacco-Johnson 2011).

To promote exploration of identity, consciousness, positionality, and practices in the preparation of ECTEs and candidates, we propose a culturally efficacious approach and responsive praxis that focus on the culture, language, and ability of the learner. Through this approach, we extend the seminal works of Ladson-Billings (1994); Gay (2010); Darder (2011); Sheets (2005); and Sleeter, Neal, and Kumashiro (2014).

Flores, Claeys, and Gist (2018) offer the Culturally Efficacious Evolution Model (CEEM) as an iterative, transformative approach in which there is a continuous exploration of self and praxis as a critical pedagogue. (See Figure 20.1.) The CEEM consists of five dimensions (Flores Claeys, & Gist 2018, 7–9):

1. Awakening Cultural Consciousness

2. Acquiring Cultural Competence

3. Developing Cultural Proficiency

4. Actualizing Cultural and Critical Responsivity

5. Realizing Cultural Efficaciousness

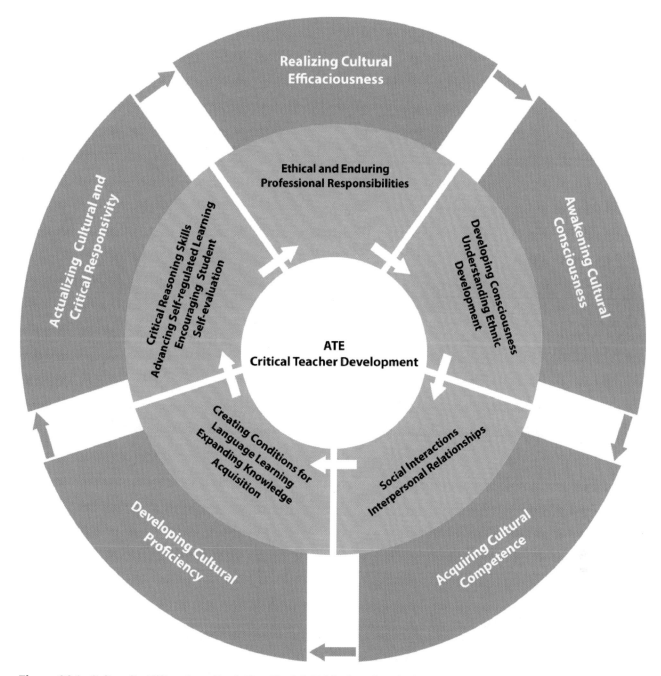

Figure 20.1. Culturally Efficacious Evolution Model: Ethical and Enduring Professional Responsibilities

Reprinted, with permission, from B.B. Flores, L. Claeys, & C. Gist, *Crafting Culturally Efficacious Teacher Preparation and Pedagogies* (Lanham, MD: Lexington Books, 2018), 31.

In retrospect, the CEEM encompasses Kroll's (2013, 53–64) postmodern notions for preparing early childhood teachers:

1. Inquiry and reflection into practice are critical for continued learning and development.

2. Learning and development are cultural and constructivist.

3. The teacher's image of the child should be as a strong and capable participant in the culture.

4. The education of young children is a community privilege and responsibility.

5. The purpose of early care and education is to enhance and support each child's daily life experience and learning in the here and now.

The subsequent section elaborates on the CEEM dimensions and offers ECTEs examples from promising, field-recommended, evidence-based, and/or research-driven practices for preparing early childhood candidates' equitable praxis. These brief yet illustrative examples will help ECTEs build the capacities of candidates for diverse, complex classrooms and settings serving young children. Importantly, each of the CEEM dimensions are aligned with initial recommendations from NAEYC's position statement on advancing equity for all involved in the early childhood field.

Alignment of CEEM and NAEYC's Position Statement Recommendations
Awakening Cultural Consciousness

> Build awareness and understanding of your culture, personal beliefs, values, and biases. [. . .] Reflect on the impacts of racism, sexism, classism, ableism, heterosexism, xenophobia, and other systems of oppression in your own life. (NAEYC 2019, 6)

Awakening cultural consciousness requires an early childhood educator (faculty, practitioners, and candidates alike) to recognize his or her own stance in terms of ethnicity, culture, gender, and other multiple forms of self and identities. The discovery of self necessitates critical reflection on the origin of biases about others as well as the disruption of personal biases. Beyond interrogating our assumptions, embracing diversity as a strength is integral to the early childhood teacher program and candidates' development of ethical professional identities (Durand 2010; Giovacco-Johnson 2011). The awakening of cultural consciousness should be intentionally interwoven throughout the program with critical discussions that recurrently build candidates' capacities for efficacy with diversity (DeVore et al. 2015). Activities should include responding to questions like *Who am I?* and *What are my cultural practices and from where do these originate?* Tracing ancestors' journeys to the

United States, interviewing grandparents, or conducting a genealogical self-study through a historical lens can also be ways of exploring self.

Acquiring Cultural Competence

> Acknowledge and seek to understand structural inequities and their impact over time. (NAEYC 2019, 6)

Awakening cultural consciousness through critical reflection allows educators to deepen their cultural competence in order to consider the impact of the existent structural inequities. A culturally competent educator knows the community, is able to comport herself or himself with various community members, and views the community as a resource. Within the early childhood teacher program, advancement of such competence can be accomplished through community ethnographic walks, community action projects, and service learning experiences. These activities require that the candidate engage in critical introspection about the community, problem solving, and the disruption of any biases that emerge (Lash & Kroeger 2018). Understanding the community prepares the early childhood educator to bring conversations into the classroom that reflect the lived experiences of the learner. Cultural competence is manifested in the classroom when the educator creates conditions for learning in which the children's languages and experiences are central to their individual learning and that of their shared classroom community.

To move candidates to enact cultural competence in the classroom, the Biography-Driven Instructional (BDI) method can be used to guide educators on how to document and leverage the learner's culturally and linguistically rooted ways of knowing (Herrera 2016). Simple activities include having candidates create a biography card for each child that documents the sociocultural, linguistic, cognitive, and academic assets he or she brings from home and community. Candidates are assisted to design an ecology where one-on-one instructional conversations are catalyzed by the language and experiences the child brings and where other techniques that value community, family, and student assets more than the scripted curriculum serve as the basis for new learning (González, Moll, & Amanti 2005; Herrera 2016).

Developing Cultural Proficiency and Actualizing Cultural and Critical Responsivity

Recognize the power and benefits of diversity and inclusivity. (NAEYC 2019, 6)

In order to develop cultural proficiency and critical responsivity, it is important to recognize the power of creating an inclusive ecology. ECTEs can help candidates acquire this capacity through a multilayered exploration of the community's cultural, historical, linguistic, political, and social status, as situated in the context of structural inequities. Beyond community activities, it is important that candidates engage in ethnographic community studies to gain an understanding of how the community constructs cultural knowledge, funds of knowledge, and other forms of knowledge, as well as the community's ways of being and distinct ways of resolving problems. Developing cultural proficiency and responsivity demands sufficient interest, buy in, and attentiveness to nuances, such that one is able to comprehend and empathize with another's perspective and actions in a given context or situation of social interaction. This requires deeper attentiveness to the beliefs, practices, and actions of another (e.g., learner, parent, or peer) whose culture is different. Similar to Achinstein and Athanases's (2005) notion of *bifocal knowledge*, early childhood educators must know and appreciate the context and the learner in order to be open to alternative viewpoints, practices, and belief systems.

Through ethnographic activities, candidates come to recognize that there are individual as well as cultural differences in both learning and development (Miller 2011). Further, they realize that knowledge building is the result of social interactions and that the solutions to problems are developed through these exchanges (Vygotsky [1930–35] 1978). ECTEs assist candidates to attend to the promotion of cognitive development of children—not from a universal perspective, but as a process of problem solving for planning lesson activities and selecting responsive literature and materials that reflect the diversity and sociocultural interactions among potential learners (Nganga 2015). Having a profound understanding of the intersectionality of cognition,

culture, and language helps candidates, as NAEYC recommends, to "uphold the unique value and dignity of each child and family" (2019, 7).

Additionally, the candidate must question how power structures affect different communities and groups. Young children's play and interactions can reflect inequities and privilege (Hyland 2010). A useful activity is exploring the power relations within the early childhood setting; for example, by documenting teachers' and children's choices, play, interactions, and role in the learning process. Using tools such as the *Early Childhood Ecology Scale-Revised* (ECES-R) observation and reflection forms (Flores, Casebeer, & Riojas-Cortez 2011; Flores & Riojas-Cortez 2015), the candidate can observe the early childhood classroom's ecology and determine if the children's cognitive, cultural, emotional, linguistic, and physical needs are being addressed.

Going beyond the classroom and into the community, candidates can explore how a new company may contribute to the gentrification of a minoritized community (or how an existing company might have done so in the past). They can also investigate the types of early childhood services available and utilized in the community, determine why services are over/underutilized, and pose solutions. It is important that ECTEs engage candidates in authentic, real-world problem-solving approaches so that they can become responsive and acquire skills that can generalize to their praxis. In attending to structural inequities, the candidate's cultural proficiency is strengthened, which aligns with the following recommendation:

View your commitment to cultural responsiveness as an ongoing process. (NAEYC 2019, 6)

ECTEs are in the best position to assist candidates as they grapple with the ever-changing demographic landscape and associated demands for adaptability and flexibility. Actualization of cultural and critical responsivity requires that the ECTE provides academic readings from scholars across the globe that challenge candidates' ways of thinking. In planning early childhood activities, the candidate should draw on the community's approaches to knowing and understanding historical perspectives that are distinct from a Western stance.

Candidates' capacities to scaffold learning are bolstered through strategies that support differentiation of contextual and situational processes and actions that involve both teachers and children, according to their levels of volition, development, and linguistic readiness (Lee & Recchia 2016; NCTE 2016). BDI strategies (Herrera 2016), which provide scaffolding opportunities for collaborative and reciprocal learning between the teacher and children, have the potential to set optimal conditions for the construction of knowledge. Early childhood educators must be prepared to select strategies that are not one-size-fits-all, or filler activities. Instead they must intentionally focus on selecting strategies that actively involve all learners and promote learner-initiated contributions, discussions, applications, and ultimately retention with meaningfulness. Cultural responsiveness begins with planning instruction focused on moving beyond the biased curriculum and scripted lessons. Preparation, reflection, and action toward reframing thinking about teaching diverse learners will require candidates to think and act outside of the traditional boundaries that perpetuate biased ways of approaching pedagogy.

Realizing Cultural Efficaciousness

Take responsibility for biased actions, even if unintended, and actively work to repair the harm.

Recognize that the professional knowledge base is changing. (NAEYC 2019, 6)

Both of these recommendations from NAEYC's position statement on advancing equity align with the candidate's attainment of cultural efficaciousness as a mindset that reflects both the confidence and capacity to enact socially just praxis that makes a difference in children's lives. The early childhood educator assumes responsibility for the experiences provided within the classroom setting (Nganga 2015). Thus, ECTEs further recognize their own vulnerabilities and engage in professional learning to influence the efficacy of candidates, who will in turn affect children's development and learning. As culturally efficacious educators themselves, ECTEs are agents of change, intentionally developing a

transformational program of study that supports candidates' agency and identity, while challenging their misconceptions through activities, readings, and inquiry approaches. In turn, candidates become better prepared to support children's agency and identity (Mackey & de Vocht-van Alphen 2016). ECTEs serve as transformative guides who assist candidates to develop a classroom ecology that promotes active engagement, fosters trusting relationships, supports the individuality of the child, and engages families. Through their preparation, candidates come to recognize the importance of developing ideological and political clarity (Bartolomé 2008).

Conclusion

The recommendations within NAEYC's "Advancing Equity in Early Childhood Education" position statement are indeed challenging goals for early childhood educators. Yet it is well-grounded in the literature of promising theory and praxis for increasingly complex and diverse schools and early childhood education classrooms. Given our current political climate, educators must be advocacy leaders, maintaining their vigilance for the educational rights of young children. Current sociopolitical contexts and their influences on the futurity and relevance of early childhood education and programs indicate that capacities for agency and advocacy among ECTEs are paramount. Further, and consistent with alignments between the CEEM and recommendations from NAEYC's position statement, candidates and practitioners should focus their readiness and capacity-building activities in three areas: praxis, agency, and advocacy. First, ECTEs need to activate their awareness of self and praxis in critically conscious ways. Second, ECTEs will benefit from professional learning that connects the outcomes of this activation with emergent cultural competency and developing cultural proficiency. Finally, ECTEs, their colleagues, organizations, and leaders best collaborate in agency for culturally responsive and sustainable practices. The CEEM for teachers' professional development, the BDI method for educators' culturally responsive teaching, and socio-constructivist principles for children's learning are all available to support early childhood educators. Each, in its own way, offers structured pathways to the innovative implementation of NAEYC's guidelines for self-reflective, culturally responsive and efficacious, and transformative early childhood education praxis.

References

Achinstein, B., & S. Athanases. 2005. "Focusing New Teachers on Diversity and Equity: Toward a Knowledge Base for Mentors." *Teaching and Teacher Education* 21 (7): 843–862.

Bartolomé, L.I., ed. 2008. *Ideologies in Education: Unmasking the Trap of Teacher Neutrality*. New York: Peter Lang.

Boutte, G.S. 2008. "Beyond the Illusion of Diversity: How Early Childhood Teachers Can Promote Social Justice." *Social Studies* 99 (4): 165–173.

Darder, A. 2011. *Culture and Power in the Classroom: A Critical Foundation for the Education of Bicultural Students*. Boulder, CO: Paradigm Press.

DeVore, S., R. Fox, L. Heimer, & B. Winchell. 2015. "Meeting in the Circle: Examining Identity, Attitudes, and Pedagogy in the Context of an Early Childhood Teacher Education Program in the United States." *Early Years: An International Journal of Research and Development* 35 (4): 394–410.

Durand, T.M. 2010. "Celebrating Diversity in Early Care and Education Settings: Moving Beyond the Margins." *Early Child Development and Care* 180 (7): 835–848.

Flores, B.B., C.M. Casebeer, & M. Riojas-Cortez. 2011. "Validation of the Early Childhood Ecology Scale-Revised: A Reflective Tool for Teacher Candidates." *Journal of Early Childhood Teacher Education* 32 (3): 266–286.

Flores, B.B., L. Claeys, & C. Gist. 2018. *Crafting Culturally Efficacious Teacher Preparation and Pedagogies*. Lanham, MD: Lexington Books.

Flores, B.B., & M. Riojas-Cortez. 2015. *Early Childhood Ecology Scale-Revised (ECES-R): Observation and Reflection Forms*. Washington, DC: APA PscyNet.

Gay, G. 2010. "Acting on Beliefs in Teacher Education for Cultural Diversity." *Journal of Teacher Education* 61 (1–2): 143–152.

Giovacco-Johnson, T. 2011. "Applied Ethics as a Foundation in Early Childhood Teacher Education: Exploring the Connections and Possibilities." *Early Childhood Education Journal* 38 (6): 449–456.

González, N., L.C. Moll, & K. Amanti. 2005. "Introduction: Theorizing Practices." In *Funds of Knowledge: Theorizing Practices in Households, Communities, and Classrooms*, eds. N. González, L.C. Moll, & K. Amanti, 1–28. Mahwah, NJ: Erlbaum.

Herrera, S. 2016. *Biography-Driven Culturally Responsive Teaching*. 2nd ed. New York: Teachers College Press.

Hyland, N.E. 2010. "Social Justice in Early Childhood Classrooms: What the Research Tells Us." *Young Children* 65 (1): 82–90.

KIDS COUNT Data Center. 2020. "Child Population by Race and Age Group in the United States," last modified September 1. https://datacenter.kidscount.org/data/tables/8446-child -population-by-race-and-age-group#detailed/1/any/false /871,870,573,869,36,868,867,133/68,69,67,12,70,66,71,13 |62/17077,17078.

Kroll, L.R. 2013. "Early Childhood Teacher Preparation: Essential Aspects for the Achievement of Social Justice." *Journal of Early Childhood Teacher Education* 34 (1): 63–72.

Lash, M.J., & J. Kroeger. 2018. "Seeking Justice Through Social Action Projects: Preparing Teachers to be Social Actors in Local and Global Problems." *Policy Futures in Education* 16 (6): 691–708.

Ladson-Billings, G. 1994. *The Dreamkeepers: Successful Teachers of African American Children*. San Francisco: Jossey-Bass.

Lee, Y.A. 2011. "What Does Teaching for Social Justice Mean to Teacher Candidates?" *The Professional Educator* 35 (2): 1–20.

Lee, Y.-J., & S.L. Recchia. 2016. "Zooming In and Out: Exploring Teacher Competencies in Inclusive Early Childhood Classrooms." *Journal of Research in Childhood Education* 30 (1): 1–14.

Mackey, G., & L. de Vocht-van Alphen. 2016. "Teachers Explore How to Support Young Children's Agency for Social Justice." *International Journal of Early Childhood* 48 (3): 353–367.

Miller, R. 2011. *Vygotsky in Perspective.* New York: Cambridge University.

NAEYC. 2019. "Advancing Equity in Early Childhood Education." Position statement. Washington, DC: NAEYC. www.naeyc.org /resources/position-statements/equity.

NCTE (National Council of Teachers of English). 2016. "Equity and Early Childhood Education: Reclaiming the Child." Research policy brief. www.ncte.org/library/NCTEFiles /EquityEarlyEdBrief.pdf.

Nganga, L. 2015. "Culturally Responsive and Anti-Biased Teaching Benefits Early Childhood Pre-Service Teachers." *Journal of Curriculum and Teaching* 4 (2): 1–16.

Sheets, R.H. 2005. *Diversity Pedagogy: Examining the Role of Culture in the Teaching-Learning Process.* Boston: Pearson.

Sleeter, C., L. Neal, & K. Kumashiro, eds. 2014. *Addressing the Demographic Imperative: Recruiting, Preparing, and Retaining a Diverse and Highly Effective Teaching Force.* New York: Routledge.

Snyder, T.D., C. de Brey, & S.A. Dillow. 2016. *Digest of Education Statistics 2014* (NCES 2016-006). Report. Washington, DC: National Center for Education Statistics, Institute of Education Sciences, US Department of Education. https://nces.ed.gov /pubs2016/2016006.pdf.

Vygotsky, L.S. [1930–35] 1978. *Mind in Society: The Development of Higher Psychological Processes.* Ed. and trans. M. Cole, V. John-Steiner, S. Scribner, & E. Souberman. Cambridge, MA: Harvard University Press.

This chapter supports recommendations from the NAEYC position statement:

Recommendations for Everyone

Item 1: Build awareness and understanding of your culture, personal beliefs, values, and biases.

Item 2: Recognize the power and benefits of diversity and inclusivity.

Item 3: Take responsibility for biased actions, even if unintended, and actively work to repair the harm.

Item 4: Acknowledge and seek to understand structural inequities and their impact over time.

Item 5: View your commitment to cultural responsiveness as an ongoing process.

Recommendations for those Facilitating Educator Preparation and Professional Development

Item 1: Prepare current and prospective early childhood educators to provide equitable learning opportunities for all children.

Item 2: Prepare prospective early childhood educators to meet the Professional Standards and Competencies for Early Childhood Educators.

Appendix: A Note on Terminology Used in this Book

Terminology and language evolve over time. As we, the editors and NAEYC staff, worked on this book, language around equity, race, and diversity was being discussed and debated, and evolving rapidly on a global scale. We engaged in this debate as we considered what terminology would be appropriate for this book and acknowledge that many of the terms used will continue to evolve and change. For the purposes of this text, we provide the following list, but not as an exhaustive glossary; instead, we have selected terms for which we feel some additional definition or explanation is required. We encourage you to also refer to the Definition of Key Terms from NAEYC's "Advancing Equity in Early Childhood Education" position statement, included on pages xix–xx in this book.

African American English Vernacular (AAEV): A variation of American English spoken by members of the African American community (Craig et al. 2003).

bias framing: A manner in which data is presented; intentional language used to describe and influence opinion and decision-making.

Black versus African American: Unless used in a direct quote, this text uses the term *Black* to refer to anyone of African descent, including indigenous Africans, African Americans, and Caribbean Black people.

codes of power: Codes or rules for participating in a culture of power; societal norms that perpetuate and maintain the status quo, such as linguistic forms, communicative strategies, ways of dressing, and ways of interacting with others. Reflection of the rules of culture of those who have power (Delpit 1988).

culturally efficacious teaching: A mindset that reflects both the confidence and capacity to enact transformative practices through critical self-reflection and dialogue (Flores, Claeys, & Gist 2018).

culturally responsive teaching: An educator's ability to reflect and draw on students' linguistic and cultural strengths and become responsive to the learning characteristics of diverse racial, ethnic, and social class groups (Gay 2010).

culturally sustaining pedagogy: The belief that educators need to sustain the cultural characteristics of students from diverse racial, ethnic, and social class groups (Paris 2012).

deficit thinking: Approaches to teaching and learning that view "the languages, literacies, and cultural ways of being of many students and communities of color as deficiencies to be overcome in learning the demanded and legitimized dominant language, literacy, and cultural ways of schooling" (Paris 2012, 93).

dual language learners: Young children who speak a language other than English and maintain their home language(s) to communicate with their families while also learning English as they begin to participate in early education programs or attend kindergarten (NASEM 2017).

Latino/a: A shortened form of the Spanish phrase *latinoamericano* (Latin American). The term refers to a person's ancestry and origin. Latino/as can be White, Black, indigenous American, Mestizo, mixed, and even of Asian descent. For the purposes of this text, the editors chose to use this term instead of *Latinx*. This decision is based on expertise from the Latin American community, who have expressed concern that the term *Latinx* is not aligned with the Latino culture. They consider *Latinx* to be a gender-neutral term created to fit a Western-dominant view and, as such, it is not culturally sound.

second-generation equity work: A "second-generation" approach to equity focuses on identifying and addressing structural barriers and root causes that prevent equitable access and outcomes for children and families of color (Neitzel 2020).

third space: Can be an intellectual and/or emotional place where people in conflict move beyond *either/or* viewpoints and embrace a spectrum of possibilities (Barrera, Kramer, & Macpherson 2012).

translanguaging: A dynamic process used by multilingual speakers to maximize communication and meaning-making. Encompasses the broader aspect of linguistic repertoire through complex and strategic employment of multiple languages (García & Wei 2014).

References

Barrera, I., L. Kramer, & T.D. Macpherson. 2012. *Skilled Dialogue: Strategies for Responding to Cultural Diversity in Early Childhood*. 2nd ed. Baltimore: Brookes Publishing.

Craig, H.K., C.A. Thompson, J.A. Washington, & S.L. Potter. 2003. "Phonological Features of Child African American English." *Journal of Speech, Language, and Hearing Research* 46 (3): 623–635. doi:10.1044/10924388 (2003/049).

Delpit, L. 1988. "The Silenced Dialogue: Power and Pedagogy in Educating Other People's Children." *Harvard Educational Review* 58 (3): 280–298.

Flores, B.B., L. Claeys, & C. Gist. 2018. *Crafting Culturally Efficacious Teacher Preparation and Pedagogies*. Lanham, MD: Lexington Books.

García, O., & L. Wei. 2014. *Translanguaging: Language, Bilingualism, and Education*. London: Palgrave Macmillan.

Gay, G. 2010. *Culturally Responsive Teaching: Theory, Research, and Practice*. New York: Teachers College Press.

NASEM (National Academies of Sciences, Engineering, and Medicine). 2017. *Promoting the Educational Success of Children and Youth Learning English*. Report. Washington, DC: National Academies Press. doi:10.17226/24677.

Neitzel, J. 2020. *Achieving Equity and Justice in Education Through the Work of Systems Change*. Lanham, MD: Lexington Books.

Paris, D. 2012. "Culturally Sustaining Pedagogy: A Needed Change in Stance, Terminology, and Practice." *Educational Researcher* 41 (3): 93–97.

About the Editors

Iliana Alanís, PhD, a native of South Texas, is professor of early childhood and elementary education in the department of interdisciplinary learning and teaching at the University of Texas at San Antonio. With over 20 years in the early childhood field, her work focuses on teaching practices in culturally and linguistically diverse early childhood contexts with an emphasis on the effect of schooling for language minority children in Spanish/English dual language programs. She is especially interested in forms of teaching that promote native language development and its correlation to second language acquisition. With over 48 refereed publications related to dual language education, her recent research focuses on higher-order cognitive and linguistic interaction found in student–student exchanges. Dr. Alanís is former president of the Texas Association for Bilingual Education and former board member for the National Latino Children's Institute. She's served as a NAEYC Governing Board member and an Early Childhood Advisory Board member for Scholastic Education. As a member of the Dual Language Training Institute, she facilitates professional development for teachers in dual language classrooms across the country. Dr. Alanís is coauthor of *The Essentials: Supporting Dual Language Learners in Diverse Environments in Preschool and Kindergarten* (NAEYC, 2021).

Iheoma U. Iruka, PhD, is research professor in public policy and founding director of the equity research action coalition at the Frank Porter Graham Child Development Institute at the University of North Carolina at Chapel Hill. Dr. Iruka is engaged in projects and initiatives focused on how evidence-informed policies, systems, and practices in early education can support the optimal development and experiences of children who are from households with low income, ethnic minorities, and immigrants. She is focused on ensuring healthy development and excellence for young diverse learners, especially Black children, through classroom and family tools, the examination of nontraditional pedagogical approaches, public policies, and publications geared toward early education practitioners and policymakers. She is an author of several books, including *Don't Look Away: Embracing Anti-Bias Classrooms* (Gryphon House, 2020). Dr. Iruka serves or has served on numerous national boards and committees, including the Brady Education Foundation, the American Psychological Association's Board of Educational Affairs Task Force on Racial and Ethnic Disparities, and the National Academies of Sciences, Engineering, and Medicine committees on Supporting Parents of Young Children and Applying Neurobiological and Socio-Behavioral Sciences from Prenatal through Early Childhood Development: A Health Equity Approach.

Susan Friedman is senior director of publications and content development at the National Association for the Education of Young Children (NAEYC). In this role, she leads the content development work of NAEYC's books and periodicals teams. Early childhood educators rely on NAEYC's award-winning content to stay current on research and best practices they can implement in their classrooms. Susan has extensive prior experience in content programming as well as editorial oversight and production with many years of experience creating content on play, developmentally appropriate uses of media, and other topics for educators and families. She has presented at numerous educational conferences, including NAEYC's Professional Learning Institute and Annual Conference, the South by Southwest Education (SXSW EDU) Conference & Festival, and the School Superintendents Association's Early Learning Cohort. Susan began her career as a preschool teacher at City and Country School in New York City. She holds degrees from Vassar College and the Harvard Graduate School of Education.

Index

Page numbers followed by an *f* refer to figures; those followed by a *t* refer to tables.